ROI FOR TECHNOLOGY PROJECTS
Measuring and Delivering Value

D0145081

ROI FOR TECHNOLOGY PROJECTS

Measuring and Delivering Value

D. BRIAN ROULSTONE
JACK J. PHILLIPS

ELSEVIER

AMSTERDAM • BOSTON • HEIDELBERG • LONDON
NEW YORK • OXFORD • PARIS • SAN DIEGO
SAN FRANCISCO • SINGAPORE • SYDNEY • TOKYO

Butterworth-Heinemann is an imprint of Elsevier

Butterworth-Heinemann is an imprint of Elsevier
30 Corporate Drive, Suite 400, Burlington, MA 01803, USA
Linacre House, Jordan Hill, Oxford OX2 8DP, UK

First edition 2008

Recognizing the importance of preserving what has been written, Elsevier prints its books
on acid-free paper whenever possible

Library of Congress Cataloging-in-Publication Data
Application submitted

British Library Cataloguing in Publication Data
A catalog record for this book is available from the British Library

ISBN: 978-0-7506-8588-7

For information on all Butterworth-Heinemann publications
visit our web site at books.elsevier.com

Printed and bound in the USA
07 08 09 10 10 9 8 7 6 5 4 3 2 1

Contents

Preface

ROI is Exploding

Calculating the return on investment (ROI) has become one of the most challenging and intriguing issues facing the information technology (IT) sector. The interest in ROI evaluation has been phenomenal, with the topic appearing on almost every IT conference and convention agenda and articles regularly featured in *CIO Magazine* and research journals. Several books have been written on the topic, and consulting firms have been formed just to tackle this important issue.

Several factors are driving this increased interest in ROI. Probably the most influential factor is the pressure from clients and senior managers to show the return on their IT investment. Competitive economic pressures are causing intense scrutiny of all expenditures, including IT and technology-focused product development costs. Total quality management, reengineering, and Six Sigma have created a renewed interest in measurement and evaluation, including weighing the effectiveness of IT. The general trend toward accountability with all staff support groups is causing some IT departments to measure their contributions. These and other drivers have created an unprecedented wave of applying the ROI process.

An Effective ROI Methodology

The challenging aspect of ROI analysis is the nature and accuracy of its development. The process often seems confusing, surrounded as it is by models, formulas, and statistics that frighten even the most capable practitioners. Coupled with this concern are the misunderstandings about the process and the gross misuse of ROI techniques in some organizations. These issues sometimes leave practitioners with a distaste for ROI evaluations. Unfortunately,

ROI cannot be ignored. To admit to clients and senior managers that the impact of IT or technology cannot be measured is to admit that IT does not add value or that IT investments should not be subjected to accountability requirements. In practice, ROI analysis must be explored, considered, and ultimately implemented in most organizations.

What is needed is a rational, logical approach that can be simplified and implemented within the current budget constraints and resources of the organization. This book presents a proven ROI Methodology based on almost 20 years of development and improvement. It is a process that is rich in tradition and refined to meet the demands facing IT and technology development projects.

The ROI Methodology described in this book meets the requirements of three important groups. First, the practitioners who have used this model and have implemented the ROI process in their organizations continue to report their satisfaction with the methodology and the success it has achieved. The ROI Methodology presented here is user-friendly, easy to understand, and has been proven to pay for itself time and time again. A second important group is the clients and senior managers who must approve IT and technology development budgets. They want measurable results, preferably expressed as a return on investment. The ROI Methodology presented in this book has fared well with these groups. Senior managers view the process as credible, logical, practical, and easy to understand from their perspectives. More important, it has their buy-in, which is critical for securing future support. The third important group is the evaluation researchers who develop, explore, and analyze new processes and techniques. When exposed to this methodology in a two-day or one-week workshop, the researchers, without exception, gave this process high praise. They often applaud the techniques for isolating the effects of IT and the techniques for converting data to monetary values. Unanimously, they characterize the process as an important—and needed—contribution to the field.

WHY WRITE THIS BOOK NOW?

This book—the first of its kind—focuses on ROI analysis for technology investments and is written for technology decision makers by a technology executive and a foremost authority on the discipline of return on investment. This book leverages the talents of both authors to provide a framework and method that can ensure greater success in mobilizing technology initiatives. No other book on the market specifically addresses the critical need to prove ROI on resource-intensive technology projects with a time-tested and industry-leading process. To date, most ROI books have focused on the areas of performance, training, marketing, and other human capital related disciplines, but the need for ROI evaluation in other areas is growing.

With increased scrutiny of technology spending by the most complex organizations in the world, technology leaders need a tool to help them prepare for hard-hitting discussions with their organizations' CFO, president, CEO, or chairman about the return they should expect from critical technology projects. Rather than focusing top managers' attention on cutting, challenging, and controlling expenditures (as many C-level accountants prefer), this approach guides technology managers in providing executives with more comprehensive, balanced information that helps all involved make better business decisions. Along the way, technology managers get help communicating more effectively with the financial decision makers within their organizations. The book also shows executives how partnering with IT leaders can help them and other managers understand the return these technology projects can provide to their organizations in increased human efficiency, automation of manual processes, unified organizational data, and other high-return results from complex and critical technology initiatives.

At the same time, executives and IT professionals must have their projects measured with balanced perspectives. While the ROI itself is important, capturing intangible benefits related to the project and information about the application and implementation of the project is important, as well. Even earlier in the cycle, gathering reaction to the technology and the extent to which individuals have learned the technology is crucial. Together, these data sets represent a balanced profile of success, with ROI at the pinnacle.

WHAT THIS BOOK COVERS

This is the first book to present the ROI Methodology for technology. This methodology generates six measures of the values of technology projects:

1. Reaction and perceived value
2. Learning and confidence
3. Application and implementation

4. Impact and consequences
5. Return on investment
6. Intangible Benefits

In addition, this methodology always has a process in place to isolate the effects of the technology solution from other solutions and factors, another critical element to ensure the credibility of the IT project's evaluation. All this is presented in a logical, systematic way, with specific standards that provide guidelines and rules for collecting data, analyzing data, and reporting results. These provide the consistency and credibility needed to secure management's buy-in of the process.

The book concludes with chapters on ROI forecasting—a critical tool for determining the value of projects *before* implementation, ways to communicate the data to stakeholders, and methods for implementing and sustaining the process.

WHO SHOULD READ THIS BOOK

This book is written primarily for managers and executives who are charged with mobilizing and executing key technology projects and initiatives within their organizations. It is also for anyone in business who is concerned about the value of technology-focused projects, programs, processes, and resources. Although executives are often committed to these projects, they need to see the value in terms that they can appreciate and understand—monetary value and ROI.

This book is also designed for technology consultants, business analysts, and practitioners who are responsible for scoping, designing, and implementing key technology initiatives within organizations. The book represents a source of basic research techniques, applications, experiences, and resources available to expose the value of key technology initiatives.

FUNCTIONAL AREAS

Designed for a spectrum of functional areas within an organization, outside the obvious IT function, professionals in the following areas represent the audience for this book:

1. IT management
2. IT planning
3. IT implementation

4. IT product development
5. Technology research & development
6. Technology consulting
7. E-learning
8. Technology PMO (project management office)
9. Finance and accounting
10. Corporate universities

STRUCTURE OF THE BOOK

This book has a unique feature that makes it a useful guide. It presents the ROI model in a step-by-step process. A chapter is devoted to each major part of the model as the pieces of the ROI Methodology are put together. At the conclusion, the reader has a clear understanding of the overall ROI process. This is critical to demystifying the ROI Methodology so it can be effectively and efficiently implemented within any organization.

Chapter 1, **Measuring the Return on Investment for Technology Initiatives**, describes how the ROI process has evolved in recent years and how organizations are currently applying this methodology to key technology investments within their organizations. Key issues and trends are briefly described. Various ROI evaluation criteria and requirements are presented, building a foundation for the remainder of the book.

Chapter 2, **The ROI Model: History and Background**, presents the ROI model. Initially conceived in the late 1970s, the model has been developed, changed, and refined during the past 25 years to arrive at what users characterize as the most logical, rational, and credible approach to calculating ROI. This chapter presents a brief summary of the model for those encountering the ROI Methodology for the first time.

Chapter 3, **Establishing the Need for the Technology Project**, discusses the approach for establishing why the organization needs the strategic technology initiative. The key components of setting up the technology project to ensure maximum buy-in from other business units are described. This approach also ensures that the project is linked to the desired outputs from the technology investments to prove maximum project return.

Chapter 4, **Collecting Data**, presents a variety of approaches to one of the most fundamental measurement issues. The most common ways to collect data at all levels—ranging from conducting user acceptance surveys to monitoring system data and implementation performance data—are described in this chapter. Useful tips and techniques for selecting the appropriate method for a specific situation are also presented.

Chapter 5, **Isolating the Strategic Effects of Strategic Technology Investments**, presents what is perhaps the most important aspect of the ROI Methodology. Ranging from the use of a control group to obtaining estimates directly from participants, the most useful techniques are presented for determining the level of improvement that can be directly linked to the technology-based initiative. The premise of this chapter is that many influences affect business performance measures, with technology being only one of them.

Chapter 6, **Exposing the Value of Technology Projects**, presents essential information for developing an economic benefit from key technology investments. Ranging from determining the profit contribution of process automation to using expert opinions to assign a value to data, the most useful techniques to convert both hard and soft data to monetary values are presented, along with many examples.

Chapter 7, **Tabulating Project Costs**, details what types of costs should be included in the ROI formula. Different categories and classifications of costs are explored in this chapter, with the goal being the development of a fully loaded cost profile for each ROI evaluation.

Chapter 8, **Calculating the Return**, describes the actual ROI calculation and presents several issues surrounding its development, calculation, use, and abuse. The most accepted ROI formulas are presented, along with examples of calculations. Common ROI myths are also dispelled.

Chapter 9, **Identifying Intangible Measures**, is a brief chapter that focuses on nonmonetary benefits from technology projects. Recognizing that not all measures can or should be converted to monetary values, this chapter shows how intangible measures are identified, monitored, and reported. More than 25 common intangible measures are examined.

Chapter 10, **ROI Forecasting**, shows how the ROI Methodology can be used to forecast the payoff of a technology initiative *before* it is implemented. Several examples are presented to highlight each concept. This chapter underscores the range of possibilities available for calculating the ROI at different times, using different types of data.

Chapter 11, **How to Communicate Results**, provides best-practice approaches to communicating the results of technology evaluations.

The chapter details how to plan for communications, select audiences and media, develop impact studies, and address typical issues that surface during communication.

Chapter 12, **Implementation Issues,** the final chapter, addresses a variety of implementation issues. Effectively implementing the ROI Methodology requires following logical steps and overcoming several hurdles. This chapter identifies the important factors that must be addressed so the ROI process is a productive, useful, and long-lasting tool within an organization.

Acknowledgments

From Brian:

This book would not have been possible without the generous partnership of Jack Phillips and the ROI Institute. Jack not only allowed me to leverage decades of research and intellectual property as a platform for this book, but he also provided the inspiration. For that, I am eternally grateful. I would also like to thank the countless technology professionals who will champion the ROI Methodology moving forward to resonate the value of their strategic technology initiatives within their organizations. Finally, I am deeply grateful for the remarkable fortune to be married to Heather Mansfield Roulstone, who provides me the support and latitude to shirk my family responsibilities to pursue personal interests such as this manuscript. To my two beautiful children, Samuel John and Ella Page, thanks for allowing your daddy to disappear for countless hours on the weekend to write a book that even a Mensa child would not enjoy.

From Jack:

Many individuals, groups, and organizations have participated in the development of this book. I owe particular thanks to the hundreds of clients I have had the pleasure to work with in the past two decades. They have helped shape, develop, mold, and refine this methodology. Their contributions are evident in this book.

I am particularly indebted to Butterworth-Heinemann for taking on this project. Ailsa Marks, ever-patient, has been a dream to work with for many years. Ailsa and her entire team have been very helpful.

I also want to thank Brian for the wealth of technical knowledge he provided for this book. I could not have asked for a better co-author for this project.

From our ROI Institute, I thank Michelle Segrest and Lori Ditoro— my publishing team—who accomplished the editing of this project under a very hectic schedule and with a demanding workload. Thanks for delivering this quality manuscript on time. Also, the support of Katherine Horton, Crystal Langford, Jaime Beard, and Carrie Luke was immeasurable.

I would also like to thank my lovely spouse, Patti, who serves as my partner, friend, and colleague in this project. She is an excellent consultant, an outstanding facilitator, a tenacious researcher, and an outstanding writer.

About the Authors

D. Brian Roulstone, a renowned authority in distance education and remote learning technologies is the chief information officer and chief technology officer of Bisk Education, a leading provider in the online postsecondary education and corporate training markets. During his tenure, he has transformed Bisk into one of the leading online education companies that has driven explosive revenue growth. Prior to joining Bisk Education, Roulstone worked in Arthur Andersen's Business Consulting practice, where his expertise included remote learning technologies, system design and implementation, management consulting, and business process improvement. His clients ranged from the Fortune 500 to technology start-ups.

Roulstone received his bachelor of science in management information systems from Florida State University and his master of business administration from the University of Florida.

Jack J. Phillips, Ph.D., a world-renowned expert on accountability, measurement, and evaluation, Dr. Jack J. Phillips provides consulting services for Fortune 500 companies and major global organizations. The author or editor of more than 50 books, Phillips conducts workshops and makes conference presentations throughout the world.

His expertise in measurement and evaluation is based on more than 27 years of corporate experience in the aerospace, textile, metals, construction materials, and banking industries. Phillips has served as training and development manager at two Fortune 500 firms, as senior human resource officer at two firms, as president of a regional bank, and as management professor at a major state university.

This background led Phillips to develop the ROI methodology— a revolutionary process that provides bottom-line figures and accountability for all types of learning, performance improvement, human resource, technology, and public policy programs.

Phillips regularly consults with clients in manufacturing, service, and government organizations in 44 countries in North and South America, Europe, Africa, Australia, and Asia.

Books most recently authored by Phillips include show me the money (Berrett-Koehler, 2007) *Building a Successful Consulting Practice* (McGraw-Hill, 2006); *Investing in Your Company's Human Capital: Strategies to Avoid Spending Too Much or Too Little* (Amacom, 2005); *Proving the Value of HR: How and Why to Measure ROI* (SHRM, 2005); *The Leadership Scorecard* (Elsevier Butterworth-Heinemann, 2004); *Managing Employee Retention* (Elsevier Butterworth-Heinemann, 2003); *Return on Investment in Training and Performance Improvement Projects*, 2nd ed. (Elsevier Butterworth-Heinemann, 2003); *The Project Management Scorecard*, (Elsevier Butterworth-Heinemann, 2002); *How to Measure Training Results* (McGraw-Hill, 2002); *The Human Resources Scorecard: Measuring the Return on Investment* (Elsevier Butterworth-Heinemann, 2001); *The Consultant's Scorecard* (McGraw-Hill, 2000); and *Performance Analysis and Consulting* (ASTD, 2000). Phillips served as series editor for ASTD's In Action casebook series, an ambitious publishing project featuring 30 titles. He currently serves as series editor for Elsevier Butterworth-Heinemann's Improving Human Performance series, and for Pfeiffer's new series Measurement and Evaluation.

Phillips has received several awards for his books and work. The Society for Human Resource Management presented him an award for one of his books and honored a Phillips ROI study with its highest award for creativity. The American Society for Training and Development gave him its highest award: Distinguished Contribution to Workplace Learning and Development. *Meeting News* named Phillips one of the 25 most influential people in the Meetings and Events industry, based on his work on ROI for the industry.

Phillips has undergraduate degrees in electrical engineering, physics, and mathematics; a master's degree in decision sciences from Georgia State University; and a Ph.D. in human resource management from the University of Alabama.

Jack Phillips has served on the boards of several private businesses—including two NASDAQ companies—and several nonprofit organizations and associations, including the American Society for Training and Development. He is chairman of the ROI Institute, Inc., and can be reached at (205) 678-8101, or by e-mail at jack@roiinstitute.net.

CHAPTER 1

Measuring the Return on Investment for Technology Initiatives: Trends and Issues

Measuring the return on investment (ROI) in information technology (IT) and technology development has consistently earned a place among the critical issues in the IT field. The topic appears routinely on conference agendas and at professional meetings. Journals and newsletters regularly embrace the concept with increasing print space. Professional organizations have been developed to exchange information on ROI evaluation. Numerous books have been written in other disciplines—such as training and development and human performance—but few deal with the IT area, even though technology and communications, spending exceeds $2.8 trillion and is nearly 7 percent of the global gross domestic product (Accenture, 2005). No wonder top executives have stepped up their appetites for ROI information as the costs of strategic technology projects have skyrocketed over the past few years.

Measuring ROI is a hotly debated topic. Rarely does any topic stir up emotions to the degree of the ROI issue. Return on investment is characterized as flawed and inappropriate by some, whereas others describe it as the only way to address their accountability concerns. The truth probably lies somewhere in between. Understanding what drives the ROI Methodology and knowing its inherent weaknesses and advantages make it possible to take a rational approach to the issue and implement an appropriate mix of evaluation strategies that includes ROI. This chapter presents the basic issues and trends concerning ROI measurement.

Although interest in the topic has heightened and much progress has been made, ROI evaluation still challenges even the most sophisticated and progressive IT departments. Whereas some professionals argue that calculating the ROI is not possible, others deliberately proceed to develop measures and ROI calculations. The latter group is gaining support from the senior management team. Regardless of the position taken on the issue, the reasons for measuring ROI still exist. Almost all IT professionals share the concern that they must eventually show a return on their IT investments. Otherwise, IT funds may be reduced, or the IT department may not be able to maintain or enhance its present status and influence within the organization.

The dilemma surrounding the ROI process is a source of frustration with many senior executives—even within the IT field itself. Executives realize that IT is a basic necessity to support the infrastructures of their organizations, but the key difference is how IT is viewed by others within the organizations. When organizations experience significant growth or increased competition, IT can provide employees with the tools they need to meet competitive challenges. IT is also important during business restructuring and rapid change, when employees must learn new processes and companies must operate more efficiently through technology automation and often find themselves doing much more work with a dramatically downsized workforce. Every large companies today make huge investments in technology regardless of its industry focus. The company does not have to be a "tech" company headquartered in Silicon Valley to have countless technology-based systems permeating the organization. The key difference is that companies are spending the money to maintain these systems, and that is exactly what they are doing—spending and spending and spending. Then there are the best-practice organizations that track the returns of their technology investments, so the organization has a system maintenance mentality and refocuses on the automation of processes that can be gained by strategic technology investments.

Most executives recognize the need for IT and technology-related research and development and intuitively feel that IT investments add value. They conclude that IT can pay off in important bottom-line measures, such as productivity improvements, quality enhancements, cost reductions, and time savings. They also believe that IT can enhance customer and partner satisfaction, improve efficiency, and increase collaboration within their organizations. Yet, the frustration comes from the lack of evidence that the process works. Although the payoffs are assumed to exist, and IT appears to be a necessity, more evidence is required, at the risk of not getting the necessary funding to truly make technology strategic within an organization. The ROI Methodology represents the most promising way to show this accountability in a logical, rational approach.

ROI PROGRESS AND STATUS

Global Measurement Trends

A few global trends about measurement and evaluation in both private and public sector organizations should be examined. The following measurement trends have been identified in our research and are slowly evolving across organizations and cultures in more than 50 countries. Collectively, these 11 trends have had a strong impact on addressing accountability:

- Technology significantly enhances the measurement and evaluation process, enabling large amounts of data to be collected, processed, analyzed, and integrated across projects.
- Evaluation is an integral part of the design, development, delivery, and implementation of projects.
- A shift from a reactive approach to a more proactive approach is developing, with evaluation addressed early and often during the cycle.
- Measurement and evaluation processes are systematic and methodical, often built into the delivery process.
- Evaluation planning has become a critical part of the measurement and evaluation cycle.
- The implementation of a comprehensive measurement and evaluation process usually leads to increased emphasis on the initial needs analysis.
- Organizations without comprehensive measurement and evaluation have reduced or eliminated their project budgets.
- Organizations with comprehensive measurement and evaluation have enhanced their project budgets.
- The use of ROI analysis is emerging as an essential part of measurement and evaluation processes.
- Many successful examples of comprehensive measurement and evaluation applications are available.

- A comprehensive measurement and evaluation process, including an ROI calculation, can be implemented for about 4 to 5 percent of the direct project budget.

Progression of ROI Evaluation Across Sectors

The ROI Methodology had its beginnings in the 1970s when it was applied to the development of a return on investment for a cooperative education program at Lockheed-Martin. Since then, it has been developed, modified, and refined to the process detailed in this book and expanded in all types of situations, applications, and sectors. Figure 1-1 shows how the process has evolved within different sectors. Applications began in the manufacturing sector, where the process was easily implemented. Its use then began in the service sector, as many major service firms, such as banks and telecommunications companies, used the ROI process to show the value of projects. Applications evolved in the health-care arena as the industry sought ways to improve educational services, human resources, quality, risk management, and case management. Nonprofit applications also emerged as these organizations pursued ways to reduce costs and generate efficient processes. Finally, applications in the public sector appeared in a variety of government organizations. Public sector implementation has intensified in recent years. An outgrowth of public sector applications includes the

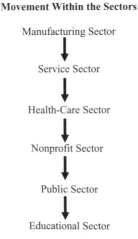

Movement Within the Sectors

Manufacturing Sector

Service Sector

Health-Care Sector

Nonprofit Sector

Public Sector

Educational Sector

Figure 1-1. Progression of ROI Implementation

use of the process in the educational field, where it is now being applied in different settings. The implementation is spreading to many different organizations and settings, including in IT and technology applications to show the value of investments in these areas.

Typical Applications

The specific types of project applications vary significantly. Table 1-1 shows a full range of current technology-focused applications representing projects from customer relationship management (CRM), enterprise resource planning (ERP), e-commerce, security, and many others. Published cases and whitepapers exist in all these areas. The process is flexible, versatile, and adaptable to almost any type of setting and environment.

Case Studies

The status of the ROI Methodology among practitioners in the technology field is difficult to pinpoint. Senior IT managers are reluctant to disclose internal practices and, even in the most progressive organizations, confess that too little progress has been made. Until recently, finding cases in the literature that showed how an organization attempted to measure its return on investment in IT was difficult.

Table 1-1
ROI Applications

• Enterprise resource planning (ERP)	• Customer relationship management (CRM)
• Information security	• Business intelligence/analytics
• Outsourcing	• System integration
• E-commerce	• Custom application development
• E-learning	• Mobile technologies
• Network infrastructure	• Process automation
• Compliance	• Hardware
• Expert systems	• Self-service applications
• Contact center applications	• Telecommunications

Research Studies

Studies indicate that the use of and interest in the ROI Methodology are growing. Research studies are continuously conducted that show the progress of ROI evaluation as well as the dilemmas concerning this level of evaluation. Accenture, a leading global technology consultancy, recently conducted a study surveying more than 300 organizations globally using 33 proprietary indicators of high, average, and low performance in managing IT (Accenture, 2005). The most compelling result of the study was that "high-performing IT organizations spend significantly less time maintaining and fixing systems and significantly more time building new systems. High performers, on average, spend 40 percent more time building and integrating systems than low performers" (Accenture, 2005).

The focus of this study was to understand IT performance in a statistically significant sample of organizations that comprise the Fortune 1000—from industries such as communications and high technology, financial services, government, resources, and products. What the survey of 310 chief information officers or the senior decision-making executive for IT within the company was *really* about was ROI! The highest-performing organizations were not the companies that spent the most on IT as a percentage of revenue, but those organizations that maximized the return on their technology investments. These are some of the other staggering results of the study:

- CIOs have more than three to four more times IT work than incremental dollars to address those technology initiatives.
- The low-performer group, on average, spent 48 percent of its time maintaining and fixing legacy systems.
- The corresponding high-performer group spent, on average, 35 percent of its time on similar activities.
- IT projects, on average, come in at a 29 percent success rate.
- The average cost overrun for projects is 56 percent.
- The average schedule delay for strategic technology initiatives is 84 percent of the original project plan.

Accenture's conclusions on the importance of IT investments are backed up by a May 2005 issue of *Barron's* featuring the "Barron's 500" performance ranking of the largest U.S. and Canadian public companies, in which the editors cited three common themes for the winners:

1. Revenue growth
2. Smart use of IT
3. Tight-fisted overhead cost management

Barron's cites the number one company in their ranking, United Health Group, as follows:

> Chief executive Bill McGuire says a number of important factors are responsible for the company's strong performance, but adds United Heath's $2 billion investment in information technology over the past four years is one of the most salient. In 2001, the company handled 4 million electronic transactions—a claim or a question from a doctor or customer, for example. Last year, it dealt with 220 million. Some 85 percent of claims and customer care transactions no longer require direct and costly human intervention. (Accenture, 2005)

These and other studies indicate two important conclusions:

1. Around the globe, interest in the ROI Methodology as an IT and technology development evaluation tool is growing.
2. Although progress has been made, much more advancement is needed to reach the desired level of use.

Global Expansion

Measuring the return on investment is becoming a global issue. Organizations around the globe are concerned about the accountability of IT and are exploring ways to credibly measure the results of IT investments. Many professional associations in the U.S. and other countries offer workshops, seminars, and dedicated conferences to the measurement issue, including ROI. Formal ROI presentations have been made in more than 70 countries, with implementation organized and coordinated in at least 50 countries. The ROI Network, a global group of practitioners who promote the science and practice of individual and organizational measurement and accountability, also holds an annual global conference.

Paradigm Shift

The progress with ROI evaluation underscores the need for IT and technology development to shift from an activity-based process to a results-based process. As depicted in Table 1-2, a significant paradigm shift has occurred, having a dramatic effect on the accountability of IT and technology development projects. Organizations have moved from IT for activity to IT as an investment, with a focus on bottom-line results, and this shift is evident from the beginning to the end of the process. The shift has often occurred because of the forces described in this chapter. In some cases, the shift is a result of progressive IT departments recognizing the need for ROI evaluation and persisting in their determination to make progress on this issue.

ROI Is Here to Stay

One thing is certain: Measuring ROI is not a fad. As long as a need for accountability of IT expenditures exists and the concept of an investment payoff is desired, the ROI Methodology will be used to evaluate major investments in IT and technology development.

Table 1-2
Paradigm Shift in IT and Technology Development

Activity Based	Results Based
Characterized by	**Characterized by**
☐ No business need for the project	☐ Project linked to specific business needs
☐ No assessment of performance issues	☐ Assessment of performance effectiveness
☐ No specific measurable objectives for application and impact	☐ Specific objectives for application and impact developed
☐ No effort to prepare project participants to achieve results	☐ Results expectations communicated to participants
☐ No effort to prepare the work environment to support application	☐ Environment prepared to support the transfer of learning
☐ No effort to build partnerships with key managers	☐ Partnerships established with key managers and clients
☐ No measurement of results or benefits/costs analysis	☐ Measurement of results and benefits/costs analysis
☐ Planning and reporting is input-focused	☐ Planning and reporting is output-focused

A *fad* is a new idea or approach or a new spin on an old approach, but the concept of ROI has been used for centuries. The 75th anniversary issue of the *Harvard Business Review* (*HBR*) tracked the tools used to measure results in organizations (Sibbet, 1997). In the early issues of *HBR*, during the 1920s, ROI was the emerging tool for placing a value on the payoff of investments.

With its adoption and use, the ROI Methodology is here to stay. Today, hundreds of organizations routinely develop ROI calculations for IT and technology projects.

Its status has grown significantly and the rate of implementation has been phenomenal. The number of organizations and individuals involved with the process underscores the magnitude of ROI implementation. Table 1-3 presents a summary of the current status. With this much evidence of the growing interest, the ROI Methodology is becoming a standard tool for project evaluation.

WHY ROI?

Return on investment has gained acceptance for many reasons. Although the viewpoints and explanations may vary, some facts are very clear. The key issues are outlined here.

Table 1-3
Summary of Current ROI Status

ROI by the Numbers

- The ROI Methodology has been refined over a 25-year period.
- The ROI Methodology has been adopted by hundreds of organizations in manufacturing, service, nonprofit, government, and technology sectors.
- Thousands of studies are developed each year using the ROI Methodology.
- Several hundred case studies are published on the ROI Methodology.
- Almost 5,000 individuals have been certified to implement the ROI Methodology in their organizations.
- Organizations in 50 countries have implemented the ROI Methodology.
- Two dozen books have been developed to support the process.
- The professional ROI Network, with hundreds of members, shares information.
- The ROI Methodology can be implemented for 4% to 5% of the IT project budget.

Increased Budgets

Most IT and technology development budgets have continued to grow year after year. In the United States alone, the cumulative average growth rate of IT expenditures in the last decade was 7.5 percent (Industry Report, 2006). The report on the state of corporate IT found that increased spending occurred primarily among medium and large organizations. Industries such as finance, insurance, real estate, transportation, public utilities, and technology spent the most on IT. Outsourced IT is increasing at a rapid rate in an attempt to leverage the technology budget to address as many projects as possible.

As organizations recognize the importance and necessity for IT and technology development, budgets continue to increase annually by organization, industry, and country. Many organizations and countries see IT as an investment instead of a cost. As a result, senior managers are willing to invest because they can anticipate a payoff for their investments.

In developing countries, increased IT is needed as new jobs are created and new plants and processes are established. Skill upgrading is required to develop the core competencies necessary for maintaining a productive labor force. In some countries, the governments require minimum levels of funding for IT to ensure that skills are developed.

The learning organization concept continues to be implemented in many organizations, requiring additional focus on learning and IT. In addition, the concern about intellectual capital and human capital has created a desire to invest more heavily in learning activities and formal IT projects. As expenditures grow, accountability becomes a more critical issue. A growing budget creates a larger target for internal critics, often prompting the development of an ROI evaluation process. The function, department, or process that shows the most value will likely receive the largest budget increase.

The Ultimate Level of Evaluation

Table 1-4 shows the five-level framework used in this book. At Level 1 (Reaction and Perceived Value), reactions to the technology from project participants is measured. At Level 2 (Learning), measurements focus on what participants learned during the technology project using tests, skill practices, simulations, group evalua-

Table 1-4
Evaluation Levels

Level	Brief Description
1. Reaction and Perceived Value	Measures participant's reaction to the technology.
2. Learning and Cofidence	Measures skills, knowledge, or attitude changes related to technology.
3. Application and Implementation	Measures actions on the job with application and implementation of the technology.
4. Impact and Consequences	Measures business impact of technology.
5. Return on Investment	Compares the monetary benefits of the impact with the costs for the project.

tions, and other assessment tools. At Level 3 (Application and Implementation), a variety of follow-up methods are used to determine if participants applied on the job what they learned in the technology project. At Level 4 (Business Impact), the measurement focuses on the changes in the impact measures directly linked to the technology project. Typical Level 4 measures include output, quality, costs, time, and customer satisfaction. At Level 5 (Return on Investment—the ultimate level of evaluation), the measurement compares the project's monetary benefits with the project's costs. The evaluation cycle is not complete until the Level 5 evaluation is conducted. As will be discussed later, however, not all evaluations will be taken to the ROI level.

Change, Quality, and Reengineering

The application of the ROI Methodology has increased because of the growing interest in organizational improvement, quality, and change projects, which have dominated organizations, particularly in North America, Europe, and Asia. Often, organizations embrace almost any trend or fad that appears on the horizon. Unfortunately, many of these efforts have not been successful and have turned out to be passing fads adopted in an attempt to improve the organization. The IT function is often caught in the middle of this activity, either by supporting the process with projects or actually coordinating the new process within these organizations. Although

ROI evaluation is an effective way to measure IT accountability, it has rarely been used in the past. A complete implementation of the process requires thorough needs assessment and significant planning. If these two elements are in place, unnecessary passing fads, doomed for failure, can be avoided. With the ROI Methodology in place, a new project that does not produce results will be exposed. Management will be aware of it early so that adjustments can be made.

Total Quality Management, Continuous Process Improvement, and Six Sigma have also brought increased attention to measurement issues. Today, organizations measure processes and outputs that were not previously measured, monitored, and reported. This focus has placed increased pressure on the IT and technology development function to develop measures of project success.

Restructuring and reengineering initiatives and the threat of outsourcing have caused IT executives to focus more directly on bottom-line issues. Many IT processes have been reengineered to align projects more closely with business needs and obtain maximum efficiencies in the IT system rollout/upgrade cycle. These change processes have brought increased attention to evaluation issues and have resulted in measuring the contribution of specific projects, including ROI.

Business Mindset of IT Managers

The business mindset of many current IT managers makes them place more emphasis on economic issues within the function. Today's IT manager is more aware of bottom-line issues in the organization and more knowledgeable about operational and financial concerns. This new business-minded manager often takes a business approach to IT and technology development, with ROI evaluation as part of the strategy.

ROI is a familiar term and concept for business managers, particularly those with business administration and management degrees. They have studied the ROI process in their academic preparation, where ROI is used to evaluate an equipment purchase, a new facility, or a new company. Therefore, they understand and appreciate ROI and are pleased to see the ROI Methodology applied to the evaluation of IT and technology development projects.

Accountability Trend

A persistent trend toward accountability in organizations has occurred around the globe. Every support function is attempting to show its worth by capturing the value that it adds to the organization. From the accountability perspective, the IT function should be no different from the other functions: It must show its contribution to the organization.

This accountability trend has developed a variety of measurement processes, sometimes causing much confusion for the potential user. As Figure 1-2 shows, many measurement possibilities have developed in recent years and have been offered to organizations as a recommended measurement of the process or scheme. Although this has created confusion, many organizations have migrated to the proven acceptance of ROI evaluation. Used for hundreds of years, and for the reasons outlined in this section, ROI analysis has become a preferred choice for IT and technology development practitioners to show the monetary payoff of technology investments.

Top Executive Requirement

ROI analysis is now taking on increased interest in the executive suite. Top executives who watched their IT budgets grow without

Figure 1-2. A Variety of Measurement Possibilities

appropriate accountability measures in place have become frustrated and, in an attempt to respond to the situation, have turned to the ROI. Top executives are now demanding return on investment calculations from departments and functions where they were not previously required. For years, IT and technology development managers convinced top executives that IT couldn't be measured, at least at the monetary contribution level. Yet, many executives are now aware that it can and is being measured in many organizations. Top executives are subsequently demanding the same accountability from their IT and technology functions.

The payoff of IT is becoming a conversation topic in top executive circles. The most critical component is holding IT accountable for the results of their strategic investments. Lacking such data, senior management develops budgets for their IT function based on blind faith that it will do *some* good and is inherently necessary for their organization. ROI analysis has been covered in many publications such as *Fortune*, *USA Today*, *Business Week*, *Harvard Business Review*, *The Wall Street Journal*, and *The Financial Times*. Executives have a never-ending desire to explore ROI analysis for their IT projects. It is not unusual for the majority of participants in an ROI workshop to attend only because it is required by the top executives, even in Europe, Africa, and Asia.

ROI CONCERNS

Although much progress has been made, the ROI Methodology is not without its share of problems and concerns. The mere presence of the process creates a dilemma for many organizations. When an organization embraces the concept and implements the process, the management team usually anxiously awaits results, only to be disappointed when they are not immediately available. For an ROI process to be useful, it must balance many issues such as feasibility, simplicity, credibility, and soundness. More specifically, three major audiences must be pleased with the ROI process to accept and use it:

- Technology project managers or consultants who design, develop, and deliver projects
- CIOs, senior managers, sponsors, and clients who initiate and support projects
- Researchers who need a credible process

IT Practitioners

For years, IT managers and consultants have assumed that the ROI of IT and technology projects could not be measured. When they examined a typical process, they found long formulas, complicated equations, and complex models that made ROI evaluation appear too confusing. With this perceived complexity, IT managers could visualize the tremendous effort required for data collection and analysis, and, more important, the increased cost necessary to make the process work. Because of these concerns, IT practitioners require an ROI evaluation process that is simple and easy to understand so that they can easily implement the steps and strategies. They also need a process that does not take too long to implement and will not consume too much precious staff time. Finally, practitioners need a process that is not too expensive. With competition for financial resources, a process that only requires a small portion of the IT budget is also needed. In summary, the ROI Methodology, from the perspective of the IT practitioner, has to save time, be user friendly, and be cost efficient.

Senior Managers, Sponsors, and Clients

Managers who must approve IT budgets, request IT projects, or live with the results of projects have a strong interest in developing the ROI of IT projects. They want a process that provides quantifiable results, using a method similar to the ROI formula applied to other types of investments. Senior managers have a never-ending desire to have it all come down to an ROI calculation. And, as do IT practitioners, they want a process that is simple and easy to understand. The assumptions made in the calculations and the methodology used in the process should reflect their point of reference, background, and level of understanding. They do not want, or need, a string of formulas, charts, and complicated models. Instead, they need a process that they can explain to others, if necessary. More important, they need a process with which they can identify, one that is sound and realistic enough to earn their confidence.

Researchers

Researchers will only support a process that stands up to their close examination. Researchers usually insist that models, formulas, assumptions, and theories are sound and based on commonly accepted practices. They also want a process that produces accurate values and consistent outcomes. If estimates are necessary, researchers want a process that provides the most accuracy within the constraints of the situation, recognizing that adjustments need to be made when there is uncertainty in the process. The challenge is to develop acceptable requirements for an ROI process that will satisfy researchers and, at the same time, please practitioners and senior managers. Sound impossible? Maybe not.

Criteria for an Effective ROI Process

To satisfy the needs of the three critical groups just described, the ROI process must meet several requirements. These are the 11 essential criteria for an effective ROI process:

1. The ROI process must be **simple,** void of complex formulas, lengthy equations, and complicated methodologies. Most ROI model attempts have failed with this requirement. In an effort to obtain statistical perfection and use too many theories, some ROI models have become too complex to understand and use. Therefore, they have not been implemented.
2. The ROI process must be **economical** and easily implemented. The process should become a routine part of IT and technology development without requiring significant additional resources. Sampling for ROI calculations and early planning for ROI evaluations are often necessary to make progress without adding new staff.
3. The assumptions, methodology, and techniques must be **credible.** Logical, methodical steps are needed to earn the respect of technology consultants, senior managers, and researchers. This requires a practical approach for the process.
4. From a research perspective, the ROI process must be **theoretically sound** and based on generally accepted practices. Unfortunately, this requirement can lead to an extensive, complicated process. Ideally, the process must strike a balance between maintaining a practical and sensible approach *and* a sound and theoretical basis. This is perhaps one of the greatest challenges to those who have developed ROI models.

5. The ROI process must **account for other factors** that may have influenced output variables. One of the most often overlooked issues—isolating the influence of the IT project—is necessary to build credibility and accuracy within the process. The ROI process should pinpoint the contribution of the IT project when compared to the other influences.

6. The ROI process must be appropriate with a **variety of IT projects**. Ideally, the process must be applicable to all types of IT projects, such as CRM, ERP, e-commerce, contact center automation, and other major process change and automation initiatives.

7. The ROI process must have the **flexibility** to be applied on a preproject basis as well as a postproject basis. In some situations, an estimate of the ROI is required before the actual project is developed. Ideally, the process should be able to adjust to a range of potential timeframes.

8. The ROI process must be **applicable for all types of data**, including hard data—which are typically represented as output, quality, costs, and time—*and* soft data—which include job satisfaction, customer satisfaction, absenteeism, turnover, grievances, and complaints.

9. The ROI process must **include the costs of the project**. The ultimate level of evaluation is to compare the benefits with the costs. Although the term *ROI* has been loosely used to express any benefit of IT, an acceptable ROI formula must include costs. Omitting or underestimating costs will only destroy the credibility of the ROI values.

10. The actual calculation must use an **acceptable ROI formula**. This is often the benefit-cost ratio (BCR) or the ROI calculation, expressed as a percent. These formulas compare the actual expenditures for the project with the monetary benefits gained from the project.

11. Finally, the ROI process must have a successful **track record** in a variety of applications. In far too many situations, models are created but never successfully applied. An effective ROI process should withstand the wear and tear of implementation and should get the results expected.

Because these criteria are considered essential, an ROI methodology should meet the vast majority of, if not all, the criteria. The bad news is that most ROI processes do not meet these criteria but the good news is that the ROI Methodology does.

Definitions and Formulas

Although definitions and formulas are presented throughout this book, several need defining early. The term *information technology (IT)* is used throughout the book to refer to a company's infrastructure focused (internal) technology organization. The term *technology development* used throughout this book describes organizations that have a technology-based product development focus. These organizations may have software or technology-related hardware as part of their enterprise product offering. Technology development projects in this context will likely have a condensed ROI timeframe because engineers creating the software or hardware (assuming the products are accepted by the marketplace) will provide a shorter ROI evaluation timeframe due to revenue being generated to offset their development costs.

It is no wonder that Microsoft has a greater than 95 percent margin on its Windows XP operating system. Although the company invested over a billion dollars creating the latest version of its operating system, Microsoft has experienced nothing short of an astronomical return. This will probably not be the case for most IT infrastructure projects, unless they happen to deploy e-commerce technologies that dramatically increase the company's revenue and drastically decrease costs. Although this has happened in many companies that we have studied, it is not expected for most technology initiatives. The good news, however, is that successful ROI evaluations have been conducted for projects with varying ROI payback periods and project returns.

The term *project* is used to reflect a software solution, hardware upgrade, enterprise system rollout, system upgrade, or any other project or initiative that is worthy of ROI analysis. In reality, IT is a dynamic and ongoing function within an organization and not a one-time event or project. However, because of the common use of the term, *project* will be used throughout the book to reflect the specific defined project (e.g., Enterprise SalesForce.com rollout), which has a specific, organization-wide initiative wrapped around it and a relatively well-defined price tag.

The term *participant* is used to refer to the individual involved in the IT project or technology development initiative. The term *sponsor* is the individual or group who initiates, approves, and supports the project or evaluation. Usually a part of senior management, this individual cares about the outcome of the ROI evaluation and is sometimes labeled the *client*.

Finally, the term *CEO* is used to refer to the top executive at a specific organizational entity. The CEO could be the chief administrator, managing director, division president, major operations executive, or other top official, and often reflects the most senior management of the organization in which the project is implemented.

Two final definitions offered in this chapter are the basic formula for return on investment and payback period. Two common formulas for ROI are offered: benefit-cost ratio (BCR) and ROI:

$$BCR = \frac{\text{Project Benefits}}{\text{Project Costs}}$$

$$ROI\,(\%) = \frac{\text{Net Project Benefits}}{\text{Project Costs}} \times 100$$

The BCR uses the total benefits and costs. In the ROI formula, the costs are subtracted from the total benefits to produce net benefits that are then divided by the costs. For example, a call center automation project at Stone Technologies (name changed to protect the innocent) produced benefits of $3,296,977 with a cost of $1,116,291. Therefore, the benefit-cost ratio is

$$BCR = \frac{\$3,296,977}{\$1,116,291} = 2.95\,(\text{or } 2.95:1)$$

As this calculation shows, for every $1 invested, $2.95 in benefits were returned. In this example, net benefits are $3,296,977 − $1,116,291 = $2,180,616. Therefore, the ROI is

$$BCR = \frac{\$2,180,616}{\$1,116,291} \times 100 = 195\%$$

This means that for each $1 invested in the project, there is a return of $1.95 in *net* benefits after costs are covered. The benefits are usually expressed as annual benefits, representing the amount saved or gained for a complete year after project completion. Although the benefits may continue after the first year if the project has long-term effects, the impact usually diminishes and is omitted from calculations. This conservative approach is used throughout the application of the ROI Methodology in this book.

Another ROI related term that will be used in this book is *payback period*. The payback period is the time it takes for the benefits returned to equal the initial project costs. This is one of the key measures of risk for a technology initiative. Given the pace of evolving technologies, the payback period should be less than one year. Some research firms use Cumulative ROI, or *cROI*. This computation takes the sum of returns over a three-year period, which often drastically overstates ROI and will not be used in this book.

Barriers to ROI Methodology Implementation

Although progress has been made in the implementation of the ROI Methodology, significant barriers can inhibit its implementation. Some of these barriers are realistic, whereas others are myths based on false perceptions. Each barrier is briefly described in this section.

Costs and Time

The ROI process will add additional costs and time to the evaluation of projects, although the added amount will not be excessive. It is possible this barrier alone stops many ROI implementations early in the process. A comprehensive ROI process can be implemented for 3 percent to 5 percent of the overall IT budget. The additional investment in ROI could perhaps be offset by the additional results achieved from these projects and the elimination of unproductive or unprofitable projects.

Lack of Skills and Orientation of IT Staff

Many IT and technology development staff members do not understand the ROI Methodology, nor do they have the basic skills necessary to apply the process within the scope of their responsibilities. Measurement and evaluation is not usually part of the job preparation. Also, the typical IT project does not focus on data-supported results but more on technology, adoption-based outcomes. Staff members attempt to measure results by measuring increased productivity surrounding a new technology deployment. Due to this, a tremendous barrier to implementation is the overall orientation, attitude change, and education of the IT staff.

Faulty Needs Assessment

Many IT projects do not have an adequate needs assessment. Some projects have been implemented for the wrong reasons based on management requests or efforts to chase a popular fad or trend in the industry. If the project is not needed, the benefits from the project will be minimal, and an ROI calculation for an unnecessary project will likely yield a negative value. This is a real barrier for many projects.

Fear

Some IT departments do not pursue ROI evaluation because of a fear of failure or fear of the unknown. Fear of failure appears in many ways. Designers, engineers, developers, and project owners may be concerned about the consequences of a negative ROI. They fear that the ROI will be a performance evaluation tool instead of a process improvement tool. The ROI process will also stir up the traditional fear of change. This fear, often based on unrealistic assumptions and a lack of knowledge, becomes another barrier to many ROI Methodology implementations.

Discipline and Planning

A successful ROI implementation requires planning and a disciplined approach for the process to stay on track. Implementation schedules, evaluation targets, ROI analysis plans, measurement and evaluation policies, and follow-up schedules are required. The IT staff may not have enough discipline and determination to remain on course. This can become a barrier, particularly when there are no immediate pressures to measure the return. If the senior management group does not require an ROI evaluation, the IT staff may not allocate time for planning and coordination. Other pressures and priorities often eat into the time necessary for ROI implementation. Only a carefully planned implementation will be successful.

False Assumptions

Many IT staff members have false assumptions about the ROI Methodology that keep them from attempting the process. Some of these assumptions are:

- The impact of an IT project cannot be accurately calculated.
- Managers do not want to see the results of IT and technology development projects expressed in monetary values.
- If the CEO does not ask for the ROI, he or she does not expect it.
- "I have a professional, competent staff. Therefore, I do not have to justify the effectiveness of our projects."
- The IT process is a complex, but necessary, activity. Therefore, it should not be subjected to an accountability process.

These false assumptions form barriers that impede the implementation of the ROI Methodology.

Benefits of the ROI Methodology

Although the benefits of adopting the ROI Methodology may appear to be obvious, several distinct and important benefits can be derived from the implementation of the ROI Methodology in an organization.

Measure Contribution

It is the most accurate, credible, and widely used process to show the impact of IT projects. The IT staff will know the specific contribution from a select number of projects. The ROI will determine if the benefits of the project, expressed in monetary values, outweighed the costs. It will determine if the project made a contribution to the organization and if it was, indeed, a good investment.

Set Priorities

Calculating the ROI in different areas will determine the projects that contribute the most to the organization, allowing priorities to be established for high-impact IT projects. Successful projects can be expanded into other areas—if the same need is present—ahead of other projects. Inefficient projects can be redesigned and redeployed.

Ineffective projects may be discontinued if they cannot be redesigned successfully.

Focus on Results

The ROI Methodology is a results-based process that focuses on results with all projects, even for those not targeted for an ROI calculation. The process requires system architects, software engineers, network and system administrators, and the technology project manager to concentrate on measurable objectives: what the project is attempting to accomplish. Therefore, this process has the added benefit of improving the effectiveness of all IT projects.

Earn the Respect of Senior Executives and Sponsor

Calculating the ROI of a project is one of the best ways to earn the respect of the senior management team and the sponsor. Senior executives have a never-ending desire to see ROI and will appreciate the efforts to connect IT to business impact and show the actual monetary value of projects. It makes them feel comfor with the process and makes their decisions easier. Sponsors see the ROI as a breath of fresh air. With it, they actually see the value of the IT, building confidence about the initial decision to go with the process.

Alter Management Perceptions of IT

The ROI Methodology, when applied consistently and comprehensively, can convince the management group that IT is an investment and not an expense. Managers will see that the IT function is making a viable contribution to their objectives, increasing the respect for the function. This is an important step in building a partnership with management and increasing management support for IT. These key benefits, inherent with almost any type of impact evaluation process, make the ROI Methodology an attractive process for the IT function within any organization.

ROI BEST PRACTICES

Continuing progress with implementations of the ROI Methodology has provided an opportunity to determine if specific strategies are common among organizations that implement the process. Several common strategies that are considered best practices for measurement and evaluation have emerged. Whether they meet the test to be labeled "best practice" will never be known, since labeling any practice a "best practice is risky." Although the following strategies are presented as a comprehensive framework, few organizations have adopted all of them. However, parts of the strategies exist in one way or another in each of the hundreds of organizations involved in ROI certification, which is discussed in Chapter 12.

Evaluation Targets

Recognizing the complexity of moving up the chain of evaluation levels, as described in Table 1-4, some organizations attempt to manage the process by setting targets for each level. A target for an evaluation level is the percent of IT projects measured at that level. Repeat sessions of the same project are counted in the total. For example, at Level 1 (Reaction), organizations achieve a high level of activity because, analysis at this level is easy. Many organizations require that 100 percent of projects are evaluated at Level 1. In these situations, a questionnaire is administered at the end of each project. Level 2 (Learning) is another relatively easy level to measure, and the target is high, usually in the 50 to 70 percent range. This target depends on the organization, based on the nature and type of projects. At Level 3 (Application) the percent drops because of the time and expense of conducting follow-up evaluations. Targets in the range of 25 to 35 percent are common. Targets for Level 4 (Impact) and Level 5 (ROI) are relatively small, because of the time and costs involved. Common targets are 10 percent for Level 4 and 5 percent for Level 5. An example of evaluation targets established for a large telecommunications company is shown in Table 1-5. In this example, half the Level 4 evaluations are taken to Level 5 (ROI).

Establishing evaluation targets has two major advantages. First, the process provides objectives for the IT staff to clearly measure accountability progress for all projects or any segment of the IT process. Second, adopting targets also focuses more attention on the accountability process, communicating a strong message about the extent of commitment to measurement and evaluation.

Micro-Level Evaluation

The evaluation of an entire IT function—such as network administration, database administration, systems administration, or systems

Table 1-5
Evaluation Targets for a Large Telecommunications Company

Level	Percent Evaluated
Level 1 Reaction and Perceived Value	100
Level 2 Learning and Confidence	60
Level 3 Application and Implementation	30
Level 4 Impact and Consequences	10
Level 5 Return on Investment	5

architecture—is difficult. The ROI Methodology is more effective when applied, at the micro level, to one project that can be linked to a direct payoff. In situations where a series of smaller projects with common objectives must be completed before the objectives are met, an evaluation of the series of projects may be appropriate. For this reason, ROI evaluation should be considered as a micro-level activity that usually focuses on a single project or a few tightly integrated projects. This decision to evaluate several projects—or just one project—should include consideration of objectives of the projects, timing of the projects, and cohesiveness of the series. Attempting to evaluate a group of projects conducted over a long period becomes difficult. The cause and effect relationship becomes more confusing and complex.

Data Collection Methods

Best-practice companies use a variety of approaches to collect evaluation data. They do not become aligned with one or two practices that dominate data collection, regardless of the situation. They recognize that each project, setting, and situation is different, and, as a result, different techniques are needed to collect the data. Interviews, focus groups, and questionnaires work well in some situations. In others, action plans, performance contracts, and performance monitoring are needed to determine the specific impact of the project. These organizations deliberately match the data collection method with the project, following a set of criteria developed internally.

Isolating the Effects of IT

One of the most critical elements of the ROI Methodology is isolating the impact of the IT project from other influences that may have occurred during the same timeframe as the project. Best-practice organizations recognize that many factors affect business impact measures. Although IT is implemented in harmony with other systems and processes, sometimes there is a need to know the direct contribution of IT projects, particularly when different process owners are involved. Because of this, after a project is conducted, IT must claim only part of the credit for improved performance.

When an ROI calculation is planned, best-practice organizations attempt to use one or more methods to isolate the effects of IT. They go beyond the typical use of a control group arrangement, which has set the standard for this process for many years. They explore the use of a variety of other techniques to arrive at a realistic, credible estimate of IT's impact on output measures.

Sampling for ROI Calculations

Because of the resources required for the process, most IT projects do not include ROI calculations. Therefore, organizations must determine the appropriate level of ROI evaluation. There is no prescribed formula, and the number of ROI evaluations depends on many variables, including the following:

- Staff expertise on evaluation
- The nature and type of IT projects
- Resources that can be allocated to the process
- Support from management for IT and technology development
- The organization's commitment to measurement and evaluation
- Pressure from others to show ROI calculations

Other variables specific to the organization may enter the process. Rarely do organizations use statistical sampling when selecting sample projects targeted for ROI calculations. For most, this approach represents far too many calculations and too much analysis. Using a practical approach, most organizations settle on evaluating one or two of their most significant technology initiatives. Still others select a project from each of its major IT segments. For example, in a large financial institution with multiple IT-focused functions (e-commerce, security, infrastructure), a project is selected each year from each function for an ROI calculation. For organizations that are implementing the ROI Methodology for the first time, the recommendation is that only one or two projects be selected for an initial calculation as a learning process.

Although being statistically sound in the approach to sampling is important, it is more important to consider a trade-off between the resources available and the level of activity management will accept for ROI calculations. The primary objective of an ROI calculation is not only to convince the IT staff that the process works but to show others (usually senior management) that IT makes a difference to the bottom line. Therefore, the sampling plan should be developed with the input and approval of senior management. In the final analysis, the selection process should yield a level of sampling so that senior management is comfortable with its accountability assessment of the IT function.

Converting Project Results to Monetary Values

Because the specific return on investment is needed, business impact data must be converted to monetary benefits. Best-practice organizations are not content to show that a project improved productivity, enhanced quality, reduced defects, or increased customer satisfaction. They convert these data items to monetary units so that the benefits can be compared to the costs resulting in the ROI. These organizations take an extra step to develop a realistic value for these data items. For hard data items, such as productivity, quality, and time, the process is relatively easy. However, for soft data items, such as removal of software defects, system uptime, and reduced system maintenance, the process is more difficult. Yet, techniques are available and are used to make these conversions as accurate as possible.

FINAL THOUGHTS

Although there is almost universal agreement that more attention is needed on developing the ROI for IT and technology development projects, it is promising to note the tremendous success of the ROI Methodology. Its use is expanding. Its payoff is huge. The approaches, strategies, and techniques are not complex and can be useful in many settings. The combined and persistent efforts of consultants, practitioners, and researchers will continue to refine the techniques and create successful applications.

References

Accenture. *IT Investing for High Performance* (Executive Summary), 2005.

Sibbet, D. "75 Years of Management Ideas and Practice, 1922–1997," *Harvard Business Review*, Supplement, 1997.

CHAPTER 2

The ROI Model: History and Background

The calculation of the return on investment follows the basic model illustrated in Figure 2-1, in which a potentially complicated process is simplified with sequential steps. The ROI model provides a systematic approach to ROI calculations. A step-by-step approach keeps the process manageable so that users can address one issue at a time. Applying the model provides consistency from one ROI calculation to another. This chapter describes the development of the complete ROI Methodology and discusses each step of the model.

BUILDING THE ROI METHODOLOGY

Building a comprehensive measurement and evaluation process is like a puzzle with the pieces developed and put into place over time. Figure 2-2 depicts this puzzle and the pieces required to build a comprehensive measurement and evaluation process. The first building block is the selection of *an evaluation framework*, which is a categorization of data. The balanced scorecard process (Kaplan & Norton, 1996) or the four levels of evaluation developed by Kirkpatrick (1975) offer the starting point for such a framework. The framework selected for the process presented here is a modification of Kirkpatrick's four levels and includes a fifth level: return on investment.

A major building block, the ROI process model (presented in Figure 2-1), is necessary to show how data are collected, processed, analyzed, and reported to various target audiences. This process model ensures that appropriate techniques and procedures are consistently used to address almost any situation.

A third building block is the development of operating standards. These standards help ensure that the results of the study are stable

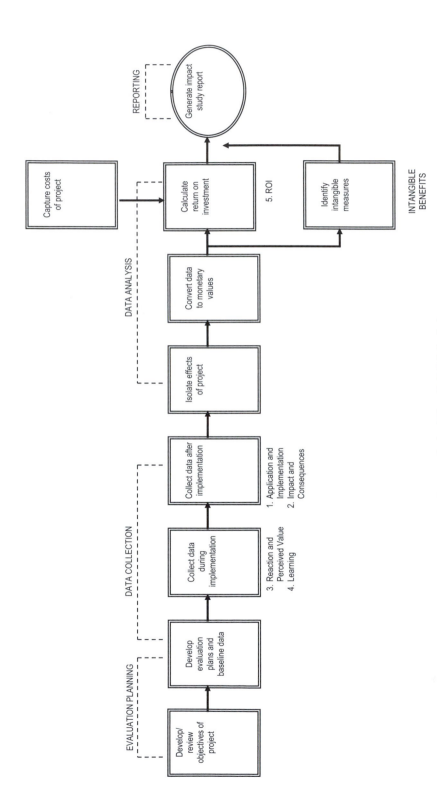

Figure 2-1. The ROI Model

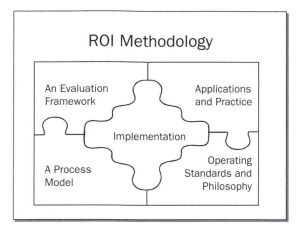

Figure 2-2. ROI: The Basic Elements

and not influenced by the individual conducting the study. Replication is critical for the credibility of an evaluation process. The use of operating standards allows for replication, so if more than one individual evaluates a specific project, the results are the same. In the ROI Methodology, the operating standards are called the 12 Guiding Principles and will be detailed later in this chapter.

Next, appropriate attention must be given to implementation issues, as the ROI Methodology becomes a routine part of IT initiatives. Several issues must be addressed involving skills, communication, roles, responsibilities, plans, and strategies.

Finally, there must be successful applications and practices that describe the implementation of the process within the organization, the value that a comprehensive measurement and evaluation process brings to the organization, and the impact that the specific project evaluated has on the organization. Although referring to studies from other organizations is helpful, having studies developed directly within the organization is more useful and more convincing.

The remainder of this chapter focuses on the individual building blocks of the ROI Methodology.

An Evaluation Framework

The concept of different levels of evaluation is both helpful and instructive for understanding how the return on investment is calculated. Table 2-1 revisits the five levels of evaluation presented in the

Table 2-1
The Five Levels of Evaluation

	Level—Chain of Impact	Measurement Focus	Value of Information	Customer Focus
1	Reaction and Perceived Value	Measures participants' reactions to the technology project	Low	Consumer
2	Learning and Confidence	Measures changes in knowledge, skills, and attitudes related to the technology		
3	Application and Implementation	Measures changes in on-the-job action and progress with planned actions		
4	Impact and Consequences	Measures changes in business impact variables		
5	Return on Investment	Compares project monetary benefits to the project costs	High	Client

Customers: Consumers = The customers who are actively involved in the IT project.
Client = The customers who fund, support, and approve the IT project.

previous chapter. It serves as the framework for evaluation, defining the types of data collected, the sequence of collection, and the approximate timing.

Level 1 (Reaction and Perceived Value) measures the reactions to the technology from project participants. Almost all organizations evaluate at Level 1, usually with a questionnaire. Although this level of evaluation is important as a customer satisfaction measure, a favorable reaction does not ensure that participants have learned new skills or knowledge.

Level 2 (Learning and Confidence) focuses on what participants learned about the technology during the project, using tests, skill practices, simulations, group evaluations, and other assessment tools. A learning check is helpful to ensure that participants have absorbed the technology, know how to use it properly, and are confident that they can apply it on the job. However, a positive measure at this level does not guarantee that what is learned will be applied on the job. The literature is laced with studies showing the failure of learning to be transferred to the job (Broad, 1997).

At Level 3 (Application and Implementation), a variety of follow-up methods are used to determine whether participants applied to their jobs what they learned. The usage of technology is an important measures at Level 3. Although Level 3 evaluation is important to gauge the success of the application of a project, it still does not guarantee that a positive business impact will occur in the organization.

Level 4 (Impact and Consequences) measures focus on the actual results achieved by project participants as they successfully apply what they have learned. Typical Level 4 measures include output, quality, costs, time, and customer satisfaction. Although the project may produce a measurable business impact, a concern might exist that the project costs too much.

Level 5 (Return on Investment), the ultimate level of evaluation, compares the monetary benefits from the project with the project costs. Although the ROI can be expressed in several ways, it is usually presented as a percentage or benefit-cost ratio. The evaluation chain of impact, illustrated in Figure 2-1, is not complete until the Level 5 (ROI) evaluation is developed, although not all projects need to be evaluated to this level.

Although some IT organizations conduct evaluations to measure satisfaction or user adoption, very few conduct evaluations to the ROI level. Perhaps the best explanation for this is that many consider ROI evaluation to be a difficult and expensive process. When business results and ROI are desired, it is also important to evaluate the other levels. A chain of impact should occur through the levels as the skills and knowledge learned (Level 2) are applied on the job (Level 3) to produce business impact (Level 4). If measurements are not taken at each level, concluding that the results achieved were actually a result of the project is difficult. Because of this, when a Level 5 evaluation is planned, evaluation must be conducted at all levels.

Another consideration is that, from the perspective of the client, the value of information increases with movement up the chain of impact. The ROI Methodology is a client-centered process that meets the data needs for the individuals who initiate, approve, and sponsor the project.

The ROI Model

The ROI model, shown in Figure 2-1, is a step-by-step approach for developing the ROI and the other measures in the ROI Methodology. Each major part of the model is described in this section.

Evaluation Planning

Several pieces of the evaluation puzzle must be explained when developing the evaluation plan for an ROI evaluation. Three specific elements are important to a successful evaluation and are outlined in this section.

Purpose

Although evaluation is usually undertaken to improve the overall IT development and delivery process, several distinct purposes can be identified:

- Improve the quality of IT implementation and delivery
- Determine whether a project is accomplishing its objectives
- Identify the strengths and weaknesses in the technology development process
- Determine the benefit-cost analysis of an IT project
- Assist in the internal marketing efforts for future IT initiatives
- Determine whether the project met the needs of the users
- Establish a database, which can assist in making quantitative decisions about projects
- Establish priorities for funding

Although there are other purposes of evaluation, these are the most important ones (Russ-Eft & Preskill, 2001). Evaluation purposes should be considered prior to developing the evaluation plan because the purposes will often determine the scope of the evaluation, the types of instruments used, and the type of data collected. For example, when an ROI calculation is planned, one of the purposes would be to compare the benefits and costs of the project. This purpose has implications for the type of data collected (hard data), type of data collection method (performance monitoring), type of analysis (thorough), and the communication medium for the results (formal evaluation report). For most projects, multiple evaluation purposes are pursued.

Feasibility

An important consideration in planning the ROI evaluation is to determine the appropriate levels for evaluation. Some evaluations will stop at Level 3, where a detailed report will determine the extent to which participants are using what they have learned. Others will be evaluated at Level 4 (Impact), where the consequences of their on-the-job application are monitored. A Level 4 evaluation will examine hard and soft data measures directly linked to the project. This level of evaluation requires that the impact of the project be isolated from other influences. Finally, if the ROI calculation is needed, two additional steps are required; (1) impact data must be converted to monetary values, and (2) the costs of the project must be captured so that the ROI can be calculated. Only a few projects should be evaluated at this level.

During the planning stage, the feasibility for a Level 4 or 5 evaluation should be examined. The following relevant questions must be addressed:

- What specific measures have been influenced by this project?
- Are those measures readily available?
- Can the effect of the project on those measures be isolated?
- Are the costs of the project readily available?
- Will it be practical and feasible to discuss costs?
- Can the impact data be converted to monetary values?
- Is the actual ROI needed?

These and other questions are important to examine during the planning process to ensure that the evaluation is appropriate for the project. Each issue will be examined in more detail as the ROI Methodology is explained.

Objectives of Projects

IT and technology development projects are evaluated at different levels, as described earlier. Corresponding to each level of evaluation are levels of objectives:

- Reaction objectives (1)
- Learning objectives (2)
- Application objectives (3)
- Impact objectives (4)
- ROI objectives (5)

Before the ROI evaluation begins, the project objectives must be developed. The objectives help determine the depth of the evaluation, meaning that they determine to what level the project will be evaluated. Historically, learning objectives are routinely developed. Application and impact objectives are not always in place, but they are necessary for proper focus on results.

Project objectives link directly to the front-end analysis. As shown in Figure 2-3, after the business need is determined, impact objectives (4), the needs analysis identifies the requirements for the IT initiative, application objectives (3), necessary to meet the business need. The skills and knowledge, learning objectives (2), needed to achieve the desired performance are identified, taking into consideration the preferences, reaction objectives (1), for the technology solution to improve efficiency, collaboration, and user adoption. In the ROI Methodology, developing objectives at each level is necessary to ensure project success and link those objectives to levels of evaluation.

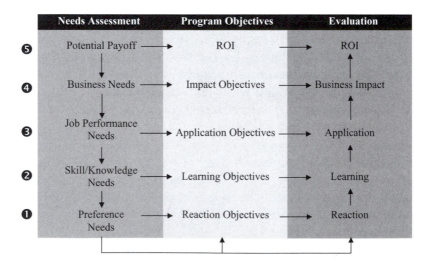

(Adapted from: Phillips, Jack J., Ron Stone, and Patricia P. Phillips. 2001. *The Human Resources Scorecard: Measuring the Return on Investment.* Boston, MA: Butterworth-Heinemann.)

Figure 2-3. Linking Needs, Objectives, and Evaluation

As Figure 2-3 illustrates, participant reaction objectives link to Level 1 evaluation, learning objectives link to Level 2 evaluation, application objectives link to Level 3 evaluation, impact objectives link to Level 4 evaluation, and ROI objectives link to the ROI outcome. If objectives at any level are not available, they have to be developed using input from several groups such as business analysts, project managers, system engineers, and technical supervisors.

Tied closely to setting objectives is the timing of data collection. In some cases, pre-project measurements are taken to compare with post-project measures, and, in some cases, multiple measures are taken. In other situations, pre-project measurements are not available and specific post-project follow-ups are still administered. The important issue in this part of the process is to determine the timing for the follow-up evaluation. For example, a major airline initiated data collection for an evaluation three months after an enterprise-wide customer relationship management system rollout. In another example, an Australian company needed three years to measure the payback for a massive custom development initiative to retire a host of legacy systems, which were intertwined with their core business processes. For most IT and technology development initiatives, a post-project follow-up should be conducted in three to six months.

Evaluation Plans

To complete the planning process, three simple planning documents are developed: the data collection plan, the ROI analysis plan, and the project plan. These documents should be completed before the evaluation is implemented—ideally, *before* the project is designed or developed. Appropriate, up-front attention will save much time later when data are actually collected.

Data Collection Plan

Figure 2-4 shows a completed data collection plan for a Salesforce automation rollout initiative. An ROI calculation was planned for a pilot of three groups.

This document provides a place for the major elements and issues regarding collecting data for each level of evaluation. Broad objectives are appropriate for planning. Specific, detailed objectives are developed later, before the project is designed. The "measures" column defines the specific measure; the "method" describes the

Program: Salesforce Automation Rollout & Training Responsibility: P. Phillips_____Date:_____

Level	Broad Program Objectives	Measures	Data Collection Method and Instruments	Data Sources	Timing	Responsibilities
❶	**Reaction Perceived Value** • Positive reaction — four out of five • Action items	• A 1–5 rating on a composite of five measures • Yes or No	• Questionnaire	• Participant	• End of project (3rd day)	• Project learning
❷	**Learning and Confidence** • Learn to use five skills	• Pass or fail on skill practice	• Observation of skill practice by facilitator	• Project leader	• Second day of project	• Project leader
❸	**Application and Implementation** • Initial use of five skills • At least 50% of participants use all skills with every customer	• Verbal feedback • 5th item checked on a 1–5 scale	• Follow-up session • Follow-up questionnaire	• Participant • Participant	• Three weeks after second day • Three months after project	• Project leader • Local manager
❹	**Impact and Consequences** • Sales Increase	• Weekly average sales per sales associate	• Business performance monitoring	• Company records	• Three months after project	• Local manager
❺	**ROI** • 50%	Comments: The ROI objective was set at a high value because of the store sample size; the executives wanted convincing data.				

Figure 2-4. Sample Data Collection Plan

technique used to collect the data; the "source" of the data is identified; the "timing" indicates when the data are collected; and the "responsibilities" column identifies who will collect the data.

The objectives for Level 1 usually include positive reactions to the IT project. If it is an ongoing project, another category, *suggested improvements*, may be included. Reaction is typically measured on a five-point scale, collected by questionnaires directly from participants, and administered by the project leader.

Level 2 evaluation focuses on the measures of learning. The specific objectives include those areas where participants are expected to change knowledge, skills, or attitudes. The measure is a pass/fail as observed by the project leader. The method of assessing the participants' absorption of the new technology is the hands-on skills and navigation observed by the project leader (source). The timing for Level 2 evaluation is usually during or at the end of the project, and the responsibility usually rests with the project leader.

For Level 3 evaluation, the objectives represent broad areas of project application, including significant on-the-job activities that should follow application. The evaluation method usually includes one post-project method, which will be described later, and is usually conducted weeks or months after project completion. Because responsibilities are often shared among several groups—including the IT and technology development staff, system trainers, business analysts, or technical managers—clarifying responsibilities early in the process is critical.

For Level 4 evaluation, objectives focus on business impact variables influenced by the project. The objectives may include the way in which each item is measured. If not, the measure is defined in the measures column. For example, if one of the objectives was to improve quality within a software development process, a specific measure would indicate how that quality is quantified, such as bugs per thousand lines of code written, usually measured by the quality assurance and testing function. The preferred evaluation method is business performance monitoring. However, other methods, such as action planning, may be appropriate. The timing of data collection depends on how quickly participants generate a sustained business impact. It is usually a matter of months after some IT rollouts. The participants, business analysts, division IT coordinators, or perhaps, an external evaluator may be responsible for Level 4 data collection in this case.

The ROI objective is determined, if appropriate. This value, most commonly expressed as a percent, defines the minimum acceptable ROI for the project. The project sponsor or the individual requesting the impact study usually provides the value. For the Salesforce automation training, the project sponsor set the ROI objective at 50 percent.

The data collection plan is an important part of the evaluation strategy and should be completed prior to moving forward with the IT project. For existing IT projects, the plan is completed before pursuing the ROI evaluation. The plan provides a clear direction of what type of data will be collected, how it will be collected, who will provide the data, when it will be collected, and who will collect it.

ROI Analysis Plan

Figure 2-5 shows a completed ROI analysis plan for the Salesforce automation training and rollout project. This planning document is the continuation of the data collection plan presented in Figure 2-4 and captures information on several key items that are required for developing the ROI calculation. In the first column, significant data items are listed, usually Level 4 (Impact), data, but in some cases could include Level 3 items. These items will be used in the ROI analysis. The method to isolate the effect of IT is listed next to each data item in the second column. In most cases, the method will be

Program: <u>Salesforce Automation Rollout & Training</u> Responsibility: <u>P. Phillips</u>   Date:_____

Data Items	Methods of Isolating the Effects of the Program	Methods of Converting Data	Cost Categories	Intangible Benefits	Communication Targets	Other Influences and Issues
• Weekly sales per associate	• Control group analysis • Participant estimates	• Direct conversion using profit contribution	• Facilitation fees • Project materials • Software (prorated) • Meals and refreshments • Facilities • Participant salaries and benefits • Cost of coordination • Evaluation	• Customer satisfaction • Employee satisfaction	• Project participants • Technology managers • Business Analysts • Senior Executives • Project staff: coordinators, designers, and managers	• Must have job coverage during training • No communication with control group

Figure 2-5. Sample ROI Analysis Plan

the same for each data item, but there could be variations. For example, if no historical data are available for one data item, then trend line analysis is not possible for that item, although it may be appropriate for other items. The method of converting data to monetary values is included in the third column.

The cost categories that will be captured for the IT project are outlined in the fourth column. Instructions about how certain costs are prorated should be noted here. Normally, the cost categories will be consistent from one project to another. However, a specific cost that is unique to the project should also be noted. The intangible benefits expected from this project are outlined in the fifth column. This list is generated from discussions about the project with sponsors and subject matter experts. Communication targets are outlined in the sixth column. Although many groups should receive the information, these four must receive the results of an ROI analysis:

1. Senior management group (sponsor)
2. Participants' managers
3. Project participants
4. IT and technology development staff

Finally, other issues or events that might influence project implementation should be highlighted in the last column. Typical items include the capability of the participants, the degree of access to data sources, and unique data analysis issues. The ROI analysis plan and the data collection plan provide detailed information on the ROI evaluation, illustrating how the process will develop from beginning to end.

Project Plan

The final plan developed for the evaluation planning phase is a project plan. A project plan consists of a description of the project and brief details about it, such as project goals, system users affected, project complexity, and scope. It also shows the implementation timeline of the project, beginning with the planning of the study to the last communication of the results. This plan becomes an operational tool and is used to keep the project on track. Sometimes, the end date drives the entire planning process. For example, a senior executive may request that the data surrounding the evaluation be developed and presented to the senior team on a particular date. With that ending point, all the other dates are added. Any appropriate project-planning tool can be used to develop the plan.

Collectively, these three planning documents (the data collection plan, the ROI analysis plan, and the project plan) provide the direction necessary for the ROI evaluation. Most of the decisions regarding the process are made as these planning tools are developed. The remainder of the project becomes a methodical, systematic process of implementing the plans. Developing these plans is a crucial step in the ROI Methodology, where valuable time allocated to this process saves precious time later.

Data Collection

Data collection is central to the ROI Methodology. Both hard data (representing output, quality, cost, and time) and soft data (user adoption and satisfaction) are collected. Data are collected using a variety of methods, including the following:

- **Surveys** are administered to determine the degrees to which participants are satisfied with the project, have learned skills and knowledge, and have used various aspects of the project. Survey responses are often developed on a sliding scale and usually represent perception data. Surveys are useful for collecting data at Levels 1, 2, and 3.
- **Questionnaires** are usually more detailed than surveys and can be used to uncover a wide variety of data. Participants provide responses to several types of open-ended and forced-response questions. Questionnaires can be used to capture data at Levels 1, 2, 3, and 4.

- **Tests** are conducted to measure changes in knowledge and skills (Level 2). Tests come in a wide variety of formal (criterion-referenced tests, performance tests, simulations, and skill practices) and informal (facilitation assessment, self assessment, and team assessment) methods.
- On-the-job **observation** captures actual application and use. Observations are particularly useful in sales and customer-service focused IT rollouts and are more effective when the observer is either invisible or transparent. Observations are appropriate for collecting Level 3 data.
- **Interviews** are conducted with participants to determine the extent to which learning has been used on-the-job. Interviews allow for probing to uncover specific applications and are usually most appropriate for collecting Level 3 data but can be used to collect data at Levels 1 and 2.
- **Focus groups** are conducted to determine the degree to which participants have applied the new technology to their job functions. Focus groups are used for collecting Level 3 data.
- **Action plans and project assignments** are developed by participants during the IT project and are implemented on the job after the project is completed. Follow-ups provide evidence of the IT project's success. Levels 3 and 4 data can be collected with action plans.
- **Performance contracts** are developed by the participant, the participant's supervisor, and the facilitator, who all agree on enhanced job performance outcomes as a result of the new technology being trained and implemented. Performance contracts are appropriate for data at Levels 3 and 4.
- **Business performance monitoring** is useful when various performance records and operational data are examined for improvement. This method is particularly useful for collecting Level 4 data.

The important challenge when collecting data is to select the method or methods appropriate for the setting and the specific project and within the time and budget constraints of the organization. Data collection methods are covered in more detail in Chapter 4.

Isolating the Effects of IT

An often overlooked issue in most evaluations is isolating the effects of a specific IT project. In this step of the methodology, specific strategies are explored that determine the amount of improvement that can be directly attributed to the project. This step is essential because many factors can influence performance data after an IT project. The isolation strategies pinpoint the amount of improvement directly related to the project, resulting in increased accuracy and credibility of the ROI calculation. The following techniques have been used by organizations to address this important issue:

- A **control group** arrangement can be used to isolate IT impact. With this strategy, one group receives a specific technology upgrade, while another similar group does not benefit from the new system. The difference in the performance of the two groups is attributed to the IT project. When properly set up and implemented, the control group arrangement is the most effective way to isolate the effects of an IT project.
- **Trend lines** are used to project the values of specific output variables if the IT project had not been implemented. The projection is compared to the actual data after the project's completion, and the difference represents the estimate of the impact for that IT initiative. Under certain conditions, this strategy can accurately isolate the IT project impact.
- When mathematical relationships between input and output variables are known, a **forecasting model** is used to isolate the effects of the IT project. With this approach, the output variable is predicted using the forecasting model with the assumption that no IT project is undertaken. The actual performance of the variable after the IT project is compared with the forecasted value, which results in an estimate of the IT project's impact.
- **Participants** estimate the amount of improvement related to the project. With this approach, participants are given the total amount of improvement, on a pre- and post-project basis, and are asked to indicate the percent of the improvement that is an actual result of the IT project.
- The **participants' supervisors** estimate the impact of the IT project on the output variables. With this approach, participants' supervisors are presented with the total amount of improvement and are asked to indicate the percent that can be directly attributed to the IT project.
- **Senior management** estimates the impact of IT. In these cases, managers provide an estimate of the portion of the improvement linked to the IT project. This may not be as

accurate as other options but gets senior management involved in the process.

- **Experts** provide estimates of the impact of IT on the performance variables. Because the estimates are based on previous experience, the experts must be familiar with the IT initiative and the specific benefits.
- When feasible, **other influencing factors** are identified, and their impact is estimated or calculated, leaving the remaining, unexplained improvement attributed to the IT project. In this case, the influence of all the other factors is developed, and the IT project remains the one variable not accounted for in the analysis.
- In some situations, **customers** may provide input on the extent to which IT has influenced their decisions to use a product or service. Although this strategy has limited applications, it can be quite useful for e-commerce and customer self-service technology applications in which customers may prefer to conduct business with an organization because of specific systems it has deployed. In cases where the company's core products are software or hardware, customer input is one of the most critical components.

Collectively, these techniques provide a comprehensive set of tools that address the critical issue of isolating the effects of IT projects. Chapter 5 is devoted to this step of the ROI Methodology.

Conversion of Data to Monetary Values

To calculate the ROI, impact data collected at Level 4 are converted to monetary values and compared to the project costs. This requires that a value is placed on each unit of data connected to the project. Many techniques are available to convert data to monetary values. The specific techniques selected usually depend on the type of data and the situation:

- **Output data** are converted to profit contributions or cost savings. When using this technique, output increases are converted to monetary values based on their unit contribution to profit or the unit of cost reduction. Standard values for these items are readily available in most organizations.
- The **cost of quality** is calculated, and quality improvements are directly converted to cost savings. Standard values for these items are available in many organizations.

- For projects in which employee time is saved, the **participants' wages and benefits** are used to develop the value for time. Because a variety of projects focus on improving the time required to complete projects, processes, or daily activities, the value of time becomes an important and necessary issue. This is a standard formula in most organizations.
- **Historical costs**, developed from cost statements, are used when they are available for a specific variable. In this case, organizational cost data establishes the specific monetary cost savings of an improvement.
- When available, **internal and external experts** may be used to estimate a value for an improvement. In this situation, the credibility of the estimate hinges on the expertise and reputation of the individual providing the estimate.
- **External databases** are sometimes available to establish the value or cost of data items. Research, government, and industry databases can provide important information. The difficulty lies in finding a specific database related to the situation.
- **Participants** estimate the value of the data item. For this approach to be effective, participants must be capable of providing a value for the improvement.
- **Supervisors and managers** provide estimates when they are both willing and capable of assigning values to the improvements. This approach is especially useful when participants are not fully capable of providing this input or in situations in which supervisors need to confirm or adjust the participant's estimate. This approach is helpful when establishing values for performance measures that are important to senior management.
- **Soft measures are linked mathematically to other measures** that are easier to measure and value. This approach is helpful when establishing values for measures that are very difficult to convert to monetary values, or intangible measures, such as customer satisfaction, employee satisfaction, grievances, and employee complaints.
- **IT staff** estimates may be used to determine a value of an output data item. In this case, the estimates must be provided on an unbiased basis.

This step in the ROI Methodology is critical for determining the monetary benefits from an IT project. The process is challenging, particularly with soft data, but can be methodically accomplished using one or more of the strategies presented in this section. Because of its importance, Chapter 6 is devoted to this step in the ROI Methodology.

Project Costs

The other part of the formula for a cost-benefit analysis is the project costs. Tabulating the costs involves monitoring or developing all the related costs of the project targeted for the ROI calculation. These are some of the cost components that should be included:

- Costs to design, develop, and implement the project, possibly prorated over the expected life of the project
- Costs of all project hardware, software, and services
- Costs for any consultants or contractors involved in the project
- Costs for facilities or data center services
- Overhead costs of the facilities (e.g., implementation "war room") for the IT project
- Travel, lodging, and meal costs for the participants, if applicable
- Salaries, plus employee benefits, of the participants
- Administrative and overhead costs of the IT function, allocated in some convenient way

In addition, specific costs related to the needs assessment and evaluation should be included, if appropriate. The conservative approach is to include all these costs so that the total is fully loaded. Chapter 7 is devoted to this step.

The Return on Investment

The ROI is calculated using the project benefits and costs. The benefit-cost ratio is the project benefits divided by the costs. In formula form, it is

$$BCR = \frac{\text{Project Benefits}}{\text{Project Costs}}$$

The ROI uses the net benefits divided by the project costs. The net benefits are the project benefits minus the costs. In formula form, the ROI is

$$ROI\,(\%) = \frac{\text{Net Project Benefits}}{\text{Project Costs}} \times 100$$

This is the same basic formula used to evaluate other investments for which the ROI is traditionally reported as earnings divided by investment. The ROI of IT projects can be huge. For example, in sales, product development, and e-commerce-related IT initiatives, the ROI can be high (frequently over 100 percent), even though the ROI value for system upgrades, legacy system migration, or data conversion may be lower. Chapter 8 is devoted to ROI calculations.

Intangible Benefits

In addition to tangible, monetary benefits, most IT projects will have intangible, nonmonetary benefits. The ROI calculation is based on converting both hard and soft data to monetary values. During data analysis, every attempt is made to convert all data to monetary values. All hard data—such as output, quality, and time—are converted to monetary values. The conversion of soft data is attempted for each data item. However, if the process used for conversion is too subjective or inaccurate, and the resulting values lose credibility in the conversion, then the data are listed as an intangible benefit, with an appropriate explanation. Intangible benefits include items such as the following:

- Increased job satisfaction
- Increased organizational commitment
- Improved teamwork
- Improved collaboration
- Improved customer service
- Reduced complaints
- Reduced conflicts

For some projects, intangible benefits are extremely valuable, often carrying as much influence as hard data items. Chapter 9 is devoted to the value of intangible benefits.

Results Reporting

The final step of the ROI Methodology is reporting the results of the evaluation. Proper attention and planning are necessary to ensure that this critical step is adequately addressed. Reporting involves developing appropriate information in impact studies and other reports. Different techniques can be used to communicate these results to a wide variety of target audiences. In most ROI studies, several audiences are interested in and need the information regarding the evaluation. Careful planning to match the communication method with the audience is essential for ensuring that the message is understood and appropriate actions follow. Chapter 11 is devoted to this critical step of the process.

OPERATING STANDARDS AND PHILOSOPHY

To ensure consistency and replication of evaluations, operating standards must be developed and applied as evaluations are conducted. The results of a study must stand alone and not vary based on who conducts the study. Operating standards detail how each step and issue of the process will be handled. Table 2-2 shows the 12 Guiding Principles that are the operating standards for the ROI Methodology.

The Guiding Principles not only serve as a way to consistently address each step, but they also provide a much-needed conservative

Table 2-2
12 Guiding Principles

1. When conducting a higher-level evaluation, collect data at lower levels.
2. When planning a higher-level evaluation, the previous level of evaluation is not required to be comprehensive.
3. When collecting and analyzing data, use only the most credible sources.
4. When analyzing data, select the most conservative alternative for calculations.
5. Use at least one method to isolate the effects of the project.
6. If no improvement data are available for a population or from a specific source, assume that little or no improvement has occurred.
7. Adjust estimates of improvements for potential errors of estimation.
8. Avoid use of extreme data items and unsupported claims when calculating ROI.
9. Use only the first year of benefits annual in ROI analysis of short-term solutions.
10. Fully load all costs of a solution project, or program when analyzing ROI.
11. Intangible measures are defined as measures that are purposely not converted to monetary values.
12. Communicate the results of ROI methodology to all key stakeholders.

approach to the analysis. A conservative approach may lower the actual ROI, but it will also build credibility with the target audience. In the remaining chapters, each guiding principle is described with an example.

IMPLEMENTATION ISSUES

Many environmental issues and events can influence the successful implementation of the ROI Methodology. These issues must be addressed early to ensure that the ROI Methodology is successful. Specific topics or actions include the following:

- A policy statement concerning results-based IT and technology development projects
- Procedures and guidelines for different elements and techniques of the evaluation process
- Meetings and formal sessions to develop staff skills with the ROI Methodology
- Strategies to improve management commitment and support for the ROI Methodology
- Mechanisms to provide technical support for questionnaire design, data analysis, and evaluation strategy
- Specific techniques to place more attention on results

The ROI Methodology can fail or succeed depending on how these implementation issues are dealt with. Chapter 12 is devoted to this important topic.

APPLICATION AND PRACTICE

It is extremely important for the ROI Methodology to be used in organizations and to develop a history of application. The ROI Methodology described in this book is rich in tradition, with application in a variety of settings and with more than 100 published case studies. In addition, thousands of case studies will soon be deposited in a website/database for future use as a research and application tool (Phillips et al., 2006).

However, success with the ROI Methodology within the organization and documenting those results in impact studies is even more important. Because of this, the IT staff is encouraged to develop their own impact studies to compare with others. Impact studies within the organization provide the most convincing data to senior management teams that IT and technology development projects add significant value and that the analysis of the data can lead to actions for improvement within the organization. Case studies also provide information needed to improve processes in the different areas of the IT function, as part of a continuous improvement process.

FINAL THOUGHTS

This chapter presented the ROI model for calculating the return on investment for IT and technology development projects. The step-by-step process takes the complicated issue of calculating ROI and breaks it into simple, manageable tasks and steps. The building blocks for the process—the pieces of the puzzle—were examined to show how the ROI Methodology has been developed and should be implemented. When the methodology is thoroughly planned, taking into consideration all potential strategies and techniques, it becomes manageable and achievable. The remaining chapters focus on the major elements of the ROI Methodology and how to implement it.

REFERENCES

Broad, M.L. (Ed.) *In Action: Transferring Learning to the Workplace.* Alexandria, VA: American Society for Training and Development, 1997.

Kaplan, R.S. and D.P. Norton. *Balanced Scorecard.* Boston, MA: Harvard Business School Press, 1996.

Kirkpatrick, D.L. "Techniques for Evaluating Training Projects," *Evaluating Training Projects.* Alexandria, VA: American Society for Training and Development, 1975, pp. 1–17.

Phillips, P.P., J.J. Phillips, R. Stone, and H. Burkett. *The ROI Field Book*, Burlington, MA: Butterworth-Heinemann, 2006.

Russ-Eft, D. and H. Preskill. *Evaluation in Organizations.* Cambridge, MA: Perseus Publishing, 2001.

CHAPTER 3

Establishing the Need
for the Technology
Project

Few things are more important in a strategic technology initiative than the initial analysis and planning, particularly the planning for accountability processes. When attempts are made to measure success after the project has been conducted; a similar conclusion is often reached: the project should have had more efficient early planning. Initial analysis and planning have many advantages and involve several key issues that will be explored in this chapter. The first issue is specifying, in detail, what the project will involve. Next, and perhaps more important, this chapter shows how to determine the success of the project—in advance, in specific detail. This chapter also examines ways to ensure that all the key measures or groups of measures are identified to reflect the success of the project, focusing on the different levels of analysis. Finally, the chapter introduces planning tools that can be helpful in setting up the initial project.

PINNING DOWN THE DETAILS:
PROJECT REQUIREMENTS

When specifying the requirements of a project, there can never be too much detail. Projects often go astray because of misunderstandings and differences in expectations about the outcomes. This section shows the key factors that must be addressed before the project begins. Depending on how an organization operates, these issues are often outlined in a project proposal developed by a business operating unit or the organization's technology function. In other cases, the project opportunities are detailed in the form of business needs,

51

which ultimately drive the scope of the project. Regardless of when or how the requirements are developed, or for what purpose, each of the areas in this section should be addressed in some way. More important, the project sponsor or business owner and the project manager within the technology development function need to reach an agreement on these requirements.

Project Objectives

For strategic technology initiatives, there are different levels of objectives. The first objectives are for the project itself, indicating specifically what will be accomplished and delivered by the IT function to the business unit sponsoring the project. The other set of objectives are the solution objectives that focus on the goals of the solution, adding value to the organization. The solution objectives will be discussed later. In this section, the focus is on the project objectives.

Every project should have a major project objective, and in many cases, multiple objectives. The objectives should be as specific as possible and focused directly on the strategic project vision, as described in the project outline or proposal. Examples of project objectives are presented in Table 3-1. As this table illustrates, the

Table 3-1
Examples of Broad Project Objectives

- Deploy an enterprise customer relationship management (CRM) application to enhance customer satisfaction and improve close rates.
- Upgrade the company's enterprise resource planning (ERP) system to leverage enhanced functionality and reduce manual processes.
- Mobilize a global business intelligence (BI) initiative to have the entire company focused on the same business metrics and key performance indicators (KPIs).
- Evaluate the feasibility of three alternative approaches to new product development and rollout. For each approach, provide data on projected success, resources required, and timing.
- Implement a new accounts payable system that will maximize cash flow and discounts and minimize late-payment penalties.
- Design, develop, and implement an automated sales-tracking system that will provide real-time information on deliveries, customer satisfaction, and sales forecasts.
- Enhance the productivity of the call center staff as measured in calls completed, without sacrificing service quality.

objectives are broad in scope, outlining what is to be accomplished overall. The details of timing, specifications, and specific deliverables will be determined in the solution objectives. The broad project objectives are critical because they bring focus to the project. Often, the beginning point of the discussion is the major project objectives, which are needed to define a project when it involves several phases and issues.

Scope

The scope of the project needs to be clearly defined. The scope pinpoints the key parameters addressed by the project. Table 3-2 shows typical scoping issues that should be defined for the project. Perhaps the project is limited to certain employee groups, a functional area of the business, a specific location, a unique type of system, or a precise timeframe. Sometimes, a constraint is placed on the type of data collected or access to certain individuals, such as customers. Whatever the scope involves, it must be clearly defined at this time.

Timing

Timing is critical for showing specifically when activities will occur. This includes the timing of the delivery of the final project report and of particular steps and events—including when data are needed, analyzed, and reported and when presentations are made. Table 3-3 shows typical events that require specific timeframes.

Table 3-2
Scoping Issues

- Project team
- Locations affected by the project
- Project timeline
- Technology architecture
- Access to project stakeholders
- Functional area for coverage
- Product line for coverage
- Type of process/activity
- Category of customers

Table 3-3
Typical Timing Events

- Start of project
- Data collection design complete
- Evaluation design complete
- Data collection begins
- Data collection complete
- Specific data collection issues (e.g., user acceptance testing)
- Data analysis complete
- Preliminary results available
- Solutions developed
- Implementation begins
- Implementation complete
- Phases complete
- Report development
- Presentation to management

Deliverables from the Project

This section describes what the organization will receive when the project is completed in terms of reports, documents, systems, processes, manuals, forms, flowcharts, or rights to new technology. Whatever the specific deliverables, they are clearly defined in the project objectives. Most projects will have a final report but often go much further, delivering process tools, software, and sometimes hardware.

Methodology

If a specific methodology is planned for the project, it should be included in the project objectives. Sometimes, a reference should be made to the appropriateness of the methodology as well as its reliability, validity, previous success, and how the methodology will accomplish the project's needs.

Steps

The specific steps of the project should be defined showing key milestones. This provides the organization with a step-by-step understanding and project tracking so that, at any given time, the organization can see not only where progress is being made but where the project is going next.

Resources Required for the Project

Specific project resources could include access to individuals, vendors, technology, equipment, facilities, competitors, or customers. All anticipated resources should be listed along with the costs and projected timing of the need for them.

Costs

The costs should be included in the project objectives and should include all the costs for the different parts and steps of the project. If outside contractors or consultants are used, they should be required to detail any fees, showing the different steps and relative cost issues.

LEVELS OF OBJECTIVES FOR SOLUTIONS

A strategic technology project is usually a solution for a particular dilemma, problem, or opportunity. In other situations, the project is designed to develop a range of different solutions. Whatever the case, all project solutions should have multiple levels of objectives. These levels of objectives, qualitative and quantitative, define precisely what should occur as a project is implemented within an organization. Table 3-4 shows the different levels of objectives. These objectives are critical to project success and need special attention in their development and use.

Reaction Objectives

For any project to be successful, the stakeholders the individuals directly involved in implementing the project, must react favorably. These stakeholders are the IT or technology development team who design and conduct the project, the participants who implement the project, the supervisors or team leaders who are responsible for the redesigned or changed process, the managers who must support or assist the process, and the executive or client who requested the project and funds it.

Table 3-5 shows some of the typical areas for reaction objectives. It is important to obtain this type of information routinely

Table 3-4
Multiple Levels of Objectives

Levels of Objectives	Focus of Objectives
Level 1 Reaction and Perceived Value	Define the expected reactions of the participants to the technology project
Level 2 Learning and Confidence	Define the skills and knowledge requirements that participants should learn during the project
Level 3 Application and Implementation	Define the key actions that participants should take when implementing the project in the workplace
Level 4 Impact and Consequences	Define the business measures that will change or improve as a result of the project's implementation
Level 5 ROI	Define the return on investment expected from the implementation of the project, comparing the benefits to the costs

Table 3-5
Typical Areas for Reaction Objectives

- Usefulness of the technology
- Relevance of the technology
- Economics of the technology
- Difficulty in understanding the technology
- Difficulty in learning the technology
- Difficulty in implementing the technology
- Difficulty in maintaining the technology
- Perceived support for the technology
- Appropriate resources for the technology
- Overall satisfaction with the technology

throughout the project so that feedback can be used to make adjustments, keep the project on track, and perhaps even redesign certain parts to improve the project. One problem with many projects is that specific objectives at this level are not developed, and data collection mechanisms are not put in place to ensure appropriate feedback for making needed adjustments for improvement.

Learning Objectives

Almost every project implementation will involve at least one learning objective. In some cases involving major change projects, the learning component is significant. To ensure that the participants have acquired the needed knowledge during the project, learning objectives are developed. Learning objectives define the expected outcomes of the project and the desired competence or performance needed to for project success. These objectives provide a basis for evaluating the learning, since they often reflect the type of measurement process. Perhaps more important, learning objectives provide a focus for participants, clearly indicating what they must learn.

The best learning objectives describe behaviors that are observable and measurable and are necessary for project success. They should be outcome-based, clearly worded, and specific. They should specify what is required of the participants as a result of the project. Learning objectives often have three components:

- Performance—what the participants will be able to do at the end of the project
- Conditions—the circumstances under which the participant will perform the tasks and processes from the project
- Criteria—the degree or level of proficiency necessary to perform a new task, process, or procedure that was learned during the project

Three types of learning objectives are often defined:

- Awareness—familiarity with the terms, concepts, and processes learned during the project
- Knowledge—general understanding of the concepts, processes, or procedures
- Performance—ability to demonstrate the skills at least on a basic level

Application Objectives

As a project is implemented in the workplace, the implementation and application objectives clearly define what is expected and to what level of performance. Application levels are similar to learning objectives but reflect the actual use of the learning on the job. Application objectives describe the expected outcomes during the time between learning the new tasks and procedures and the actual improvements within the organization, the business impact. Implementation objectives describe how participants should perform or the state of the workplace after the technology project is implemented. They provide the basis for the evaluation of on-the-job changes and performance. The emphasis is on what has occurred on the job as a result of the project learning objectives.

The best application objectives identify behaviors that are observable and measurable or that are action steps in a process. They specify what the participants will change or have changed as a result of the technology process. As with learning objectives, implementation objectives may have three components:

- Performance—describes what the participants have changed or have accomplished during a specified timeframe after the implementation of the technology project
- Condition—specifies the circumstances under which the participants have performed or are performing the tasks or implementing the skills learned during the project
- Criteria—indicates the level of proficiency under which the project is implemented, the task is being performed, or the steps are completed

There are two types of application objectives: knowledge-based—in which the general use of concepts, processes, and procedures is important—and behavior-based—in which the participant must be able to demonstrate the use of skills, accomplishment of particular tasks, or completion of milestones. Table 3-6 shows typical, key

Table 3-6
Typical Questions When Developing Application Objectives

- What new or improved knowledge will be applied on the job?
- What is the frequency of application?
- What specific new task will be performed?
- What new steps will be implemented?
- What action items will be implemented?
- What new procedures will be implemented or changed?
- What new guidelines will be implemented?
- What new processes will be implemented?
- Which meetings need to be held?
- Which tasks, steps, or procedures will be discontinued?

questions asked when developing application and implementation objectives.

Application objectives have almost always been included to some degree in technology projects, but they have not been as specific as they should be. To be effective, they must clearly define how the work environment should be after the project is successfully implemented.

Impact Objectives

Every project should result in improved business impact. Business impact represents the key business measures that should improve as the implementation objectives are achieved. The impact objectives are critical to measuring business performance because they define the ultimate expected outcome from the project. They describe business-unit performance that should be connected to the project. Above all, they place emphasis on achieving bottom-line results that key business groups expect and demand.

The best impact objectives contain measures that can be linked to the technology initiative. They should describe measures that are easily collected and are well known to the business group. They should also be results-based and clearly worded, specifying what the participants have accomplished in the business unit as a result of the project.

The four major categories of hard data impact objectives are output, quality, cost, and time. The major categories of soft data impact objectives are customer service, work climate, and work habits.

ROI Objectives

The fifth, and final, level of objectives for project solutions is the expected return on investment. These objectives define the expected payoff from the technology project and compare the project costs to the monetary benefits. This is typically expressed as a desired ROI percentage: the annual monetary benefits minus the costs, divided by the costs, multiplied by 100. A 0 percent ROI indicates a break-even investment. A 50 percent ROI indicates that the costs of the project are recaptured and an additional 50 percent "earnings" are achieved.

For many technology initiatives, the ROI objective will be larger than the ROI of other expenditures, such as the purchase of a new company, a new building, or major equipment, but the two are related. In many organizations the technology project's ROI objective is set slightly higher than the ROI expected from other projects because of the relative newness of applying the ROI concept to technology projects. For example, if the expected ROI from the purchase of a new company is 20 percent, then the ROI from a technology project might be 25 percent. The important point to consider is that the ROI objective should be established up front and in discussions with executives in the organization.

THE IMPORTANCE OF SPECIFIC OBJECTIVES

Developing specific objectives at different levels for technology projects provides important benefits. First, specific objectives provide on-track direction to the IT or technology team directly involved in the project. Objectives define exactly what is expected at different timeframes, from different individuals, and with different types of data. Also, they provide guidance to the support staff and management so that they fully understand the ultimate goal and planned impact of the project. They also provide important information and motivation for all stakeholders. In most technology projects, the stakeholders are actively involved and will influence the solution results. Specific objectives also provide goals and motivation for participants so that they will clearly see the gains that should be achieved. More important, objectives provide critical information for the key business groups so that they clearly understand what the landscape will look like when the project is implemented. Finally, from an evaluation perspective, the objectives provide a basis for measuring success.

HOW IS IT ALL CONNECTED? LINKING EVALUATION WITH NEEDS

A distinct link exists between evaluation objectives and the original needs that drove a project. The earlier material in this chapter showed the importance of setting project objectives. The objectives define the specific improvements sought. In this section, the objectives will be connected to the original needs assessment. Figure 3-1 shows the connection between the evaluation and the needs assessment. This figure shows the important link from the initial problem or opportunity that created the need for evaluation and measurement.

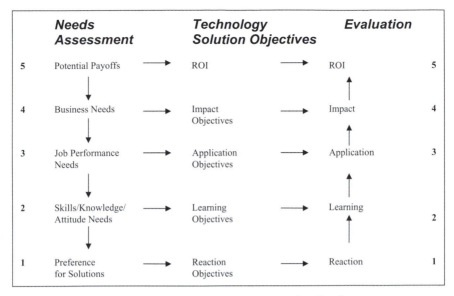

*Figure 3-1. Connection Between the Evaluation
and the Needs Assessment*

Level 5 defines the potential payoff and examines the possibility of a positive ROI before the project is even pursued. Level 4 analysis focuses directly on the business needs that precipitated the technology project. At Level 3, the specific issues in the workplace focus on job performance in detail. At Level 2, the specific knowledge, skills, or attitude deficiencies are uncovered as learning needs are identified. Finally, the preferences for the structure of the project define the Level 1 needs. These connections are critical to understanding all the elements that must be included in an effective technology implementation.

An example will help illustrate this link. Figure 3-2 shows an example of linking the needs assessment with the evaluation of a project involving a reduction in order entry error rate. As the figure shows, the first step is to see if the problem is great enough at Level 5. However, the problem may need to be evaluated using Level 4 data. Four benchmarks are used to compare the current error rate problem:

- Error rate is higher than it used to be.
- Error rate is higher than at other locations within the company.
- Error rate is higher than at other facilities in the local area.
- Error rate is higher than the general manager desires.

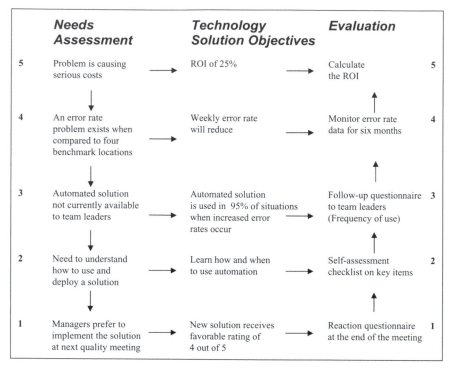

Figure 3-2. Example of Linking the Needs Assessment of a Project

With confirmation at Level 4 that a problem exists, a potential payoff is estimated. This involves estimating the cost of order entry error rates and estimating the potential reduction that can come from a more automated technology solution. This develops a profile of potential payoff to see if the problem is worth solving.

At Level 3, the causes of the excessive error rate are explored using a variety of techniques. One uncovered issue is that an automated solution is not currently available to team leaders. A learning component is also uncovered, as the team leaders need to understand how and when to use the automated solution. Finally, the specific way in which the solution should be implemented is explored in terms of preferences. In this case, managers preferred that the automated technology solution be implemented at the next quality meeting.

These five levels provide an overall profile for determining if the problem is worth solving to begin with, as well as aligning problems with key measures and data necessary to develop the project objectives. The project solution objectives for each level are also shown in the figure, as is the evaluation method needed to verify that the appropriate change did occur. This process is important to the development and implementation of a project solution. Many projects are focused on developing and implementing the final solution, as is the case in this particular example. When this occurs, the preceding link connects the needs to actual objectives and then to evaluation.

The solution to the problem or opportunity is an important part of this link. Some projects may be involved in uncovering needs with the initial analysis to determine the actual causes of the problem and then recommending solutions. It is up to the business to then implement the solution, or implementation becomes part of another project. In either case, the solutions are ultimately developed for a complete technology project. If this has not been accomplished, multiple levels of analysis may be necessary. Although other references focus specifically on the performance analysis to uncover different levels of needs, a brief summary is presented here.

Payoff Needs

The first part of the process is to determine if the problem is worth solving or the opportunity is large enough to warrant serious consideration. In some cases, this is obvious when serious problems are affecting the organization's operations and strategy. Still others may not be so obvious. At Level 5, the business measures at Level 4, which need to improve, must be identified and converted to monetary values so the actual improvement can be seen to financial measures. The second part of the process is to develop an approximate cost for the entire project. This could come from a detailed proposal, or it may be a rough estimate. At this stage it is only an estimate, as the projected cost of the project is compared to the potential benefits to roughly determine if a payoff is possible if the issue is pursued. This step may be omitted in some situations when the problem must be solved regardless of the cost or if it becomes obvious that it is a high-payoff activity. Still other projects may be initiated, and the potential payoff is not expected to be developed. For example, as an organization strives to become a technology leader, placing a value on that goal may be difficult.

Business Needs

In conjunction with Level 5, actual business data are examined to determine which measures need to improve. This includes an examination of organizational records and involves examining all types of hard and soft data. The measure that must improve is usually one of the data items and its performance triggers the project assignment. For example, market share is not as much as it should be, costs are excessive, quality is deteriorating, or productivity is not as high as it should be. These are the key issues that come directly from the data in the organization and are often found in the operating reports or records.

The supporting data may not only come from the operating reports, but annual reports, marketing data, industry data, major planning documents, or other important information sources that clearly indicate performance in terms of operation or strategy.

Performance Needs

The Level 3 analysis involves workplace needs. The task is to determine the cause of the problem as determined at Level 4 (i.e., what is causing the business measure not to be at the desired level or to be inhibited in some way). The different types of needs can vary considerably and may include, among others, the following:

1. Ineffective or inappropriate processes
2. Dysfunctional work teams
3. Ineffective systems
4. Improper process flow
5. Ineffective procedures
6. Unsupported culture
7. Inappropriate technology
8. Unsupportive environment

These and other types of needs will have to be uncovered using problem-solving or analysis techniques. This may involve the use of data collection techniques discussed in this book, such as surveys, questionnaires, focus groups, or interviews. It may involve a variety of problem-solving or analysis techniques, such as root-cause analysis and fishbone diagrams. Leave as is. Whatever is used, the key is to determine all the causes of the problem so that solutions can be developed. Often, multiple solutions are appropriate.

Learning Needs

Most problem analysis from Level 3 uncovers specific systems-related learning needs. Learning inefficiencies, in terms of knowledge and skills, may either contribute to the problem or be the major cause of it. In other situations, the solution applied may need a learning component as participants learn how to implement a new process, procedure, or system. The extent of learning required will determine if formalized training is needed or if more informal, on-the-job methods can be used to build the necessary skills and knowledge. The learning would typically involve acquisition of knowledge or the development of skills necessary to improve the situation. In some cases, perceptions or attitudes may need to be altered to make the process successful in the future.

Preference Needs

The final level is to consider the preference for the solution. This involves determining the preferred way in which those involved in the process prefer to have it changed or implemented. It may involve implementation preferences and/or systems preferences. Preferences may involve decisions, such as expected timing for the implementation, the amount of training needed, how it is presented, and the overall costs. Implementation preferences may involve issues such as timing, support, expectation, and other key factors. The important point is to try to determine the specific preferences to the extent possible so that the complete profile of the solution can be adjusted accordingly.

PLANNING FOR MEASUREMENT AND EVALUATION

An important ingredient in the success of the ROI methodology is to properly plan early in the project cycle. Appropriate up-front attention will save time later when data are collected and analyzed, thus improving accuracy and reducing the cost of the process. It also avoids any confusion surrounding what will be accomplished, by whom, and at what time. Two planning documents are key and should be completed before the project is designed or developed.

Data Collection Plan

Table 3-7 shows a completed data collection plan for a customer data collection initiative. The project was initiated to improve the data monitored on the organization's customers through improved systems. An ROI calculation was planned to show the value of this project.

This document provides a place for the major elements and issues regarding data collection for the five evaluation levels. In the first column, broad areas for planning objectives are stated. Specific, detailed objectives are developed later, before the project is designed. In the second column, the specific measures or data descriptors are indicated when they are necessary to explain the measures linked to the objectives. In the next column, the specific data collection method is briefly described using standard terminology. Next, the source of the data is entered. Data sources will vary considerably, but they usually include participants, team leaders, and company records. In the next column, the timeframe for data collection is usually referenced from the beginning of the project. Finally, the responsibility for data collection is described.

The reaction objectives usually include positive reactions to the project and suggested improvements. Planned actions may be included in the input. Reaction and perceived value data may be collected at different intervals. In this example, feedback is taken only at one time: at the end of the solution's implementation.

Because Level 2 evaluation focuses on the measures of learning, specific objectives include those areas where participants are expected to learn new systems, tasks, knowledge, skills, or attitudes. The evaluation method is the specific way in which learning is assessed. In this case, the method used is a test and observation of skill practice by the facilitator of the meeting. The timing for Level 2 evaluation is at the end of the implementation.

For application and implementation evaluation, the objectives represent broad areas, including on-the-job activities and implementation steps. In this example, the data collection methods include questionnaires, surveys, and monitoring company records. This information is usually collected months after the implementation. Because responsibilities are often shared among several groups, including the project staff, clarifying this issue early in the process is important. In this example, four groups share the responsibilities.

For impact evaluation, objectives focus on business impact measures influenced by the project. The measures/data column includes

Table 3-7
Example of Completed Data Collection Plan

Project: Improve Customer Data Collection **Responsibility:** _____ Date: _____

Data Collection Plan

Level	Broad Objectives	Measures/Data	Data Collection Method	Data Sources	Timing	Responsibilities
1. Reaction and Perceived Value	• Obtain a positive reaction to project • Obtain input for suggestions for improvement • Identify planned actions		• Questionnaire	• Project participants	• End of Implementation	• Project coordinator
2. Learning and Confidence	• Knowledge of techniques for data capture • Skills to capture data through existing systems	• True/false statements • Skill practices	• Pre- and Posttest • Observation	• Project participants • Project participants	• Beginning of project and end of implementation • During Session	• Project leader
3. Application and Implementation	• Administer system • Conduct meeting with employees to explain system and techniques	• Completed meeting records	• Questionnaire • Customer survey (25% sample)	• Project participants • Project participants	• 6 months after project • 6 months after project	• Project evaluator • Employee communications
4. Impact and Consequences	• Improve data quality • Reduce internal complaints • Enhance employee performance • Improve close rates	• Formal metrics and reporting on historical customer data gaps	• Performance monitoring • Questionnaire	• Company records • Supervisors	• Monthly for 1 year before and after project • 6 months after project	• Project evaluator

the way in which each item is measured. For example, if one of the objectives is to improve quality, a specific measure would indicate how that quality is measured, such as defects per thousand units produced. Two sources of data are used at this level: company records and questionnaires. The timing depends on how quickly the project can generate a sustained impact on the three measures. It is usually a matter of months after the project is completed. In this example, data were collected at six-month intervals. A project evaluator is responsible for data collection at this level. If appropriate, an ROI objective (Level 5) is included. It was not considered appropriate for this example.

The data collection plan is an important part of the evaluation strategy and should be completed prior to moving forward with the systems project; the plan is completed before pursuing an ROI evaluation. The plan provides a clear direction of the types of data to be collected, how they will be collected, where they will be collected, when they will be collected, and who will collect them.

ROI Analysis Plan

Table 3-8 shows a completed ROI analysis plan for the same customer data collection project. This planning document is the continuation of the data collection plan presented in Table 3-7, and it captures information on several key items that are necessary to develop the ROI calculation. In the first column, data items are listed, usually business impact measures (Level 4 data items), but in some cases they could include Level 3 data. These items will be used during the ROI analysis. The method for isolating the effects of the project is listed next to each data item in the second column. For most projects, the method will be the same for each data item, but there could be variations. For example, if no historical data are available for one data item, then trend line analysis is not possible for that item, although it may be appropriate for other items. In this example, a control group arrangement was not feasible, but a trend line analysis was. Participant estimates were used as a backup.

The method for converting data to monetary values is included in the third column. In this example, complaints are converted to monetary values with two approaches: using costs in the company records and collecting expert input directly from the staff involved in the process. The cost categories planned for capture are outlined in the fourth column. Instructions about how certain costs should be

Table 3-8
Example of Completed ROI Analysis Plan

Project: <u>Improve Customer Data Collection</u>   Responsibility: _____   Date: _____

ROI Analysis Plan

Data Items	Methods of Isolating the Effects of the Project	Data	Cost Categories	Intangible Benefits	Communication Targets	Other Influences/ Issues
Formal internal complaints of inaccurate customer data	• Trend line analysis • Participant estimation (as a backup)	• Historical costs with estimation from marketing and sales	• Initial analysis and assessment solution	• Job satisfaction	• All employees (condensed info.)	• Several initiatives to reduce system error rates were implemented during this project
External complaints by customers	• Trend line analysis • Participant estimation (as a backup)	• Historical costs with estimation from marketing, sales, and operations	• Solution development • Coordination/ facilitation • Company time for and project • Materials • Salaries and benefits for participants • Evaluation and reporting	• Stress reduction • Public image	• Senior executives (summary report with detailed backup) • All managers (brief report) • IT/consulting staff (full report)	• Must not duplicate benefits from both internal and external complaints

prorated are noted here. Normally, the cost categories will be consistent from one project to another. However, a specific cost that is unique to this project is also noted. The anticipated intangible benefits expected from this initiative are outlined in the fifth column. This list is generated from discussions about the project with sponsors and subject matter experts.

Communication targets are outlined in the sixth column. Although many groups could receive the information, four target groups are always recommended: senior management, managers of participants, project participants, and the project staff. Each of these four groups needs to be informed about the results of the ROI analysis. Finally, other issues or events that might influence project implementation are highlighted in the seventh column. Typical items include the capability of participants, the degree of access to data sources, and unique data analysis issues.

The ROI analysis plan, when combined with the data collection plan, provides detailed information on calculating the ROI, illustrating how the process will develop from beginning to end. When completed, these two plans should provide the direction necessary for an ROI evaluation and should integrate with the overall project plan.

Shortcut Ways to Plan for the Evaluation

This chapter presents a comprehensive approach to planning the evaluation of a systems project. The process is thorough, which is often needed in most major technology initiatives. When a major project involves an investment of hundreds, thousands, or even millions of dollars, allocating the appropriate time and budgets for developing the project ROI is important. For smaller-scale projects, a more simplified process is appropriate. Four key issues should be addressed when taking a shortcut approach to evaluation planning.

Define Expectations and Requirements

Even in small-scale, simple projects, The specific requirements for the project to be successful should be detailed and the expectations should be clearly defined. Here, the business should be as specific as possible in terms of the desired conduct and expectations of the technology project. The highest level of detail possible is recommended. This can be included in the business requirements or a brief working document, but it should highlight the key issues that can cause the process to go astray.

Define Workforce Changes

The anticipated changes at the work site—changes that will be driven by the project and, more specifically, the opportunities from the technology solution—should be defined. Thinking through the changes often will help identify potential barriers and enablers to the process. It will define what the employees and other stakeholders will experience or be expected to do to make the project successful. Perhaps a checklist of concerns would be appropriate to ensure that both business and IT agree on the anticipated changes and the work flow, work process, working conditions, and the workplace environment.

Define Expected Outcomes

The levels of objectives are helpful for the simplest projects. Some consideration should be given to developing multiple levels of objectives. More important, the ultimate impact expected should be clearly defined in terms of the measures that should change or improve if the project is successful. Along with this definition would be the parameters around collecting data and the methods to isolate the effects of the project. The results will be more focused when the anticipated outcomes are clearly defined.

Develop a Plan

Although the two documents presented in Tables 3-7 and 3-8 may be too much detail for a simple project, there is no substitute for detailing these issues. Even a project with a $50,000 price tag is worth a few hours of planning to make sure that the key issues are covered. Shortcut ways to develop some of those processes are possible and are described later in this book. The important point here is to develop some type of simplified plan, even if the document is less detailed than the two formal planning documents presented. Overall, this step is critical and should not be ignored.

FINAL THOUGHTS

This chapter presented the initial analysis and planning for the evaluation of a strategic technology initiative. The rationale for initial analysis and objectives was explored. The links between the levels of evaluation, objectives, and initial needs was also outlined. This connection greatly simplifies the project accountability process. Next, evaluation planning tools were introduced. When the ROI process is thoroughly planned, taking into consideration all potential strategies and techniques, it becomes manageable and achievable.

CHAPTER 4

Collecting Data

Collecting data during and after the IT project has been conducted is the first operational phase of the ROI methodology. This step is usually the most time consuming of all steps and is also the part of the ROI process that can be the most disruptive to the organization. Fortunately, a variety of methods are available to capture data at the appropriate time. This chapter defines the sources of data and outlines the common approaches for collecting post-project data.

SOURCES OF DATA

When considering the possible data sources that will provide input on the success of an IT project, several categories are easily defined.

Organizational Performance Records

The most useful and credible data source for ROI analysis is the organization's records, reports and systems. Whether individualized or group-based, the records reflect the performance in a work unit, department, division, region, or overall organization. This source can include all types of measures, which are usually available in abundance throughout the organization and sometimes embedded in software. Collecting data from this source is preferred for Level 4 evaluation, since it usually reflects business impact data, and it is relatively easy to obtain. Sloppy record keeping by some organizations, however, may add to the difficulty of locating particular reports.

Participants

The most widely used data source for an ROI analysis is the project participants. Participants are frequently asked about their reactions to a new enterprise system, the extent of learning, and how skills and knowledge for the new application have been applied on the job. Sometimes, they are asked to explain the impact of those actions. Participants are a rich source of data for Levels 1, 2, 3, and 4 evaluations. They are credible because they are the individuals who have been involved in the project and achieved the performance. Also, they are often the most knowledgeable about the processes and other influencing factors. The challenge is to find an effective and efficient way to capture the data in a consistent manner.

The good news is there are many inexpensive or free Web-based survey tools (e.g., SurveyMonkey.com) that can help create flexible and interactive surveys. These can easily be electronically mailed to all survey participants, regardless of the survey population size. These tools have solid reporting and analytics, making it easy to manipulate the data or create additional pivot tables to draw correlations between various elements of the questionnaire or survey. Whether the number of people being surveyed is 5 in a small operational department or 5,000 across the enterprise, every effort should be made to leverage a technology-enabled survey tool so that the data reside in a database. This will help maintain the accuracy and reliability of the data. Paper-based surveys are old-school and have no place in the IT field.

Managers of Participants

Another important source of data is those individuals who directly supervise the project participants. This group will often have a vested interest in the evaluation process because they approved the individuals' participation in the implementation of the technology project. In many situations, they observe the participants as they attempt to use the knowledge and skills acquired during the project. Therefore, they can report on the success linked to the project as well as the difficulties and problems associated with application. Although supervisor input is usually best for Level 3 data, it can be useful for Level 4 as well. However, supervisors must maintain objectivity when assessing the project participants.

Team/Peer Group

Those individuals who serve as team members with the participant or who occupy peer-level positions within the organization are another source of data for a few types of projects. In these situations, peer group members provide input on perceived changes (Level 3 data). This source of data is more appropriate when all team members participate in the project and, are able to report on the collective efforts of the group or changes of specific individuals. Because of the subjective nature of this process and the lack of opportunity to fully evaluate the application of skills, this source of data can be limited.

Internal/External Groups

In some situations, internal or external groups (such as the IT and technology development staff, project managers, system architects, or external consultants) may provide input on the success of the individuals when they learn and apply the acquired skills and knowledge learned in the project. Sometimes, technology project managers or business analysts may be used to measure learning (Level 2 data). This source may be useful for on-the-job observation (Level 3 data) after the completion of the IT project. Collecting data from this source has limited uses. Because internal groups may have a vested interest in the outcome of evaluation, their input may lose credibility.

QUESTIONNAIRES AND SURVEYS

Probably the most common data collection method is the questionnaire (Alreck & Settle, 1995). Ranging from short reaction forms to detailed follow-up tools, questionnaires can be used to obtain subjective information about participants, as well as to objectively document the measurable business results of an ROI analysis. With this versatility and popularity, the questionnaire is the preferred method for capturing Levels 1, 2, 3, and 4 data in some organizations.

Surveys represent a specific type of questionnaire with several applications for measuring IT success. They are often used in situations in which attitudes, beliefs, and opinions are captured. However, a questionnaire has much more flexibility and captures data ranging from attitude to specific improvement statistics. The principles of survey construction and design are similar to questionnaire design. The development of both instruments is covered in this section.

Types of Questions

In addition to the particular data sought, the types of questions asked distinguish surveys from questionnaires. Surveys can have yes or no responses when an absolute agreement or disagreement is required, or a range of responses may be used from strongly disagree to strongly agree. A five-point scale is common.

A questionnaire may contain any or all of these types of questions:

- *Open-ended question:* has an unlimited answer. The question is followed by ample blank space for the response.
- *Checklist:* provides a list of items where a participant is asked to check those that apply in the situation.
- *Two-way question:* has alternate responses, a yes/no or other possibilities.
- *Multiple-choice question:* has several choices, and the participant is asked to select the most applicable one.
- *Ranking scale:* requires the participant to rank a list of items.

Questionnaire Design Steps

Questionnaire design is a simple and logical process. There is nothing more confusing, frustrating, and potentially embarrassing than a poorly designed or an improperly worded questionnaire. The following steps can ensure that a valid, reliable, and effective instrument is developed (Robson, 2002).

Determine the Specific Information Needed

As a first step in questionnaire design, the knowledge, skills, or reaction to the new enterprise system are reviewed for potential items for the questionnaire. Developing this information in outline form is sometimes helpful so that related questions or items can be grouped. Other issues related to the project's application are explored for inclusion in the questionnaire.

Involve Management in the Process

To the extent possible, management should be involved in this process, either as a client, sponsor, supporter, or interested party. If possible, managers most familiar with the project or process should provide information on specific issues and concerns that often frame the questions planned for the questionnaire. In some cases, managers want to provide input on specific issues or items. Not only is manager input helpful and useful during questionnaire design, but it also builds ownership in the measurement and evaluation process.

Select the Type(s) of Questions

Using the previous five types of questions, the first step in questionnaire design is to select the type(s) that will best result in the data needed. The planned data analysis and kind of data to be collected should be considered when deciding which questions to use.

Develop the Questions

The next step is to develop the questions based on the type of questions planned and the information needed. Questions should be simple and straightforward to avoid confusion. Questions should not lead the participant to a desired response. A single question should only address one issue. If multiple issues must be addressed, separate the questions into multiple parts or simply develop a separate question for each issue. Terms or expressions unfamiliar to the participant should be avoided.

Check the Reading Level

To ensure that the questionnaire can be easily understood by the target audience, it is helpful to assess the reading level. Most word processing programs have features that will evaluate the reading difficulty according to grade level. This provides an important check to ensure that the reading level of the target audience matches the questionnaire design.

Test the Questions

Proposed questions should be tested for understanding. Ideally, the questions should be tested on a sample group of participants. If this is not feasible, the sample group of employees should be at approximately the same job level as participants. From this sample group, feedback, critiques, and suggestions are sought to improve questionnaire design.

Address the Anonymity Issue

Participants should feel free to respond openly to questions without fear of reprisal. The confidentiality of responses is important because there is usually a link between survey anonymity and accuracy. Therefore, surveys should be anonymous unless there are specific reasons why individuals need to be identified. In situations where participants must complete the questionnaire in a captive audience or submit a completed questionnaire directly to an individual, a neutral third party should collect and process the data, ensuring that the identity is not revealed. In cases where identity must be known (e.g., to compare output data with the previous data or to verify the data), every effort should be made to protect the respondents' identities from those who may be biased.

Design for Ease of Tabulation and Analysis

Each potential question should be considered in terms of data tabulation, data summary, and analysis. If possible, the data analysis process should be outlined and reviewed in a mock-up form. This step avoids the problems of inadequate, cumbersome, and lengthy data analysis caused by improper wording or design.

Develop the Completed Questionnaire and
Prepare a Data Summary

The questions should be integrated to develop an attractive questionnaire with proper instructions so that it can be administered effectively. In addition, a summary sheet should be developed so that the data can be tabulated quickly for analysis. Virtually all Web-based survey creation tools have a number of design templates to ensure that the layout will be visually appealing to the respondent.

Questionnaire Content: During Project

The areas of feedback used on reaction questionnaires depend, to a large extent, on the organization and the purpose of the evaluation. Some questionnaires are simple, and others are detailed and require a considerable amount of time to complete. A feedback questionnaire should be designed to supply the information necessary to satisfy the purpose of evaluation. The following is a comprehensive list of the most common types of feedback solicited:

- *System functionality.* Are the features and functions of the system meeting the business user's needs?
- *Intuitive interface.* Can the system be easily navigated, and does the screen interface layout inherently make sense?
- *Increased productivity.* Does this new piece of technology increase efficiency while providing empowerment to complete tasks?
- *Enhanced system data.* Can key system data be reconciled in ways that were previously impossible?
- *Progress with objectives.* To what degree were the original objectives for the technology initiative met?
- *Help systems.* Are the online help systems useful and easy to navigate?
- *Instructional components.* Are the system training materials useful?
- *Method of delivery.* Was the method of training delivery (remote or in-person) appropriate for the objectives?
- *Instructor/facilitator.* Was the facilitator effective?
- *New information.* How much new information was included?
- *Motivation to learn.* Was there motivation to learn this new system or process?
- *Relevance.* Was the project relevant?
- *Importance.* How important is this content to the job success?
- *Facilities.* Did the training environment help or hinder learning?
- *Potential barriers.* What potential barriers exist for the long-term user acceptance of the new system?
- *Planned improvements/use of material.* How will new knowledge be applied?
- *Recommendations for target audiences.* What is the appropriate audience for this project?
- *Overall evaluation.* What is the overall rating of the project?

Objective questions covering each of these areas will ensure thorough feedback from participants. This feedback can be extremely useful in making adjustments to a project and/or assist in predicting performance after the project.

In most medium- to large-size organizations where there is significant IT and technology development project activity, the Level 1 instrument is usually created as a Web-based survey, as discussed earlier. Typical Level 1 questions can and should easily be developed for an online survey that has numerous canned reports to help present and understand the data. Some organizations create their own Web-based survey utilities so that the data can more cleanly be integrated and related to other operational data. Ultimately, this is a decision for the organization, but thorough research of the options is useful. Many of the survey technologies today have the necessary application programming interface (API) or Webservice to make integration with existing corporate databases a straightforward task.

Collecting learning data using a questionnaire is common. Most types of tests, whether formal or informal, are questionnaire-based and are described in more detail in this chapter. However, several questions can be developed to use with the reaction form to gain insight into the extent of learning during the project. Answers to these questions can help ensure that the participant will be an effective user of the system. These are some possible areas to explore on a reaction questionnaire, all aimed at measuring the extent of learning:

- Skill enhancement
- Knowledge gain
- Ability
- Capability
- Competence
- Awareness

Other questions can focus indirectly on the learning issue, such as the complexity of the system or confidence in using what is learned. These questions are developed using a format similar to the reaction part of the questionnaire. They measure the extent to which learning has taken place, usually based on confidence and perception.

Questionnaire Content: Post-project

The following items represent a comprehensive list of questionnaire content possibilities for capturing follow-up data. Figure 4-1 presents a questionnaire used in a follow-up evaluation of a leadership development project. The evaluation was designed to capture data for an ROI analysis, with this questionnaire as the primary data collection method. This example will be used to illustrate many of the issues involving potential content items for questionnaire design, with emphasis on application (Level 3) and impact (Level 4).

Customer Relationship Management (CRM) Project Impact Questionnaire

Are you currently in a supervisory or management role/capacity? Yes ❑ No ❑

1. Listed below are the objectives of the CRM Project. After reflecting on the project, please indicate your degree of success in achieving these objectives. *Please check the appropriate response beside each item.*

Skill/Behavior	No Success	Very Little Success	Limited Success	Generally Successful	Completely Successful
A. Intuitive user interface	❑	❑	❑	❑	❑
B. Improved reporting and analytic tools	❑	❑	❑	❑	❑
C. 360° view of Lead > Prospect > Suspect > Customer information	❑	❑	❑	❑	❑
D. Ad hoc search and query functionality within the system	❑	❑	❑	❑	❑
E. Integration with back-end accounting system for end-to-end view of account history	❑	❑	❑	❑	❑
F. Tracking of customer demographic and psychographic data for advanced customer segmentation	❑	❑	❑	❑	❑
G. Integrated Miller Heiman sales process	❑	❑	❑	❑	❑
H. Data validation on key system fields and attributes	❑	❑	❑	❑	❑
I. Explorer view online help systems	❑	❑	❑	❑	❑

2. Did you implement on-the-job action plan as part of the CRM Project?   Yes ❑   No ❑

If yes, complete and return your action plan with this questionnaire. If not, please explain why you did not complete your action plan. _____

_____

Figure 4-1. Impact Questionnaire

Progress with Objectives

Sometimes, it is helpful to assess progress with the objectives in the follow-up evaluation, as is illustrated in Question 1 of Figure 4-1. Although this issue is usually assessed during the project (because it is Level 1 data), it can be helpful to revisit the objectives after the participants have had an opportunity to apply what has been learned.

3. Have you used the materials and/or online help systems since you participated in the project?

     Yes ❑   No ❑

     Please explain. _____

4. For the following skills, please indicate the extent of improvement during the last few months as influenced by your participation in the CRM Project. *Check the appropriate response beside each item.*

Skill Area	No Opportunity to Apply	No Change	Some Change	Moderate Change	Significant Change	Very Significant Change
A. ORGANIZING						
1. Prioritizing daily activities	❑	❑	❑	❑	❑	❑
2. Tracking sales funnel	❑	❑	❑	❑	❑	❑
3. Organizing daily activities	❑	❑	❑	❑	❑	❑
4. Increased contact-to-close metrics	❑	❑	❑	❑	❑	❑
B. WORK CLIMATE						
1. Applying coaching	❑	❑	❑	❑	❑	❑
2. Applying techniques/initiatives that influence motivational climate	❑	❑	❑	❑	❑	❑
3. Implementing actions that influenced retaining customers	❑	❑	❑	❑	❑	❑
4. Implementing job enrichment opportunities for valued associates	❑	❑	❑	❑	❑	❑
5. Implementing better control and monitoring systems	❑	❑	❑	❑	❑	❑
6. Applying techniques that influenced better teamwork	❑	❑	❑	❑	❑	❑
7. Realizing improved written communications	❑	❑	❑	❑	❑	❑
8. Improved communication through use of collaboration tools	❑	❑	❑	❑	❑	❑
9. Working personal performance plan	❑	❑	❑	❑	❑	❑

Figure 4-1. Continued

Action Plan Implementation

If an action plan is required, the questionnaire should reference the plan and determine the extent to which it has been implemented. If the action plan requirement is low-key, perhaps only one question would be devoted to the follow-up on the action plan, as illustrated in Question 2 in Figure 4-1. If the action plan is comprehensive and contains abundant Level 3 and 4 data, then the questionnaire takes

5. List the three (3) uses from the above list that you have used most frequently as a result of the project.

A. _____

B. _____

C. _____

6. What has changed about you or your work as a result of your participation in this project? (Specific behavior change, such as better visibility of sales pipeline, improved communication with customers, employee participation in sales forecasting, improved close rates, etc.)

_____

_____

_____

7. How has your organization benefited from your participation in the project? Please identify specific business accomplishments or improvements that you believe are linked to participation in this project. Think about how the improvements actually resulted in influencing business measures, such as increased revenue, increased overall shipments, improved customer satisfaction, improved employee satisfaction, decreased costs, saved time, etc.

_____

_____

_____

_____

8. Reflect on your specific business accomplishments/improvements as stated above and think of specific ways that you can convert your accomplishments to a monetary value. Along with the monetary value, please indicate your basis for the value.

Estimated monetary amount $ _____

Indicate if the above amount is weekly, monthly, quarterly, or annually.

    ○ Weekly   ○ Monthly   ○ Quarterly   ○ Annually

What is your basis for your estimates? (What influenced the benefits/savings, and how did you arrive at the value above?) _____

_____

_____

_____

_____

_____

_____

9. What percentage of the improvement above was influenced by the application of the *CRM Project*?

_____ % (0% = None, and 100% = All)

Figure 4-1. Continued

a secondary role, and most of the data collection process will focus directly on the status of the completed action plan.

Use of Project Materials and Handouts

If participants are given materials to use on the job, determining the extent to which these materials are used is helpful. This is particularly helpful when system user guides, "cheat sheets" for desktop shortcuts, and job aids have been distributed and explained during

10. What level of confidence do you place on the above estimation?

           _____ % *Confidence* (0% = No Confidence, and 100% = Certainty)

11. Do you think this *CRM Project* represented an appropriate investment for the company?

    Yes ❑   **No** ❑

    Please explain. _____

    _____

12. Indicate the extent to which you think your application of the *CRM Project* had a positive influence on the following business measures in your own work or your work unit. *Please check the appropriate response beside each measure.*

Business Measure	Not Applicable	Applies But No Influence	Some Influence	Moderate Influence	Significant Influence	Very Significant Influence
A. Work output	❑	❑	❑	❑	❑	❑
B. Quality	❑	❑	❑	❑	❑	❑
C. Cost control	❑	❑	❑	❑	❑	❑
D. Efficiency	❑	❑	❑	❑	❑	❑
E. Response time to customers	❑	❑	❑	❑	❑	❑
F. Cycle time of products	❑	❑	❑	❑	❑	❑
G. Sales	❑	❑	❑	❑	❑	❑
H. Employee turnover	❑	❑	❑	❑	❑	❑
I. Employee absenteeism	❑	❑	❑	❑	❑	❑
J. Employee satisfaction	❑	❑	❑	❑	❑	❑
K. Employee complaints	❑	❑	❑	❑	❑	❑
L. Customer satisfaction	❑	❑	❑	❑	❑	❑
M. Customer complaints	❑	❑	❑	❑	❑	❑
N. Other (please specify)	❑	❑	❑	❑	❑	❑

Please cite specific examples or provide more details: _____

_____

_____

Figure 4-1. Continued

the project, and participants are expected to use them on the job. Question 3 in Figure 4-1 addresses this issue.

Application of Knowledge/Skills

As shown in Question 4 of Figure 4-1, determining the level of improvement in skills directly linked to the project is important. A

_____

_____

13. What barriers, if any, have you encountered that have prevented you from using the CRM?
    Check all that apply.

    ❑ I have had no opportunity to use the CRM.
    ❑ I have not had enough time to apply the CRM.
    ❑ My work environment does not support the use of these CRM.
    ❑ My supervisor does not support this type of project.
    ❑ This CRM does not apply to my job situation.
    ❑ Other (please specify): _____

If any of the above are checked, please explain if possible. _____

_____

_____

14. What enablers, if any, are present to help you use the CRM? Please explain.

_____

_____

15. What additional support could be provided by management that would influence your ability to use the CRM?

_____

16. What additional benefits have been derived from this project? _____

_____

_____

17. What additional solutions do you recommend that would help achieve the same business results that the
    CRM Project has influenced? _____

_____

_____

18. Would you recommend the *CRM Project* to others?   **Yes** ❑   **No** ❑
    Please explain. If no, why not. If yes, what groups/jobs and why? _____

_____

_____

19. What specific suggestions do you have for improving this project? _____

_____

_____

20. Other Comments:

_____

Figure 4-1. Continued

more detailed variation of this question is to list each skill and indicate their frequency and effectiveness of use. For many skills, frequent use quickly after acquisition is important so the skills become internalized. In this example, Question 5 addresses the skill frequency issue.

Changes with Work

Sometimes, the specific participant work activities or processes that have changed as a result of the project must be determined. As Question 6 in Figure 4-1 illustrates, the participant explores how the skill applications (listed previously) have changed work habits, processes, and output.

Improvements/Accomplishments

Question 7 in Figure 4-1 begins a series of four impact questions that are appropriate for most follow-up questionnaires. This question seeks specific accomplishments and improvements directly linked to the project and focuses on specific measurable successes that can be easily identified by the participants. Since this question is open-ended, it can be helpful to provide examples that indicate the nature and range of responses requested. However, examples can also limit the responses.

Monetary Impact

Perhaps the most difficult question (Number 8 in Figure 4-1) asks participants to provide monetary values for the improvements identified in Question 7. Only the first-year improvement is sought. Participants are asked to specify net improvements so that the actual monetary values will represent gains from the project. An important part of the question is the basis for the calculation, where participants specify the steps taken to develop the annual net value and the assumptions made in the analysis. The basis must be completed with enough detail to understand the process.

Improvements Linked with Project

The next question in the impact series (Question 9 of Figure 4-1) isolates the effects of the IT project. Participants indicate the percent of the improvement that is directly related to the project. As an alternative, participants may be provided with the factors that have influenced the results and asked to allocate percentages to each factor.

Confidence Level

To adjust for the uncertainty of the data provided in Questions 8 and 9, participants are asked to offer a level of confidence for the estimation, expressed as a percentage, with a range of 0 to 100 percent, as shown in Question 10 in Figure 4-1. This input allows participants to reflect any uncertainty with this process.

Investment Value

The value of the project, from the viewpoint of the participant, can be useful information. As illustrated in Question 11 in Figure 4-1, participants are asked if they perceive this project to be an appropriate investment. Another option for this question is to present the actual cost of the project so that participants can respond more accurately from an investment perspective. It may be useful to express the cost per participant. Also, the question can be divided into two parts: one reflecting the investment of funds by the company and the other the investment of the participant's time in the project.

Link with Output Measures

Sometimes, determining the degree to which the project has influenced certain output measures, as shown in Question 12 in Figure 4-1, can be helpful. In some situations, a detailed analysis may reveal specifically which measures this project has influenced. However, when this issue is uncertain, it may be helpful to list the potential business performance measures influenced by the project and seek input from the participants. The question should be worded so that the frame of reference is for the time period after the project was conducted.

Barriers

Barriers can influence the successful application of the skills and knowledge learned during the IT project. Question 13 in Figure 4-1 asks participants to identify these barriers. As an alternative, the perceived barriers are listed and participants check all that apply. Still another variation is to list the barriers with a range of responses, indicating the extent to which the barrier inhibited results.

Enablers

Just as important as barriers are the enablers. These are the issues, events, or situations that enable the process to be applied successfully on the job. Question 14 is open-ended and applies to enablers. The same options are available with this question as in the question on barriers.

Management Support

For most projects, management support is critical to the successful application of newly acquired skills. At least one question should be included about the degree of management support, such as Question 15. Sometimes, this question is structured so that descriptions of management support are detailed. Participants check the one that applies to their situations. This information is beneficial to help remove or minimize barriers.

Other Benefits

In most projects, additional benefits will begin to emerge, particularly intangible benefits. Participants should be asked to detail any benefits not presented elsewhere. In this example, Question 16 is an open-ended question for additional benefits.

Other Solutions

An IT project is only one of many potential solutions to a performance problem. If the needs assessment is faulty or if alternative approaches to developing the desired skills or knowledge are available, other potential solutions could be more effective and achieve the same success. In Question 17, the participant is asked to identify other solutions that could have been effective in obtaining the same or similar results. This information can be particularly helpful as the IT function is perceived as a business transformation function.

Target Audience Recommendations

Sometimes, participants' input about the most appropriate target audience for this project should be obtained. In Question 18, the participants are asked to indicate which groups of employees would benefit the most from leveraging the technology being implemented during the project.

Suggestions for Improvement

As a final wrap-up question, participants are asked to provide suggestions for improving any part of the project. As illustrated in Question 19, the open-ended structure is intended to solicit qualitative responses to be used to make improvements.

Improving the Response Rate for Questionnaires and Surveys

The content items represent a wide range of potential issues to explore in a follow-up questionnaire or survey. Obviously, asking all the questions could cause the response rate to be reduced considerably. The challenge, therefore, is to tackle questionnaire design and administration for maximum response rate. This is a critical issue when the questionnaire is the primary data collection method and most of the evaluation hinges on questionnaire results. The following actions can be taken to increase response rates.

Provide advance communication. If appropriate and feasible, participants should receive advance communications about the requirement to complete the questionnaire. This minimizes some of the resistance to the process, provides an opportunity to explain the evaluation in more detail, and positions the follow-up evaluation as an integral part of the project, not an add-on activity.

Communicate the purpose. Participants should understand the reason for the questionnaire, including who or what has initiated this evaluation. Participants should know if the evaluation is part of a systematic process or a special request for this project.

Explain who will see the data. Participants need to know who will see the data and the results of the questionnaire. If the questionnaire is anonymous, it should clearly be communicated to participants what steps will be taken to ensure anonymity. Participants should know if senior executives will see the combined results of the study.

Describe the data integration process. Participants should understand how the questionnaire results will be combined with other data, if applicable. The questionnaire may be only one of the data collection methods used. Participants should know how the data is weighted and integrated in the final report.

Keep the questionnaire as simple as possible. While a simple questionnaire does not always provide the full scope of data necessary for an ROI analysis, a simplified approach should always be a goal.

When questions are developed and the total scope of the questionnaire is finalized, every effort should be made to keep it as simple and as brief as possible.

Simplify the response process. To the extent possible, responding to the questionnaire should be easy. E-mailing a link to a secure Web-based survey is the most efficient way of reaching all your participants. This will maximize your response rate as participants can complete the survey in detail in a convenient setting.

Use local manager support. Management involvement at the local level is critical to response rate success. Project managers can electronically distribute the questionnaires themselves, refer to the questionnaire during staff meetings, follow up to see if questionnaires have been completed, and show general support for completing the questionnaire. This direct supervisor support will cause some participants to respond.

Let the participants know they are part of the sample. If appropriate, participants should know they are part of a carefully selected sample and their input will be used to make decisions regarding a much larger target audience. This action often appeals to a sense of responsibility from participants to provide usable, accurate data for the questionnaire.

Consider incentives. Different types of incentives can be offered, and they usually fall into three categories. First, an incentive can be provided in exchange for the completed questionnaire. For example, if participants return the questionnaire personally, they will receive a small gift, such as a mouse pad or coffee mug. If anonymity is an issue, a neutral third party can provide the incentive. In the second category, the incentive can be provided to make participants feel guilty about not responding. Examples are a dollar bill (or equivalent currency) or online gift certificate attached to the questionnaire, or a pen enclosed in the envelope. Participants are asked to "Take the money, buy a beverage, and fill out the questionnaire," or "Please use this pen to complete the questionnaire." A third group of incentives is designed to obtain a quick response. This approach is based on the assumption that a quick response will ensure a greater response rate. Once an individual starts to procrastinate about completing the questionnaire, the odds of it ever being completed diminish considerably. The initial group of respondents may receive a more expensive gift, or they may be part of a drawing for an incentive. For example, in one study involving 75 participants, the first 25 returned questionnaires were placed in a drawing for a $500 gift card. The next 25 were added to the first 25 for another drawing. After the first 50, there was no incentive. The longer a participant waited, the lower the odds of winning. Incentives work particularly well with online surveys because a large audience of respondents may act quickly, providing rapid access to statistically significant data.

Have an executive send the introductory e-mail. Participants are always interested in who sent the e-mail with the questionnaire. For maximum effectiveness, a senior executive who is responsible for a major area should send the e-mail. Employees may be more willing to respond to a senior executive than a member of the IT or technology development staff.

Use follow-up reminders. A follow-up reminder should be sent one week after the questionnaire is received and another sent a week later. Depending on the questionnaire and the situation, these times could be adjusted. In some situations, a third follow-up is recommended. Sometimes, the follow-up should be sent through different media. For example, a questionnaire may be sent through e-mail, whereas the first follow-up reminder is an e-mail from the immediate supervisor, and the second follow-up reminder is sent through instant messaging or comparable corporate communication tool.

Send a copy of the results to the participants. Even if it is an abbreviated form, participants should see the results of the impact study. More important, participants should understand that they will receive a copy of the impact study when asked to provide the data. This promise will often increase the response rate, because some individuals want to see the results of the entire group.

Review the questionnaire in the session. Participants must understand the questionnaire as much as possible. To help, they should see a copy in advance of the data collection. Ideally, the questionnaire should be distributed and reviewed during the first session of the project. Each question should be briefly discussed and any issues or concerns about the questions need to be clarified. This not only helps the response rate, but it also improves the quality and quantity of data.

Consider a captive audience. The best way to have an extremely high response rate is to consider a captive audience. In a follow-up session, a routine meeting, or a session designed to collect data, participants meet and provide input, usually during the first few minutes of the meeting. Sometimes, a routine meeting (such as a sales, technology, or management meeting) provides a good opportunity to collect data. This approach is ideal in a major project with a series of different courses. Each subsequent course is an opportunity to collect data about the previous course.

Communicate the timing of data flow. Participants should be given deadlines for providing the data. They also need to know when they will receive results. The best approach is to provide the exact date that the last questionnaires will be accepted, the date that the analysis will be complete, the date that they will receive the results of the study, and the date that the sponsor will receive the results. The specific timing builds respect for the entire process.

Select the appropriate media. The medium for the survey (whether Web-based, e-mail, or paper-based) should match the culture of the group and not necessarily selected for the convenience of the evaluator. Sometimes, an optional response media will be allowed. The important thing is to make it fit the audience.

Consider making the input anonymous. Anonymous data is often more objective and sometimes more free-flowing. If participants believe that their input is anonymous, they will be more constructive and candid in their feedback, and response rates will generally be higher.

Treat data with confidence. Confidentiality is an important part of the process. A confidentiality statement should be included, indicating that participants' names will not be revealed to anyone other than the data collectors and those involved in analyzing the data. In some cases, it may be appropriate to indicate specifically who will actually see the raw data. Also, the steps that are taken to ensure the confidentiality of the data should be detailed. As a side note, for the technology savvy individual with experience using online survey tools, the IP address of the respondents can be captured when the survey is accessed. To ensure complete anonymity, this tracking feature should be disabled so there is no temptation to find a respondent who provided less-than-stellar feedback on a system carefully designed, developed, and delivered.

Pilot testing. Consider using a pilot test on a sample audience. This is one of the best ways to ensure that the questionnaire is designed properly and the questions are understood. Pilot testing can be accomplished quickly with a small sample size and can be revealing.

Explain how long it will take to complete the questionnaire. Although this is a simple issue, participants need to have a realistic understanding of how long completing the questionnaire will take. There is nothing more frustrating than to grossly underestimate the time needed to complete the questionnaire. The pilot test should provide the information needed to adequately allocate time for the response.

Personalize the process, if possible. Participants will respond to personal messages and requests. If possible, the e-mail with the questionnaire should be personalized. Also, a personal phone call can be a helpful follow-up reminder. The personal touch brings appropriate sincerity and responsibility to the process.

Provide an update. In some cases, providing an update on current response totals and the progress on the entire project can. It is helpful for individuals to understand how others are doing. Sometimes this creates a subtle pressure and reminder to provide data.

Collectively, these items help boost response rates of follow-up questionnaires. Using all of these strategies can result in a 50 to 60 percent response rate, even with lengthy questionnaires that might take 45 minutes to complete.

TESTS

Testing is important for measuring learning as it relates to the new features and functionality in the system. Pre- and post-implementation comparisons using systems competency tests are common. An improvement in test scores shows the change in skills, knowledge, or attitudes attributed to the project. The principles of test development are similar to those for the design and development of questionnaires and attitude surveys. This section presents additional information on types of tests and test construction (Westgaard, 1999).

Types of Tests

Several types of tests, which can be classified in three ways, are used for properly measuring IT and technology development skills assessment. The first is based on the medium used for administering the test.

Norm-Referenced Test

Norm-referenced tests compare participants with each other or to other groups rather than to specific instructional objectives. They are characterized by using data to compare the participants to the "norm" or average. Although norm-referenced tests have only limited use in some IT evaluations, they may be useful in projects involving large numbers of participants in which average scores and relative rankings are important. In some situations, participants who score highest on the exams are given special recognition or awards or made eligible for other special activities.

Criterion-Referenced Test

The criterion-referenced test (CRT) is an objective test with a predetermined cut-off score. The CRT is a measure against carefully written objectives for the IT project. In a CRT, the interest lies in whether participants meet the desired minimum standards, not how that participant ranks with others. The primary concern is to measure, report, and analyze participant performance as it relates to the instructional objectives.

Criterion-referenced testing is a popular measurement instrument in IT (Shrock & Coscarelli, 2000). Its use is becoming widespread and is frequently used in e-learning and other key technology initiatives. It has the advantage of being objective-based, precise, and relatively easy to administer. It does, however, require projects with clearly defined objectives that can be measured by tests.

Performance Testing

Performance testing allows the participant to exhibit a skill (and occasionally knowledge or attitudes) that has been learned during an IT project. The skill can be manual, verbal, analytical, or a combination of the three. Performance testing is used frequently in job-related IT projects where the participants are allowed to demonstrate what they have learned. In supervisory- and management-focused IT projects, performance testing comes in the form of skill practices or system demonstrations. Participants are asked to demonstrate discussion or problem-solving skills they have acquired.

For a performance test to be effective, the following steps are recommended for its design and administration:

- The test should be a representative sample of the IT project, and it should allow the participant to demonstrate as many skills taught during the project as possible.
- Every phase of the test should be thoroughly planned, including the time, the preparation of the participant, the collection of necessary materials and tools, and the evaluation of results.
- Thorough and consistent instructions are necessary. As with other tests, the quality of the instructions can influence the

outcome of a performance test. All participants should be provided the same instructions.

- Acceptable standards must be developed for a performance test so that employees know in advance what has to be accomplished to be considered satisfactory and acceptable for test completion.
- Information that may lead participants astray should not be included.

With these general guidelines, performance tests can be developed into effective tools for project evaluation. Although more costly than written tests, performance tests are essential when a high degree of fidelity is required between work and test conditions.

Simulations

Another technique to measure learning is job simulation. This method involves the construction and application of a procedure or task that simulates or models the activity for which the IT project is being conducted. The simulation is designed to represent, as closely as possible, the actual job situation. Simulation may be used as an integral part of the IT project as well as for evaluation. In evaluation, participants are provided an opportunity to try out their performance in the simulated activity and have it evaluated based on how well the task was accomplished. Simulations may be used during the project, at the end of the project, or as part of the follow-up evaluation. A variety of simulation techniques are used to evaluate project results.

Automated Simulation

This technique uses process automation software to mimic the keystrokes and processes that a live user would input into the system to simulate real-life user interaction with the new application.

Task Simulation

This approach involves the performance of a simulated task as part of an evaluation.

Business Games

Business games have grown in popularity in recent years. They represent simulations of part or all of a business enterprise in which participants change the variables of the business and observe the effect of those changes. The game not only reflects the real-world situation, but it also represents the synopsis of the IT project of which it is a part. Business games can also be a great tool for simulating quirky processes that may not have been tested thoroughly during the quality assurance process. This allows business users to input atypical transactions into the system in a simulated environment and witness the results. The feedback generated from this process can prove valuable to the technology development team.

Case Study

A possibly less effective, but still popular, technique is a case study. A case study gives a detailed description of a problem and usually contains a list of several questions. The participant is asked to analyze the case and determine the best course of action.

Role Playing

In role playing, sometimes referred to as skill practice, participants practice a newly learned skill as they are observed by other individuals. Participants are given an assigned role with specific instructions, which sometimes includes an ultimate course of action. The participant then practices the skill with all the corresponding system inputs with other individuals to accomplish the desired objectives.

In summary, simulations come in many varieties. They offer an opportunity for participants to practice what is being taught in an IT project and have their performance observed in a simulated job condition. They can provide extremely accurate evaluations if the performance in the simulation is objective and can be clearly measured.

Informal Tests

In some situations, an informal learning check that provides assurance that participants have acquired skills, knowledge, or perhaps some changes in attitudes is acceptable. This approach is appropriate when other levels of evaluation are pursued. For example, if a Level 3 on-the-job application evaluation is planned, it might not be critical to have a comprehensive Level 2 evaluation. An informal assessment of learning may be sufficient. After all, resources are scarce and a comprehensive evaluation at all levels becomes expensive. The following are some alternative approaches to measuring learning that might suffice when inexpensive, low-key, informal assessments are needed.

Features/Functions/Fixes

Many IT projects contain specific features, functions, or fixes that must be scoped, developed, and deployed during the project. These items should each be captured during the business requirements phase of the project and should have ample documentation detailing their specific business needs and benefits. When these are integrated into the project, there are several ways to measure the success of a technology initiative:

- The results of the system functionality enhancements can be submitted for review and evaluated by the project manager.
- The results can be discussed in a group with a comparison of approaches and solutions. The group can reach an assessment of how much each user will benefit from the enhanced system processes.
- The system feature enhancements can be shared with the group, and the participant can provide a self-assessment indicating the degree to which skills and knowledge have been obtained from additional system functionality.
- The business analyst or technology project manager can review the individual progress or success of each participant to determine the relative success.

Self-Assessment

In many applications, a self-assessment may be appropriate. Participants are provided an opportunity to assess the extent of skills and knowledge acquisition. This is particularly applicable when Level 3, 4, and 5 evaluations are planned, and it is important to know if user competency with the technology application has improved. A few techniques can ensure that the process is effective:

- The self-assessment should be made on an anonymous basis so that individuals feel free to express a realistic and accurate assessment of what they have learned or additional skills they have gained.
- The purpose of the self-assessment should be explained, along with the plans for the data—specifically, if there are implications for system design or redesign as a result of user feedback.
- If no improvement has occurred or the self-assessment is unsatisfactory, some explanation should be given as to what that means and the resulting implications. This will help ensure that accurate and credible information is provided.

Project Manager Assessment

A final technique is for the technology project manager to provide an assessment of the systems adoption that has taken place. Although this approach is subjective, it may be appropriate when a Level 3, 4, or 5 evaluation is planned. One of the most effective ways to accomplish this is to provide a checklist of the specific skills that need to be acquired in the course. Project managers can then check off their assessment of the skills individually. Also, if a particular body of knowledge needs to be acquired, the categories could be listed with a checklist for assurance that the individual has a good understanding of those items.

INTERVIEWS

Another helpful data collection method is interviews, although they are not used in evaluation as frequently as questionnaires are. The IT staff, the participant's supervisor, or an outside third party can conduct interviews. Interviews can secure data not available in performance records or data that are difficult to obtain through written responses or observations (Kvale, 1996). Also, interviews can uncover success stories that can be useful in communicating evaluation results. Participants may be reluctant to describe their results in a questionnaire but will volunteer the information to a skillful interviewer who uses probing techniques. Although the interview process uncovers reaction, learning, and impact, it is primarily used with application data. A major disadvantage of the interview is that it is time consuming and requires interviewer preparation to ensure that the process is consistent.

Types of Interviews

Interviews usually fall into two basic types: structured and unstructured. A structured interview is much like a questionnaire. Specific questions are asked with little room to deviate from the desired responses. The primary advantages of the structured interview over the questionnaire are that the interview process can ensure completion and that the interviewer understands the responses supplied by the participant.

The unstructured interview allows for probing for additional information. This type of interview uses a few general questions that can lead to more detailed information as important data are uncovered. The interviewer must be skilled in the probing process.

Interview Guidelines

The design issues and steps for interviews are similar to those of the questionnaire. A few key issues need emphasis.

Develop questions to be asked. After the type of interview is determined, specific questions need to be developed. Questions should be brief, precise, and designed for easy response.

Try out the interview. The interview should be tested on a small number of participants. If possible, the interviews should be conducted as part of the trial run of the IT project. The responses should be analyzed and the interview revised, if necessary.

Prepare the interviewers. The interviewer should have the appropriate level of core skills, including active listening, asking probing questions, and collecting and summarizing information.

Provide clear instructions to the participant. The participant should understand the purpose of the interview and know how the information will be used. Expectations, conditions, and rules of the interview should be thoroughly discussed. For example, the participant should know if statements will be kept confidential.

Administer the interviews according to a scheduled plan. As with the other evaluation instruments, interviews need to be conducted according to a predetermined plan. The timing of the interview, the individual who conducts the interview, and the location of the interview are all issues that become relevant when developing a plan. For a large number of participants, a sampling plan may be necessary to save time and reduce evaluation costs.

FOCUS GROUPS

An extension of the interview, focus groups are particularly helpful when in-depth feedback is needed for a Level 3 evaluation. The focus group involves a small group discussion conducted by an experienced facilitator. It is designed to solicit qualitative judgments on a planned topic or issue. Group members are all required to provide their input because individual input builds on group input (Subramony et al., 2002).

When compared to questionnaires, surveys, tests, or interviews, the focus group strategy has several advantages. The basic premise of using focus groups is that when quality judgments are subjective, several individual judgments are better than one. The group process, where participants stimulate ideas in others, is an effective method for generating qualitative data. It is inexpensive and can be quickly planned and conducted. Its flexibility makes it possible to explore an IT or technology development project's unexpected outcomes or applications.

Applications for Evaluation

The focus group is particularly helpful when qualitative information is needed about the success of an IT project. For example, the focus group can be used in the following situations:

- Evaluate the reactions to specific features, functionality, fixes, or other components of an IT project
- Assess the overall effectiveness of the project implementation and rollout
- Assess the impact of the project in a follow-up evaluation after the project is completed

Essentially, focus groups are helpful when evaluation information is needed but cannot be collected adequately with questionnaires, interviews, or quantitative methods.

Guidelines

Although there are no set rules on how to use focus groups for evaluation, the following guidelines are helpful.

Ensure that management buys into the focus group process. Because this is a relatively new process for technology project evaluation, it might be a foreign concept to management surrounding this type of initiative. Managers need to understand focus groups and their advantages. This should raise confidence levels in the information obtained from group sessions.

Plan topics, questions, and strategy carefully. As with any evaluation instrument, planning is critical. The specific topics, questions, and issues to be discussed must be carefully planned and sequenced. This enhances the comparison of results from one group to another and ensures that the group process is effective and stays on track.

Keep the group size small. Although there is no magic group size, a range of 8 to 12 is appropriate for most focus group applications. A group must be large enough to ensure different points of view but small enough to provide every participant with a chance to freely exchange comments.

Use a representative sample of the target population. If possible, groups should be selected to represent the target population. The group should be homogeneous in experience, rank, and job level in the organization.

Facilitators must have appropriate expertise. The success of a focus group rests with the facilitator who must be skilled in the focus group process. Facilitators must know how to control aggressive members of the group and diffuse the input from those who want to dominate the group. Also, facilitators must be able to create an environment in which participants feel comfortable in offering comments freely and openly. Because of this, some organizations use external facilitators.

In summary, the focus group is an inexpensive and quick way to determine the strengths and weaknesses of IT projects, particularly with management and supervisory IT-focused initiatives. However, for a complete evaluation, focus group information should be combined with data from other instruments.

OBSERVATIONS

Another potentially useful data collection method is observing participants and recording any changes in their behavior. The observer may be a member of the IT staff, the participant's supervisor, a member of a peer group, or an external party. The most common observer, and probably the most practical, is a member of the IT staff.

Guidelines for Effective Observation

Observation is often misused or misapplied to evaluation situations, leaving some to abandon the process. The effectiveness of observation can be improved with the following guidelines.

The observations should be systematic. The observation process must be planned so that it is executed effectively without any surprises. The persons observed should know in advance about the observation and why they are being observed, unless the observation is planned to be invisible. The timing of observations should be a part of the plan. If a participant is observed when times are not normal (i.e., in a crisis), the data collected may be useless.

The observers should know how to interpret and report what they see. Observations involve judgment decisions. The observer must analyze which behaviors are being displayed and what actions the participants are taking. Observers should know how to summarize behavior and report results in a meaningful manner.

The observer's influence should be minimized. Except for mystery observers and electronic observations, completely isolating the overall effect of an observer is impossible. Participants may display the behavior they think is appropriate, and they will usually be at their best, which is referred to as "the big brother effect." The presence of the observer must be minimized. To the extent possible, the observer should blend into the work environment or extend the observation period.

Select observers carefully. Observers are usually independent of the participants, typically a member of the training or quality assurance staff. The independent observers are usually more skilled at recording behavior and making interpretations of behavior. They are usually unbiased in these interpretations. Using them enables the technology department to bypass IT observers and relieves the line organization of that responsibility. On the other hand, this type of observer has the appearance of an outsider checking the work of others. There may be a tendency for participants to overreact and possibly resent this kind of observer. Sometimes, it might be more plausible to recruit observers from outside the organization. This approach has an advantage of neutralizing the prejudicial feelings entering the decisions.

Observers must be fully prepared. Observers must fully understand what information is needed and what skills were covered during the project. They must be trained for the assignment and provided a chance to practice observation skills.

Observation Methods

Five methods of observation are used, depending on the circumstances surrounding the type of information needed. Each method is described briefly.

Behavior Checklist and Codes

A behavior checklist can be useful for recording the presence, absence, frequency, or duration of a participant's behavior as it occurs. A checklist will not usually provide information on the quality, intensity, or possibly the circumstances surrounding the behavior observed. The checklist is useful because an observer can identify exactly which behaviors should or should not occur. Measuring the duration of a behavior may be more difficult, and it requires a stopwatch and a place on the form to record the time interval. This factor is usually not as important when compared to whether a particular behavior was observed and how often. The number of behaviors listed in the checklist should be small and in a logical sequence. A variation of this approach involves a coding of behaviors on a form. This method is less time consuming because the code is entered identifying a specific behavior.

Delayed Report Method

With a delayed report method, the observer does not use any forms or written materials during the observation. The information is either recorded after the observation is completed or at predetermined time intervals during an observation. The observer attempts to reconstruct what was observed during the observation period. The advantage of this approach is that the observer is not as noticeable, and there are no forms being completed or notes being taken during the observation. The observer can blend into the situation and be less distracting. An obvious disadvantage is that the information written may not be as accurate and reliable had the information been collected as it occurred. A variation of this approach is the 360-degree feedback process in which surveys are completed on other individuals based on observations within a specific timeframe.

Call Recording

Monitoring conversations of participants who are using the skills taught during the IT project is an effective observation technique. For example, in a large communication company's telemarketing department, sales representatives were trained to sell equipment by telephone. To determine if employees were using the skills properly, telephone conversations were monitored on a selected and sometimes random basis. Although this approach may stir some controversy, it is an effective way to determine if skills are being applied consistently and effectively. For it to work smoothly, it must be fully explained and the rules clearly communicated.

Computer Monitoring

For employees who work regularly with a keyboard, computer monitoring is becoming an effective way to "observe" participants as they perform job tasks. The computer monitors times, sequences of steps, and other activities to determine if the participant is performing the work according to what was learned during the IT project. As technology use continues to increase, computer monitoring holds the promise of observing actual applications on the job. This is particularly helpful when collecting Level 3 data.

BUSINESS PERFORMANCE MONITORING

Data to measure performance are available in every organization. Monitoring performance data enables management to measure performance in terms of output, quality, costs, and time. In determining the use of data during the evaluation, the first consideration should be existing databases and reports. In most organizations, performance data suitable for measuring the improvement resulting from a project are available. If not, additional record-keeping systems will have to be developed for measurement and analysis. At this step, as with many other steps in the process, the question of economics enters. Is it economical to develop the record-keeping system necessary to evaluate an IT project? If the costs are greater than the expected return for the entire project, then it is meaningless to develop them.

Using Current Measures

The recommended approach is to use existing performance measures, if available. Specific guidelines are recommended to ensure that current measurement systems are easily developed.

Identify appropriate measures. Performance measures should be researched to identify those that are related to the proposed objectives of the project. Frequently, an organization will have several performance measures related to the same item. For example, the efficiency of a production unit can be measured in a variety of ways:

- Number of electronic transactions per hour
- Number of on-schedule shipments
- Percent utilization of the system
- Percent of system downtime
- Labor cost per transaction
- Overtime required per unit of sale
- Total unit cost

Each of these, in its own way, measures the efficiency or effectiveness of the production system. All related measures should be reviewed to determine those most relevant to the IT project.

Convert current measures to usable ones. Occasionally, existing performance measures are integrated with other data, and it may be difficult to keep them isolated from unrelated data. In this situation, all existing related measures should be extracted and retabulated to be more appropriate for comparison in the evaluation. At times, conversion factors may be necessary. For example, the average number of new sales orders per month may be presented regularly in the performance measures for the sales department. In addition, the sales costs per sales representative are also presented. However, in the evaluation of an IT project, the average cost per new sale is needed. The two existing performance records are required to develop the data necessary for comparison.

Develop a collection plan. A data collection plan defines the data to be collected, the source of the data, when data are collected, who will collect them, and where they will be collected. A blank copy of the plan is shown in Figure 4-2. This plan should contain provisions

Data Collection Plan

Program _____   Responsibility _____   Date _____

Level	Objective(s)	Measures/Data	Data Collection Method	Data Sources	Timing	Responsibilities
1	Reaction/ Perceived Value					
2	Learning and Confidence					
3	Application/ Implementation					
4	Impact and Consequences					
5	ROI	Comments: _____ _____ _____				

Figure 4-2. Evaluation Plan: Data Collection

for the evaluator to secure copies of performance reports in a timely manner so that the items can be recorded and available for analysis.

Developing New Measures

In some cases, data are not available for the information needed to measure the effectiveness of an IT project. The IT staff must work with the participating organization to develop record-keeping systems, if this is economically feasible. In one organization, a new e-learning-based employee systems training program was implemented on a company-wide basis. Several measures were planned, including employee productivity and early turnover representing the percentage of employees who left the company during the first six months of employment. An improved e-learning-based system training program should influence this measure. At the time of the project's inception, this measure was not available. When the project was implemented, the organization began collecting productivity and early turnover figures for comparison. Here are some typical questions when creating new measures:

- Which department will develop the measurement system?
- Who will record and monitor the data?

- Where will it be recorded?
- Will forms be used?

These questions will usually involve other departments or a management decision that extends beyond the scope of the IT department. Possibly the administration division, the training department, or human resources organization will be instrumental in helping to determine if new measures are needed and, if so, how they will be collected.

ACTION PLANNING AND FOLLOW-UP ASSIGNMENTS

In some cases, follow-up assignments can develop Level 3 and Level 4 data. In a typical follow-up assignment, the participant is instructed to meet a goal or complete a particular task or project by the determined follow-up date. A summary of the results of these completed assignments provides further evidence of the project's impact.

The action plan is the most common type of follow-up assignment and is fully described in this section. With this approach, participants are required to develop action plans as part of the project. Action plans contain detailed steps to accomplish specific objectives related to the project. The plan is typically prepared on a printed form such as the one shown in Figure 4-3. The action plan

Name _____ Instructor Signature _____ Follow-up Date _____
Objective _____ Evaluation Period _____ to _____
Improvement Measure _____ Current Performance _____ Target Performance _____

Action Steps	Analysis
1 _____	A. What is the unit of measure? _____
2 _____	B. What is the value (cost) of one unit? $ _____
3 _____	C. How did you arrive at this value? _____
4 _____	_____
5 _____	_____
6 _____	D. How much did the measure change during the evaluation period? (monthly value) _____
7 _____	E. What percent of this change was caused by this program? _____ %
Intangible Benefits	F. What level of confidence do you place on the above information? (100% = Certainty; and 0% = No Confidence) _____ %

Comments _____
_____
_____
_____

Figure 4-3. Action Plan

shows what is to be done, by whom, and the date by which the objectives should be accomplished. The action plan is a straightforward, easy-to-use method for determining how participants have changed their behavior on the job and achieved success with the project. The approach produces data and answers such questions as the following:

- What steps or action items have been accomplished and when?
- What on-the-job improvements or accomplishments have been realized since the project was conducted?
- How much of the improvement is linked to the project?
- What may have prevented participants from accomplishing specific action items?
- What is the monetary value of the improvement?

With this information, IT professionals can decide if a project should be modified and in what ways, while managers can assess the findings to evaluate the project's worth.

Developing the Action Plan

The development of the action plan requires two tasks: (1) determining the areas for action and (2) writing the action items. Both tasks should be completed during the project. The areas or measures for action should originate from the need for the project and the content of the project and, at the same time, be related to on-the-job activities. Participants can independently develop a list of potential areas for action, or a list may be generated in group discussions. The list may include a measure needing improvement or represent an opportunity for increased performance. The following are some typical categories:

- Productivity
- Sales, revenue
- Quality/process improvement
- Efficiency
- Time savings
- Cost savings
- Complaints
- Job satisfaction
- Work habits

- Customer satisfaction
- Customer service

The specific action items support the business measure and are usually more difficult to write than the identification of the action areas. The most important characteristic of an action item is that it is written clearly. One way to help achieve this goal is to use specific action verbs. Here are some examples of action items:

- *Learn* how to enter an order into the new Enterprise Resource Planning (ERP) system by *(date)*
- *Identify* and *secure* a new customer account in the new Customer Relationship Management (CRM) system by *(date)*
- *Handle* every workflow document electronically to improve my personal time management by *(date)*
- *Learn* to communicate with my work team, using the new electronic collaboration tools by *(date)*

The following are some typical questions when developing action steps:

- How much time will this action take?
- Are the skills for accomplishing this action item available?
- Who has the authority to implement the action plan?
- Will this action have an effect on other individuals?
- Are there any organizational constraints for accomplishing this action item?

If appropriate, each action item should have a completion date and indicate other individuals or resources required for completion. Also, planned behavior changes should be observable. It should be obvious to the participant and others when it happens. Action plans, as used in this context, do not require the prior approval or input from the participant's supervisor, although it may be helpful.

Using Action Plans Successfully

The action plan process should be an integral part of the project and not an add-on or optional activity. To gain maximum effectiveness from action plans and to collect data for ROI evaluations the following steps should be implemented.

Communicate the action plan requirement early. One of the most negative reactions to action plans is the surprise factor often inherent in the way the process is introduced. When project participants realize that they must develop an unexpected detailed action plan, there is often immediate, built-in resistance. Communicating to participants in advance that the process is an integral part of the project, will often minimize resistance. When participants fully realize the benefits before they attend the first session, they take the process more seriously and usually perform the extra steps to make it more successful. In this scenario, the action plan is positioned as an application tool, not an evaluation tool.

Describe the action planning process at the beginning of the project. When the project begins, action plan requirements should be discussed, including an explanation of the purpose of the process, why it is necessary, and the basic requirements during and after the project. Some facilitators furnish tablet PCs for participants to collect ideas and useful techniques for their action plans. This is a productive way to focus more attention and effort on the process.

Teach the action planning process. An important prerequisite for action plan success is an understanding of how it works and how specific action plans are developed. A portion of the project's agenda is allocated to teaching participants how to develop plans. In this session, the requirements are outlined, special forms and procedures are discussed, and a completed example is distributed and reviewed. Sometimes an entire project module is allocated to this process so that participants will fully understand it and use it. Any available support tools, such as key measures, charts, graphs, suggested topics, and sample calculations, should be used in this session to help facilitate the plan's development.

Allow time to develop the plan. When action plans are used to collect data for an ROI calculation, participants must be allowed enough time to develop their plans during the project. Sometimes, it having participants work in teams is helpful, so they can share ideas. In these sessions, facilitators often monitor the progress of individuals or teams to keep the process on track and to answer questions. In some management and executive development projects, action plans are developed in an evening session, as a scheduled part of the project.

Have the facilitator approve the action plans. It is essential for the action plan to be related to project objectives and, at the same time, represent an important accomplishment for the organization when it is completed. It is easy for participants to stray from the intent and purposes of action planning and not give it the attention it deserves. Therefore, it is helpful to have the facilitator or project director actually sign off on the action plan, ensuring that the plan reflects all of the requirements and is appropriate for the project. In some cases, a space is provided for the facilitator's signature on the action plan document.

Require participants to assign a monetary value for each improvement. Participants are asked to determine, calculate, or estimate the monetary value for each improvement outlined in the plan. When the actual improvement has occurred, participants will use these values to capture the annual monetary benefits of the plan. For this step to be effective, it may be helpful to provide examples of typical ways in which values can be assigned to the actual data.

Ask participants to isolate the effects of the project. Although the action plan is initiated as part of the IT project, the actual improvements reported on the action plan may be influenced by other factors. Therefore, the action planning process should not take full credit for the improvement. For example, an action plan to increase sales rep efficiency could take only partial credit for an improvement because of the other variables that influenced the efficiency rate. Even with at least nine ways to isolate the effects of IT performance, participant estimation is usually more appropriate in the action planning process. The participants are asked to estimate the percent of the improvement actually related to this particular project. This question can be asked on the action plan or on a follow-up electronic questionnaire.

Ask participants to provide a confidence level for estimates. Since the process to convert data to monetary values may not be exact and the amount of the improvement directly related to the project may not be precise, participants are asked to indicate their level of confidence in those two values, collectively. On a scale of 0 to 100 percent, where 0 percent means "no confidence" and 100 percent means "complete confidence," this value provides participants a mechanism to express their uneasiness with their ability to be exact with the process.

Require action plans to be presented to the group. There is no better way to secure commitment and ownership of the action planning process than to have a participant describe his or her action plan in front of fellow participants. Presenting the action plan helps to ensure that the process is thoroughly developed and will be implemented on the job. Sometimes, the process spurs competition among the group. If the number of participants is too large for individual presentations, perhaps one participant can be selected from the team (if the plans are developed in teams). Under these circumstances, the team will usually select the best action plan for presentation to the group, raising the bar for others.

Explain the follow-up mechanism. Participants must leave the session with a clear understanding of the timing of the action plan implementation and the planned follow-up. The method in which the data will be collected, analyzed, and reported should be openly discussed. Five options are common:

1. The group is reconvened to discuss the progress on the plans.
2. Participants meet with their immediate manager and discuss the success of the plan. A copy is forwarded to the IT department.
3. A meeting is held with the project evaluator, the participant, and the participant's manager to discuss the plan and the information contained in it.
4. Participants send the plan to the evaluator, and it is discussed in a conference call.
5. Participants send the plan directly to the evaluation with no meetings or discussions. This is the most common option.

Although there are other ways to collect the data, it is important to select a mechanism that fits the culture, requirements, and constraints of the organization.

Collect action plans at the predetermined follow-up time. Because it is critical to have an excellent response rate, several steps may be necessary to ensure that the action plans are completed and the data are returned to the appropriate individual or group for analysis. Some organizations use follow-up reminders by mail or e-mail. Others call participants to check progress. Still others offer assistance in developing the final plan. These steps may require additional resources, which have to be weighed against the importance of having more data. When the action plan process is implemented as outlined in this chapter, the response rates will normally be high—in the 60 to 90 percent range. Usually participants will see the importance of the process and will develop their plans in detail before leaving the project.

Summarize the data and calculate the ROI. If developed properly, each action plan should have annualized monetary values associated with improvements. Also, each individual has indicated the percent of the improvement that is directly related to the project. Finally, each participant has provided a confidence percentage to reflect their uncertainty with the process and the subjective nature of some of the data that may be provided.

Because this process involves some estimates, it may not appear credible. Several adjustments during the analysis make the process credible and believable. The following adjustments are made:

Step 1: For those participants who do not provide data, it is assumed that they had no improvement to report. This is a conservative assumption. (Guiding Principle 6)

Step 2: Each value is checked for realism, usability, and feasibility. Extreme values are discarded and omitted from the analysis. (Guiding Principle 8)

Step 3: Because the improvement is annualized, it is assumed that the project had no improvement after the first year. Some projects should add value at year two and three. (Guiding Principle 9)

Step 4: The improvement from Step 3 is then adjusted by the confidence level, multiplying it by the confidence percent. The confidence level is actually an error suggested by the participants. (Guiding Principle 7) For example, a participant who indicates 80 percent confidence with the process is reflecting a 20 percent error possibility. In a $10,000 estimate with an 80 percent confidence factor, the participant is suggesting that the value could be in the range of $8,000 to $12,000. To be conservative, the lower number is used. Therefore, the confidence factor is multiplied by the amount of improvement.

Step 5: The new values are then adjusted by the percent of the improvement related directly to the project using multiplication. This isolates the effects of the IT project. (Guiding Principle 5)

The monetary values determined in these five steps are totaled to arrive at a total project benefit. Since these values are already annualized, the total of these benefits becomes the annual benefits for the project. This value is placed in the numerator of the ROI formula to calculate the ROI.

Application

The impact of the action plan process is impressive. In a medium-sized circuit manufacturing facility, an IT project was developed for first-level supervisors that focused on a streamlined order entry process in a new online order entry application and on improving electronic collaboration skills (instant messaging, e-mail, and electronic workflow) with employees. Several of the areas addressed were system navigation, job efficiency, paperless order processing, system order accuracy, and customer satisfaction. These areas were discussed thoroughly and supervisors learned skills to make improvements in each area. Supervisors were required to develop action plans for improvement and report the results in a follow-up six months after the project. In this situation, the improvement measures were predetermined from the needs assessment. The following results were documented from a pilot group:

- The department unit hour was increased from 65 to 75. This is a basic measure of productivity, where a unit hour of 60 is considered to be average and acceptable work.
- Order rework was reduced from 11 to 7.4 percent. This data shows that users are comfortable with the navigation and process flow of systems.
- Order entry errors were reduced from 7 to 3.25 percent. This is a sign that the automated validation of data fields being entered into the system is working properly and that users are mastering the system.
- Order entry time was reduced from 7 to 3.25 percent. These data points also demonstrate a streamlined process for completing their job function within the system.
- Lost time during order processing was reduced 95 percent. This is a job efficiency measure.

These results were achieved because supervisors practiced what they had learned and reporting results of their action plans. Although these results are impressive, three additional steps are needed to develop the ultimate evaluation: the ROI. First, the amount of the improvement that is actually linked to the project must be determined, working with each measure. In this situation, supervisors estimated the percent of the improvement directly linked to the project. For example, while the order entry error improvement showed an overall decrease of 3.75 percent, the supervisors collectively estimated that only 46 percent of the error reduction was linked to the project. Therefore, a 3.75 percent order entry error reduction became 1.725 percent. This figure can be further adjusted by factoring in a confidence level (provided by supervisors when they supplied the estimate). In this example, supervisors were 84 percent confident of their allocation of the order entry error improvement. This adjustment meant that 1.725 percent then became 1.45 percent when adjusted for the 84 percent confidence level. These two adjustments isolated the effects of the IT project on the output measure and will be fully described in the next chapter.

The second step to develop the ROI is to convert the data to monetary values. A value for a single error must be determined and used to calculate the annual benefit of the improvement. There are at least ten ways to place values on data, and they are fully described in Chapter 5. In this example, supervisors had developed an estimated value of one order entry error, which was used previously in several applications where the cost of a single entry error was needed. Therefore, the total number of errors avoided was calculated and multiplied by the value of one error to obtain the IT project's annual impact on order entry error reduction in the system. This process shows clearly the economic value of the project on that specific output measure. These two steps, isolating the effects of the IT project and converting data to monetary values are performed for each of the six improvement measures, and the total value represents the annual economic benefit of the project.

The third step necessary to move to an ROI is to develop the fully loaded costs of the project. In this step, the costs related to the needs assessment and project development were prorated. In addition, all direct IT costs were captured, along with the cost of the participants' salaries and benefits for the time they were participating in the IT project. The fully loaded cost for all participants reflected the total investment in this project for this group. (This process is discussed in more detail in Chapter 6.) With these three additional steps, the ROI can be calculated using the formulas described in Chapter 3 (net benefits divided by costs). In this example, total annual benefits directly attributed to the project after converting all improvement items to monetary values were $775,000. The fully loaded costs for the project, where needs assessment, project development, and the cost for the evaluation were included, resulted in a value of $65,000. Therefore, the ROI was:

$$ROI = \frac{\text{Net Project Benefits}}{\text{Project Costs}} \quad \frac{\$775,000 - \$65,000}{\$65,000} \times 100 = 1,092\%$$

This impressive ROI has credibility because of the conservative nature of the adjustments made to the data. Without these three additional steps, the target audience may be left wondering how much of the results were actually linked to the IT project and how much the benefits exceeded the costs.

Advantages/Disadvantages

Although there are many advantages, there are at least two problems with action plans. The process relies on direct input from the participant, usually with no assurance of anonymity. As such, the information may be biased and unreliable. Also, action plans can be time consuming for the participant, and if the participant's supervisor is not involved in the process, there may be a tendency for the participant not to complete the assignment.

As this section has illustrated, the action plans have many inherent advantages. Action plans are simple and easy to administer; easily understood by participants; used with a wide variety of projects; appropriate for all types of data; able to measure reaction, learning, behavior changes, and results; and may be used with or without other evaluation methods. The two disadvantages may be overcome with careful planning and implementation. Because of the tremendous flexibility and versatility of the process and the conservative adjustments that can be made in analysis, action plans have become an important data collection tool for the ROI analysis.

PERFORMANCE CONTRACTS

The performance contract is essentially a slight variation of the action planning process with a pre-project commitment. Based on the principle of mutual goal setting, a performance contract is a written agreement between a participant and the participant's supervisor. The participant agrees to improve performance in an area of mutual concern related to the content of the IT project. The agreement is in the form of a project to be completed or a goal to be accomplished soon after project completion. The agreement spells out what is to be accomplished, at what time, and with what results.

Performance contracting is administered much the same way as the action planning process. Although the steps can vary according to the specific kind of contract and the organization, a common sequence of events is as follows:

- With supervisor approval, the employee (participant) decides to participate in an IT project.
- The participant and manager mutually agree on a topic for improvement with specific measure(s).
- Specific, measurable goals are set.
- The participant is involved in the project where the contract is discussed and plans are developed to accomplish the goals.
- After the project, the participant works on the contract against a specific deadline.
- The participant reports the results to his or her immediate manager.
- The supervisor and participant document the results and forward a copy to the IT department along with appropriate comments.

The individuals mutually select the topic/measure to be improved prior to project inception. The process of selecting the area for improvement is similar to the process used in the action planning process. The topic can cover one or more of the following areas:

- *Routine performance*—includes specific improvements in routine performance measures such as production targets, efficiency, and error rates.
- *Problem solving*—focuses on specific problems such as an unexpected increase in system error rate, a decrease in efficiency, or a loss of productivity.
- *Innovative or creative applications*—includes initiating changes or improvements in work practices, methods, procedures, techniques, and processes.

- *Personal development*—involves learning new information or acquiring new skills to increase individual effectiveness.

The topic selected should be stated in terms of one or more objectives. The objectives should state what is to be accomplished when the contract is complete. These objectives should be all of the following:

- Written
- Understandable (by all involved)
- Challenging (requiring an unusual effort to achieve)
- Achievable (something that can be accomplished)
- Largely under the control of the participant
- Measurable and dated

The details required to accomplish the contract objectives are developed following the guidelines under the action plans presented earlier. Also, the methods for analyzing data and reporting progress are essentially the same, as with the action planning process.

SELECTING THE APPROPRIATE METHOD

This chapter has presented a variety of methods to capture post-project data for an ROI analysis. Collectively, they offer a wide range of opportunities to collect data in a variety of situations. Several issues should be considered when deciding which method is appropriate for a situation.

Type of Data

Perhaps one of the most important issues to consider when selecting the method is the type of data to be collected. Some methods are more appropriate for Level 4, whereas others are best for Level 3. Still others are best for Level 2 or 1. Table 4-1 shows the most appropriate type of data for a specific method. Questionnaires and surveys, observations, interviews, and focus groups are suited for all levels. Tests are appropriate for Level 2. Questionnaires and surveys are best for Level 1, although interviews and focus groups can be used, but they are often too costly. Performance monitoring, performance contracting, action planning, and questionnaires can easily capture Level 4 data.

Table 4-1
Data Collection Methods

	Level 1	Level 2	Level 3	Level 4
❑ Questionnaires/surveys	✓	✓	✓	✓
❑ Tests		✓		
❑ Interviews			✓	
❑ Focus groups			✓	
❑ Observations		✓	✓	
❑ Action planning			✓	✓
❑ Performance contracting			✓	✓
❑ Performance monitoring				✓

Participants' Time for Data Input

Another important factor in selecting the data collection method is the amount of time that participants must take with data collection. Time requirements should always be minimized, and the method should be positioned so that it is value-added activity (i.e., the participants understand that this activity is something they perceive as valuable so they will not resist). This requirement often means that sampling is used to keep the total participant time to a reasonable length. Some methods, such as business performance monitoring, require no participant time, although others, such as interviews and focus groups, require a significant investment in time.

Management's Time for Data Input

The time that a participant's immediate manager must allocate to data collection is another important issue in the method selection. This time requirement should always be minimized. Some methods, such as performance contracting, may require much involvement from the manager prior to, and after, the project. Other methods, such as questionnaires administered directly to participants, may not require any manager time.

Cost of Method

Cost is always a consideration when selecting the method. Some data collection methods are more expensive than others.

For example, interviews and observations are very expensive. Surveys, questionnaires, and performance monitoring are usually inexpensive.

Disruption of Normal Work Activities

Another key issue in selecting the appropriate method, and perhaps the one that generates the most concern with managers, is the amount of disruption the data collection will create. Routine work processes should be disrupted as little as possible. Some data collection techniques, such as performance monitoring, require little time and distraction from normal activities. Questionnaires generally do not disrupt the work environment and can often be completed in only a few minutes, or even after normal work hours. On the other extreme, some items such as observations and interviews may be too disruptive for the work unit.

Accuracy of Method

The accuracy of the technique is another factor when selecting the method. Some data collection methods are more accurate than others. For example, performance monitoring is usually very accurate, and questionnaires can be distorted and unreliable. If actual on-the-job behavior must be captured, unobtrusive observation is clearly one of the most accurate processes.

Built-in Design Possibility

The relative ease at which the method can be built into the project is important; it must become an integral part of the project. Some methods, such as action plans, can be easily built into the design of the project. Other methods, such as observation, are more difficult.

For some situations, the project is redesigned to allow for a follow-up session where evaluation is addressed along with additional IT-focused training on the new system. For example, a technology-focused interactive selling skills project (a consecutive, three-day project) was redesigned as a two-day workshop to build skills, followed by a one-day session three weeks later. Therefore, the follow-up session provided an opportunity for additional IT training and evaluation. During the first part of the last day, Level 3 evaluation data was collected using a focus group process. Also, specific barriers and problems encountered in applying the skills were discussed. The second half of the day was devoted to additional skill building and refinement, along with techniques to overcome the particular barriers to using the skills. In effect, the redesigned project provided a mechanism for follow-up.

Utility of an Additional Method

Because many different data collection methods are available, it is tempting to use too many data collection methods. Multiple data collection methods add time and costs to evaluation and may result in little additional value. *Utility* refers to the added value of the use of an additional data collection method. When more than one method is used, this question should always be addressed. Does the value obtained from the additional data warrant the extra time and expense of the method? If the answer is no, the additional method should not be implemented.

Cultural Bias for Data Collection Method

The culture or philosophy of the organization can dictate which data collection methods are used. For example, some organizations are accustomed to using questionnaires and prefer to use them in their culture. Other organizations will not use observation because their culture does not support the potential "invasion of privacy" associated with it.

DATA TABULATION ISSUE

Data must be collected using one or more of the methods outlined in this chapter. As the data are collected, several other issues need to be addressed and clarified.

Use the Most Credible Source

This is a principle discussed earlier, but it is worth repeating. The data used in the analysis must be the most credible data available.

If data are collected from more than one source, the most credible one is used if there is a clear difference. This leads to a guiding principle.

> **Guiding Principle 3**
> When collecting and analyzing data, use only the most credible sources.

Missing Data

It is rare for all the participants to provide data in a follow-up evaluation. The philosophy described in this chapter is to use only the data available for the total benefits. This philosophy is based on making every attempt possible to collect data from every participant, if at all possible. In reality, the return rate of questionnaires or the participation rate of other data collection methods will probably be in the 60 to 80 percent range. Below 50 percent should be considered questionable because of the extreme negative impact it will have on the results. This leads to a guiding principle:

> **Guiding Principle 6**
> If no improvement data are available from a specific source, it is assumed that little or no improvement has occurred.

Data Summary

Data should be tabulated and summarized, ready for analysis. Ideally, tabulation should be organized by evaluation levels and issues. Tables can be summarized, analyzed, and then reported in the impact study.

Extreme Data

As data are entered, there should be some review of the data for its reasonableness. Extreme data items and unsupported claims should be omitted. This leads to a guiding principle:

> **Guiding Principle 8**
> Extreme data items and unsupported claims should not be used in ROI calculations.

These rules for initially adjusting, summarizing, and tabulating data are critical in preparing for the analysis. They take a conservative approach and, as a result, build credibility with the target audience. More use on these principles will be presented later.

Final Thoughts

This chapter provided an overview of collection approaches that can be used in the ROI analysis. A variety of options are available, which can usually match any budget or situation. Some methods are gaining more acceptance for ROI calculations. In addition to performance monitoring, follow-up questionnaires and action plans, as described in this chapter, are regularly used to collect data for an ROI analysis. Other methods can be helpful to develop a complete picture of application of the IT and subsequent business impact.

References

Alreck, P.L. and R.B. Settle. *The Survey Research Handbook: Guidelines and Strategies for Conducting a Survey*, 2nd ed. New York: McGraw-Hill, 1995.

Kvale, S. *InterViews: An Introduction to Qualitative Research Interviewing*. Thousand Oaks, CA: Sage Publications, 1996.

Robson, C. *Real World Research: A Resource for Social Scientists and Practitioner-Researchers*, 2nd ed. Malden, MA: Blackwell Publishers, 2002.

Shrock, S. and W.C.C. Coscarelli. *Criterion-Referenced Test Development: Technical and Legal Guidelines for Corporate Training and Certification*, 2nd ed. Washington, D.C.: International Society for Performance Improvement, 2000.

Subramony, D.P. et al. "Using Focus Group Interviews," *Technology Development*. International Society for Performance Improvement, September 2002.

Westgaard, O. *Tests That Work: Designing and Delivering Fair and Practical Measurement Tools in the Workplace*. San Francisco, CA: Jossey-Bass/Pfeiffer, 1999.

CHAPTER 5

Isolating the Effects of Strategic Technology Investments

The following situation is often repeated. A significant increase in performance is noted after a major IT project is completed, and the two events appear to be linked. A key manager asks, "How much of this improvement was a result of the IT project?" When this potentially embarrassing question is asked, it is rarely answered with any degree of accuracy and credibility. Although the change in performance may be linked to the IT project, non-IT factors usually have also contributed to the improvement. This chapter explores the techniques used to isolate the effects of IT. These strategies are used in many successful organizations because they attempt to measure the return on investment in IT and technology development.

The cause-and-effect relationship between IT and performance can be confusing and difficult to prove. However, it can be accomplished with an acceptable degree of accuracy. The challenge is to develop one or more specific strategies to isolate the effects of IT early in the process, usually as part of an evaluation plan. Up-front attention ensures that appropriate strategies will be used with minimum costs and time commitments.

PRELIMINARY ISSUES

The Need for Isolating the Effects of IT

Isolating the effects of IT projects seems to be a logical, practical, and necessary issue, but it is still controversial. Some professionals argue that isolating the effects of IT goes against everything taught in systems thinking. Others argue that the only way to link IT to actual business results is to isolate its effect on those business measures. Much of the debate centers around misunderstandings and the challenge of isolating the effects of the process. The first point in the debate is the issue of complementary processes. It is true that specific IT projects are often implemented as part of a total systems plan or part of an even higher-level strategic business plan. There are always other influences that must work in harmony with IT to improve business results. It is often an issue not of whether IT is part of the mix but how much IT is needed, what specific projects are needed, and the most effective method to drive IT's involvement in the overall business strategy.

The issue of isolating the effects of IT is not meant to suggest that IT should stand alone as a single, influencing factor that drives business performance. The isolation issue comes into play, however, when different process owners are influencing business results and they must have more information about relative contribution. In many situations, the question that must be addressed is "How much of the improvement was caused by IT?" Without an answer or a specific method to address the issue, tremendous credibility is lost, particularly with the senior-management team.

The other debated point is the difficulty of achieving the isolation. The classic approach is to use control group arrangements in which one group receives the latest functionality enhancements from a specific technology initiative and another does not. This is one of the techniques described in this chapter, and it is the most credible. However, the control group may not be appropriate in the majority of studies. Therefore, other methods must be used. Researchers sometimes use time-series analysis (also discussed in this chapter as trend line analysis). Beyond that, many researchers either give up and suggest it cannot be addressed credibly or choose to ignore the issue in hopes that it will not be noticed by the project sponsor. Neither of these responses is acceptable to the senior management team attempting to understand the link between IT and business success. A credible estimation, adjusted for error, will often satisfy the requirements. It is important to *always* address this issue, even if an expert estimation is used with an error adjustment. In this way, the issue of isolating the effects of IT becomes an essential step in the analysis. A guiding principle is established on this issue.

Guiding Principle 5
At least one method must be used to
isolate the effects of the project.

Isolating the effects of IT is a required step. Nine different techniques are used to address this issue, and at least one of them will *always* be used.

Chain of Impact: The Initial Evidence

Before presenting the techniques, the chain of impact must be examined. As illustrated in Figure 5-1, the chain of impact must be in place for the project to drive business results.

Measurable business impact achieved from an IT initiative should be derived from the application of skills/knowledge on the job, over a specified period of time, after a project has been conducted. This on-the-job application of what has been learned during the implementation and training of a specific technology project is referred to as Level 3 in the five evaluation levels described in Chapter 2 and reported elsewhere. Continuing with this logic, successful application of project material on the job should stem from participants learning new skills or acquiring new knowledge surrounding the IT initiative, which is measured as a Level 2 evaluation. Therefore, for a business results improvement (Level 4), this chain of impact implies that measurable on-the-job applications are realized (Level 3) and new knowledge and skills are learned (Level 2). Without the preliminary

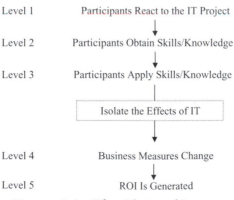

Figure 5-1. The Chain of Impact

evidence of the chain of impact, it is difficult to isolate the effects of a defined IT project. If there is no learning or application of the enhanced systems functionality on the job, it is virtually impossible to conclude that the IT project provided any material improvements. This chain of impact requirement with the different levels of evaluation is supported in the literature. From a practical standpoint, this issue requires data collection at four levels for an ROI calculation. If data are collected on business results, they should also be collected for the other levels of evaluation to ensure that the IT project helped to produce the business results. This issue is so critical that it becomes the first guiding principle for the ROI Methodology.

Guiding Principle 1
When a higher-level evaluation is conducted, data must be collected at the lower levels.

This approach is consistent with the approach practiced by leading organizations that embrace the ROI Methodology and have years of experience highlighting the returns on their strategic technology investments. It was reported that most organizations that collected Level 4 data on business results also collected data at the previous three levels. The chain of impact does not prove that there was a direct connection to IT. The isolation is necessary to make this connection and pinpoint the amount of improvement caused by IT. Many research efforts have attempted to develop correlations between the different levels. This research basically states that if a significant correlation exists, the chain of impact is in place. If a significant correlation does not exist, there were many barriers that caused the process to break down. This is logical when the chain of impact is considered.

Most research in this area adds little to the understanding of evaluation. Correlations between two levels show the connection (or disconnect) between the two. It does not mean that the levels are flawed but that some factor prevented the learning process from adding value. For example, most of the breakdowns occur between Levels 2 and 3. Much research has shown that as much as 90 percent of what was learned is not used on the job (Kauffman, 2002).

Barriers can impede the transfer of the learning to the job. Many barriers may exist and readily inhibit the success of IT initiatives. It does not mean that the next level of evaluation (Level 3) is inappropriate, only that some factor is preventing the skills and knowledge learned during systems training from transferring to the job. Therefore, a correlation analysis between the levels adds little understanding to what must occur in practice for IT to add business value. Also, correlation analysis does not show the cause-and-effect relationship. Even if there is a strong correlation, the critical step of isolating the effects of an IT project must be undertaken to ensure a causal relationship between the IT project and the business improvement.

Identifying Other Factors: A First Step

As a first step in isolating IT's impact on performance, all the key factors that may have contributed to the improved business processes should be identified. This step reveals other factors that may have influenced the results, underscoring that the IT project is not the sole source of improvement. Therefore, the credit for improvement is shared with several possible sources, an approach that is likely to gain the respect of management.

Several potential sources identify major influencing variables. The sponsors may be able to identify factors that should influence the output measure if they have requested the project. The client will usually be aware of other initiatives or projects that may impact the output. Even if the project is operational, the client may have much insight into the other influences that may have driven the performance improvements.

Project participants are often aware of other influences that may have caused business process improvements. After all, it is the impact of their collective efforts being monitored and measured. In many situations, they witness previous movements in the performance measures and can pinpoint the reasons for changes. They are normally the experts in this issue.

Analysts and project developers are another source for identifying variables that have an impact on results. The needs analysis will routinely uncover these influencing variables. Project designers typically analyze these variables while addressing the IT transfer issue.

In some situations, participants' supervisors may be able to identify variables that influence the performance improvement. This is particularly useful when IT project participants are entry-level or low-skill employees (operatives) who may not be fully aware of the variables that can influence performance.

Finally, middle and top management may be able to identify other influences based on their experience and knowledge of the situation. Perhaps they have monitored, examined, and analyzed the other influences. The authority positions of these individuals often increase the credibility and acceptance of the data.

Taking the time to focus attention on variables that may have influenced performance brings additional accuracy and credibility to the process. It moves beyond the scenario where results are presented with no mention of other influences, a situation that often destroys the credibility of an IT impact study. It also provides a foundation for some of the techniques described in this book by identifying the variables that must be isolated to show the effects of IT. Caution is appropriate here. Halting the process after this step would leave many unknowns about actual IT impact and might leave a negative impression with the client or senior management, since it may have identified variables that management did not previously consider. Therefore, it is recommended that the IT staff go beyond this initial step and use one or more of the techniques that isolate the impact of IT.

Use of Control Groups

The most accurate approach to isolating the impact of IT is the use of control groups in an experimental design process (Wang, 2002). This approach involves the use of an experimental group that attends IT training during the rollout of a new system and a control group that does not. The composition of both groups should be as similar as possible, and, if feasible, the selection of participants for each group should be on a random basis. When this is possible and both groups are subjected to the same environmental influences, the difference in the performance of the two groups can be attributed to the IT project.

As illustrated in Figure 5-2, the control group and experimental group do not necessarily have preproject measurements. Measurements are taken after the project is implemented. The difference in the performance of the two groups shows the amount of improvement that is directly related to the IT project.

Control group arrangements appear in many settings, including both private and public sectors. For example, in an impact study to measure the return on investment for call center automation technol-

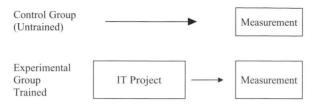

Figure 5-2. Posttest Only, Control Group Design

ogy, a global communications company used both an experimental group and a control group. The IT project was designed to improve contact center rep productivity and also provide a suite of Web-based customer self-service applications, which were designed to reduce the overall number of calls that escalated to the supervisory level. The difference between the two groups revealed the extent to which the skills were transferred to the job (Level 3) and also the impact it was having in the workplace (Level 4). Therefore, control group differences can be used to isolate the effects on Level 3 and Level 4 data.

In another example, a Customer Relationship Management (CRM) project for a leading provider of online education used a control group and an experimental group to try and isolate the effects of the CRM initiative. The experimental group was compiled of individuals in a legacy division of the company who were accustomed to not receiving the best enhancements to most of the organization's enterprise systems. The members of the experimental group operated under a completely different set of business and systems rules than the core business. The control group was carefully selected to match the experimental group in terms of job function, tenure with the organization, and level of education. The control/experimental group differences were dramatic, showing the impact of the Customer Relationship Management project.

One caution: The use of control groups may create an image that the IT staff is creating a laboratory setting, which can cause a problem for some administrators and executives. To avoid this stigma, some organizations run a project using pilot participants as the experimental group and do not inform the nonparticipating control group. Another example will illustrate this approach. An international specialty manufacturing company developed a Workforce Optimization project for its customer service representatives who sell directly to the public. The project was designed to improve selling skills through automated call scripting and computer telephone integration to produce higher levels of sales. Previously, sales skills acquisition was informal, on the job, or by trial and error. The IT manager was convinced that formal IT-enabled processes would significantly increase sales. Management was skeptical and wanted proof—a familiar scenario.

The project was pilot-tested by automating the rep dialing and call scripting process to 16 customer service representatives randomly selected from the 32 most recently hired. The remaining 16, who were virtual call center agents working remotely from their home, served as a control group and did not receive the IT enhancements. Prior to the additional IT functionality, performance was measured using average daily sales (sales divided by number of days) for 30 days (or length of service, if shorter) for each of the two groups. After the IT improvements, the average daily sales were recorded for another 30 days. A significant difference in the sales of the two groups emerged, and because the groups were almost identical and were subjected to the same environmental influences, it was concluded that the sales differences were a result of the IT process automation and not other factors. In this setting, the pilot group was the experimental group. The comparison group (control group) was easily selected. The technique was used without the publicity and potential criticism that is typical when using the control group arrangement.

The control group process does have some inherent problems that may make it difficult to apply in practice. The first major problem is that the process is inappropriate for many situations. For some types of IT projects, it is not proper to withhold IT enhancements from one particular group while the upgrades are given to another. This is particularly important for critical skills that are needed immediately on the job. For example, in entry-level positions, employees need basic computer skills to perform their jobs. It would be improper to withhold system enhancements from a group of new employees just so they can be compared to a group that receives the technology upgrades. Although this would reveal the impact of initial system enhancements, it would be devastating to those individuals who are struggling to learn necessary skills, trying to cope with the job situation. In the previous example, a control group is feasible. The IT upgrades provided were not necessarily essential to the job, and the organization was not completely convinced that it would add value in terms of the actual sales.

This particular barrier keeps many control groups from being implemented. Management is not willing to withhold IT in one area to see how it works in another. However, in practice, many opportunities for a natural control group may develop in situations where IT is implemented throughout an organization. If it will take several months for everyone in the organization to receive the IT upgrades, there may be enough time for a parallel comparison between the initial group being trained and rolled out with the latest version of an enterprise system and the last group upgraded. In these cases, it is critical to ensure that the groups are matched as closely as possible so the first two groups are similar to the last two groups. These naturally occurring control groups often exist during large-scale IT project implementation. The challenge is to address this issue early enough to influence the implementation schedule so that similar groups can be used in the comparison.

The second major problem is the selection of the groups. From a practical perspective it is virtually impossible to have identical control and experimental groups. Dozens of factors can affect employee performance, some of them individual and others contextual. To tackle the issue on a practical basis, it is best to select three to five variables that will have the greatest influence on performance. For example, in a sales force automation project in a retail chain, three groups were trained, and their performances were compared to three similar groups, which were the control groups. The selection of the groups was based on four variables that store executives thought would influence performance most from one store to another: previous sales performance, actual market area, store size, and customer traffic. In this example, there were dozens of variables that could affect store performance, ranging from individual differences (e.g., sales experience, education, and tenure) to managerial and leadership differences within the department and store (e.g., leadership style and managerial control), as well as in-store policies on merchandising and marketing.

Perhaps the most differences occur externally with the market area and surrounding competition. The challenge was to take a realistic approach and to address a reasonable number of measures. In this example, the regional store executives selected the four measures that probably account for at least 80 percent of the differences. Using the 80-20 rule, the challenge of selecting groups is manageable. When the output can be influenced by as many as 40 to 50 measures, it is almost impossible to consider all the measures with a store sample size of 420. Therefore, the practical use of the control group must take into consideration the constraints in a work setting and focus on the most critical influences, besides IT, that will make a difference in the output measure.

A third problem with the control group arrangement is contamination, which can develop when participants in the IT project instruct others in the control group. Sometimes the reverse situation occurs when members of the control group model the behavior from the trained group. In either case, the experiment becomes contaminated because the influence of IT filters to the control group. This can be minimized by ensuring that control groups and experimental groups are at different locations, have different shifts, or are on different floors in the same building. When this is not possible, it is sometimes helpful to explain to both groups that one group will receive IT enhancements now and another will receive the system updates at a later date. Also, it may be helpful to appeal to the sense of responsibility of those being trained and ask them not to share the information with others.

Closely related to the previous problem is the issue of time. The longer a control group and experimental group operate, the greater the likelihood of other influences affecting the results. More variables will enter into the situation, contaminating the results. On the other end of the scale, there must be enough time so that a clear pattern can emerge between the two groups. The timing for control group comparisons must strike a delicate balance of waiting long enough for their performance differences to show but not so long that the results become seriously contaminated.

A fifth problem occurs when the different groups function under different environmental influences. Because they may be in different locations, the groups may have different environmental influences. Sometimes, the selection of the groups can help prevent this problem from occurring. Also, using more groups than necessary and eliminating those with some environmental differences is another tactic.

A sixth problem with using control groups is that it may appear to be too research-oriented for most business organizations. For example, management may not want to take the time to experiment before proceeding with a project, or they may not want to withhold IT from a group just to measure the impact of an experimental project. Because of this concern, some IT leaders do not entertain the idea of using control groups. When the process is used, however, some organizations conduct it with pilot participants as the experimental group and nonparticipants as the control group. Under this arrangement, the control group is not informed of their control group status.

Because this is an effective approach for isolating the impact of IT, it should be considered as a strategy when a major ROI evaluation is planned. In these situations, it is important for the project impact to be isolated to a high level of accuracy. The primary advantage of the control group process is accuracy. About one-third of the first 100 published studies on the ROI Methodology use the control group process.

Trend Line Analysis

Another useful technique for approximating the impact of strategic IT initiatives is trend line analysis. With this approach, a trend line is drawn, using previous performance as a base, and extending the trend into the future. When IT upgrades are deployed, actual performance is compared to the projected value: the trend line. Any improvement of performance over what the trend line predicted can then be reasonably attributed to the IT enhancements if two conditions are met:

1. The trend that has developed prior to the project is expected to continue if the project had not been implemented to alter it (i.e., if the IT project had not been implemented, would this trend continue on the same path established before the IT?). The process owner(s) should be able to provide input to reach this conclusion. If the answer is "no," the trend line analysis will not be used. If the answer is "yes," the second condition is considered.
2. No other new variables or influences entered the process after the IT project was deployed. The key word is *new*, realizing that the trend has been established because of the influences already in place and no additional influences enter the process beyond the IT or technology development project. If the answer is "yes," another method would have to be used. If the answer is "no," the trend line analysis develops a reasonable estimate of the impact of IT.

Figure 5-3 shows an example of this trend line analysis taken from a shipping department in a large distribution company. The percent reflects the level of actual shipments compared to scheduled shipments. Data are presented before and after an IT project was implemented in July. As shown in the figure, there was an upward trend on the data prior to conducting the systems project. Although the project apparently had a dramatic effect on shipment productivity, the trend line shows that improvement would have continued

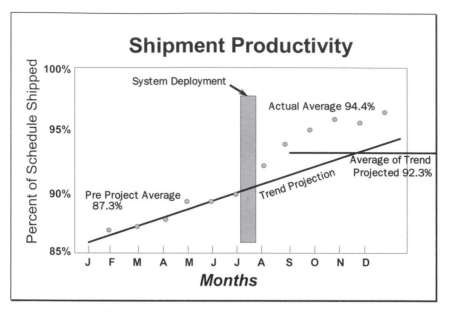

Figure 5-3. Trend Line of Productivity

anyway, based on the trend that had been established. It is tempting to measure the improvement by comparing the average six-months shipments prior to the project (87.3 percent) to the average of six months after the project (94.4 percent) yielding a 6.9 percent difference. However, a more accurate comparison is the six-month average after the project compared to the trend line (92.3 percent). In this example, the difference is 2.1 percent. In this case, the two preceding conditions were met (yes on the first; no on the second). Therefore, using this more modest measure increases the accuracy and credibility of the process to isolate the impact of the project.

Preproject data must be available before this technique can be used, and the data should have some reasonable degree of stability. If the variance of the data is high, the stability of the trend line becomes an issue. If this is an extremely critical issue and the stability cannot be assessed from a direct plot of the data, more detailed statistical analyses can be used to determine if the data are stable enough to make the projection (Salkind, 2000).

The trend line, projected directly from the historical data using a straight edge, may be acceptable. If additional accuracy is needed, the trend line can be projected with a simple routine that is available in many calculators and software packages, such as Microsoft Excel™.

The use of the trend line analysis becomes more dramatic and convincing when a measure, moving in an undesired direction, completely turns around following the IT project. For example, Figure 5-4 shows a trend line of the order entry errors from an online retailer. As the figure presents, the entry errors were increasing in a direction undesired by the organization. The data validation enhancements and other subsequent activities connected with the project turned the situation around so that the actual results are in the other direction. The trend line process shows when a dramatic improvement has occurred. The trend line projected value shows a number that is higher than the actual results and the prepost differences.

A primary disadvantage of the trend line approach is that it is not always accurate. The use of this approach assumes that the events that influenced the performance variable prior to the project are still in place after the project, except for the implementation of the IT project (i.e., the trends that were established prior to IT enhancements will continue in the same relative direction). Also, it assumes that no new influences entered the situation at the time IT upgrades were conducted. This is seldom the case.

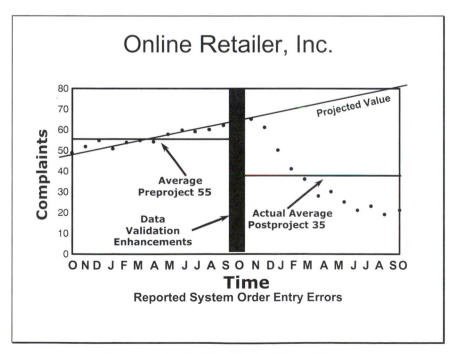

Figure 5-4. Online Order-Entry Errors

The primary advantage of this approach is that it is simple and inexpensive. If historical data are available, a trend line can quickly be drawn and differences estimated. Although not exact, it does provide a quick assessment of IT's potential impact. About 15 percent of the first 100 published studies on the ROI Methodology use the trend line analysis technique. When other variables enter the situation, additional analysis is needed.

FORECASTING METHODS

A more analytical approach to trend line analysis is the use of forecasting methods that predict a change in performance variables. This approach represents a mathematical interpretation of the trend line analysis just discussed above when other variables entered the situation at the time of IT deployment. The basic premise is that the actual performance of a measure, related to IT, is compared to the forecasted value of that measure. The forecasted value is based on the other influences. A linear model, in the form of $y = ax + b$, is appropriate when only one other variable influences the output performance and that relationship is characterized by a straight line. Instead of drawing the straight line, a linear equation is developed that calculates a value of the anticipated system related performance improvement.

An example will help explain the application of this process. A large retail chain with a strong sales culture implemented a metrics-based salesforce automation application (SFA) for its sales associates. The SFA application was designed to enhance and measure sales skills and prospecting techniques. The application of the metrics focused automated processes should increase the sales volume for each associate. An important measure of the project's success was the sales per employee six months after the project compared to the same measure prior to the project. The average daily sales per employee before implementing the SFA application, using a one-month average, were $1,100 (rounded to the nearest $100). Six months after the project, the average daily sales per employee were $1,500 (the sixth month). These sales numbers were average values for a specific group of participants. Two related questions must be answered: "Is the difference in these two values attributable to the sales force automation project?" and "Did other factors influence the actual sales level?"

After reviewing potential influencing factors with several store executives, only one factor—the level of advertising—appeared to have changed significantly during the period under consideration. When reviewing the previous sales per employee data and the level of advertising, a direct relationship appeared to exist. As expected, when advertising expenditures were increased, the sales per employee increased proportionately.

The advertising staff had developed a mathematical relationship between advertising and sales. Using the historical values, a simple linear model yielded the following relationship: $y = 140 + 40x$, where y is the daily sales per employee and x is the level of advertising expenditures per week (divided by 1,000). This equation was developed by the marketing department using the method of least squares to derive a mathematical relationship between two columns of data (i.e., advertising and sales). This is a routine option on some calculators and is included in many software packages. Figure 5-5 shows the linear relationship between advertising and sales.

The level of weekly advertising expenditures in the month preceding the SFA rollout was $24,000, and the level of expenditures in the sixth months after the rollout was $30,000. Assuming that the other factors possibly influencing sales were insignificant, store executives determined the impact of the advertising by plugging in the new advertising expenditure amount, 30, for x and calculating the daily sales, which yielded $1,340. Therefore, the new sales level caused by the increase in advertising was $1,340, as shown in Figure 5-5. Since the new actual value was $1,500, then $160 (i.e., 1,500 − 1,340) must be attributed to the IT project. The effect of both the IT project implementation and advertising is shown in the figure.

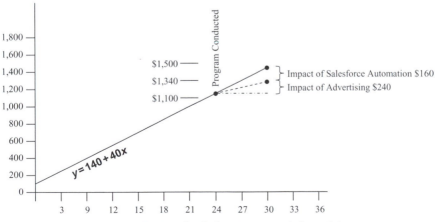

Figure 5-5. Daily Sales Versus Advertising

A major disadvantage with this approach occurs when several variables enter the process. The complexity multiplies, and the use of sophisticated statistical packages for multiple variable analyses is necessary. Even then, a good fit of the data to the model may not be possible. Unfortunately, some organizations have not developed mathematical relationships for output variables as a function of one or more inputs. Without them, the forecasting method is difficult to use.

The primary advantage of this process is that it can accurately predict business performance measures without IT, if appropriate data and models are available. The presentation of specific methods is beyond the scope of this book and is contained in other works (Armstrong, 2001). Approximately 5 percent of the first 100 published studies on the ROI Methodology used the forecasting technique.

PARTICIPANT ESTIMATE OF IT's IMPACT

An easily implemented method to isolate the impact of IT is to obtain information directly from project participants. The effectiveness of this approach rests on the assumption that participants are capable of determining or estimating how much performance improvement is related to the IT project. Because their actions have produced the improvement, participants may have accurate input on the issue. They should know how much of the change was caused by applying what they have learned in the project. Although an estimate, this value will typically have credibility with management because participants are at the center of the change or improvement.

When using this technique, several assumptions are made:

1. An IT project (or technology development initiative) has been conducted with a variety of different enhancements, upgrades, and functionality improvements, all focused on improving performance.
2. One or more business measures have been identified prior to the IT project and have been continually monitored following the process. Data monitoring has revealed an improvement in the business measure.
3. There is a need to link the IT initiative to the specific amount of performance improvement and develop the monetary impact of the improvement. This information forms the basis for calculating the actual ROI.

With these assumptions, the participants can pinpoint the actual results linked to the IT project and provide data necessary to develop the ROI. This can be accomplished using a focus group or a questionnaire.

Focus Group Approach

The focus group works extremely well for this challenge if the group size is relatively small—for example, in the 8 to 12 range. If much larger, the groups should be divided into multiple groups. Focus groups provide the opportunity for members to share information equally, avoiding domination by any one individual. The process taps the input, creativity, and reactions of the entire group.

The meeting should take about one hour (slightly more if there are multiple factors affecting the results or there are multiple business measures). The facilitator should be neutral to the process (i.e., the same individual spearheading the IT initiative should not conduct this focus group). Focus group facilitation and input must be objective.

The task is to link the business results of the specific IT project to business performance. The group is presented with the improvement and provides input on isolating the effects of the project.

The following steps are recommended to arrive at the most credible value for IT impact:

Explain the task. The task of the focus group meeting is outlined. Participants should understand that there has been performance improvement. Although many factors could have contributed to the performance, the task of this group is to determine how much of the improvement is related to the specific IT project.

Discuss the rules. Each participant should be encouraged to provide input, limiting his or her comments to two minutes (or less) for any specific issue. Comments are confidential and will not be linked to a specific individual.

Explain the importance of the process. The participant's role in the process is critical. Because it is their performance that has improved, the participants are in the best position to indicate what has caused this improvement. They are the experts in this determination. Without quality input, the contribution of this IT upgrade (or any other processes) may never be known.

Select the first measure and show the improvement. Using actual data, show the level of performance prior to and following the system implementation. In essence, the change in business results— the Δ—is reported.

Identify the different factors that have contributed to the performance. Using input from experts—others who are knowledgeable about the improvements—identify the factors that have influenced the improvement (e.g., the volume of work has changed, a new system has been implemented, or technology has been enhanced). If these are known, they are listed as the factors that may have contributed to the performance improvement.

The group is asked to identify other factors that have contributed to the performance. In some situations, only the participants know other influencing factors and those factors, should surface at this time.

Discuss the link. Taking each factor one at a time, the participants individually describe the link between that factor and the business results. For example, for the IT influence, the participants would describe how the IT project has driven the actual improvement by providing examples, anecdotes, and other supporting evidence. Participants may require some prompting to provide comments. If they cannot provide dialogue of this issue, there's a good chance that the factor had no influence.

The process is repeated for each factor. Each factor is explored until all the participants have discussed the linkage between all the factors and the business performance improvement. After this linkage has been discussed, the participants should have a clear understanding of the cause-and-effect relationship between the various factors and the business improvement.

Allocate the improvement. Participants are asked to allocate the percent of improvement to each of the factors discussed. Participants are provided a pie chart that represents a total amount of improvement for the measure in question and are asked to carve up the pie, allocating the percentages to different improvements with a total of 100 percent. Some participants may feel uncertain with this process but should be encouraged to complete this step using their best estimate. Uncertainty will be addressed later in the meeting.

Provide a confidence estimate. The participants are then asked to review the allocation percentages and, for each one, estimate their level of confidence in the allocation estimate. Using a scale of 0 to 100 percent, where 0 percent represents no confidence and 100 percent is certainty, participants express their level of certainty with their estimates in the previous step. A participant may be more comfortable with some factors than others, so the confidence estimate may vary. This confidence estimate serves as a vehicle to adjust results.

Table 5-1
Example of a Participant's Estimation

Factor That Influenced Improvement	Percent of Improvement Caused By	Confidence Expressed as a Percent
IT project upgrades	50	70
Change in procedures	10	80
Adjustment in standards	10	50
Revision to incentive plan	20	90
Increased management attention	10	50
Other _____	—	—
Total	100	

Participants are asked to multiply the two percentages. For example, if an individual has allocated 35 percent of the improvement to IT and is 80 percent confident, he or she would multiply 35 percent times 80 percent, which is 28 percent. In essence, the participant is suggesting that at least 28 percent of the teams' business improvement is linked to the IT project. The confidence estimate serves as a conservative discount factor, adjusting for the error of the estimate. The pie charts with the calculations are collected without names and the calculations are verified. Another option is to collect pie charts and make the calculations for the participants.

Report results. If possible, the average of the adjusted values for the group is developed and communicated to the group. Also, the summary of all of the information should be communicated to the participants as soon as possible.

Participants who do not provide information are excluded from the analysis. Table 5-1 illustrates this approach with an example of one participant's estimations. The participant allocates 50 percent of the improvement to IT upgrades. The confidence percentage is a reflection of the error in the estimate. A 70 percent confidence level equates to a potential error range of ±30 percent (100% − 70% = 30%). The 50 percent allocation to IT upgrades could be 30 percent more (50% + 15% = 65%) or 30 percent less (50% − 15% = 35%) or somewhere in between. Therefore, the participant's allocation is in the range of 35 to 65 percent. In essence, the confidence estimate frames an error range. To be conservative, the lower side of the range is used (35%). This leads to another guiding principle:

Guiding Principle 7
Estimates of improvement should be
adjusted for the potential error of
the estimate.

This approach is equivalent to multiplying the factor estimate by the confidence percentage to develop a usable IT factor value of 35 percent (50% × 70%). This adjusted percentage is then multiplied by the actual amount of the improvement (postproject minus pre-project value) to isolate the portion attributed to IT. The adjusted improvement is now ready for conversion to monetary values and, ultimately, used in developing the return on investment.

This technique provides a credible way to isolate the effects of IT when other methods will not work. It is often regarded as the low-cost solution to the problem because it takes only a few focus groups and a small amount of time to arrive at this conclusion. In most of these settings, the actual conversion to monetary value is not conducted by the group but developed in another way. For most data, the monetary value may already exist as a standard, acceptable value. The issue of converting data to monetary value is detailed in the next chapter. However, if participants must provide input on the value of the data, it can be approached in the same focus group meeting as another phase of the process, where the participants provide input into the actual monetary value of the unit. To reach an accepted value, the steps are similar to the steps for isolation.

Questionnaire Approach

Sometimes, focus groups are not available or considered unacceptable for data collection use. The participants may not be available for a group meeting or the focus groups become too expensive. In these situations, it may be helpful to collect similar information via a questionnaire. With this approach, participants must address the same issues as those addressed in the focus group but now on a series of impact questions imbedded into a follow-up questionnaire.

The questionnaire may focus solely on isolating the effects of an IT project, as detailed in the previous example, or it may focus on the monetary value derived from the project, with the isolation issue being only a part of the data collected. This is a more versatile approach for using questionnaires when it is not certain exactly how participants will provide business impact data. In some projects, the precise measures that will be influenced by the project may not be known. This is sometimes the case in projects that involve leadership, team building, communications, negotiations, problem solving, innovation, and other types of IT or technology development initiatives. In these situations, it is helpful to obtain information from participants on a series of impact questions, showing how they have used what they have learned and the subsequent impact in the work unit. It is important for participants to know about these questions before they receive the questionnaire. The surprise element can be disastrous in data collection. (More on this issue later.) The recommended series of questions are as follows:

Impact Questions

1. How have you and your job changed as a result of this technology project?
2. What impact do these changes bring to your work unit?
3. How is this impact measured (specific measure)?
4. How much did this measure change after you used the technology (monthly, weekly, or daily amount)?
5. What is the unit value of the measure?
6. What is the basis for this unit value? Please indicate the assumptions made and the specific calculations you performed to arrive at the value.
7. What is the annual value of this change or improvement in the work unit (for the first year)?
8. Recognize that many other factors influence output results in addition to IT enhancements. Please identify the other factors that could have contributed to this performance.
9. What percent of this improvement can be attributed directly to the use of the technology (0–100%)?
10. What confidence do you have in the preceding estimate and data, expressed as a percent (0% = no confidence; 100% = certainty)?
11. What other individuals or groups could estimate this percentage or determine the amount?

Perhaps an illustration of this process can reveal its effectiveness and acceptability. In a large global organization, the impact of a business intelligence application to drive dashboard-level reporting for senior managers was being assessed. Because the decision to calculate the impact of the business intelligence application was made after the project had been conducted, the control group arrangement was not feasible as a method to isolate the effects of this project. Also, before the project was implemented, no business impact data (Level 4) were specified that were directly linked to the project. Participants could drive one or more of a dozen business performance measures. Therefore, it was not appropriate to use trend line analysis. Estimates from the senior managers who were the focus of this project proved to be the most useful way to assess the impact of this IT investment on the business performance. In a detailed follow-up questionnaire, participants were asked a variety of questions regarding the applications of what was learned from the project. As part of the project, the senior managers were asked to develop action plans and implement them, although there was no specific follow-up plan needed. The preceding series of impact questions provided an estimation of the impact. Although this series of questions is challenging, when set up properly and presented to participants in an appropriate way, they can be effective for collecting impact data. Table 5-2 shows a sample of the calculations from these questions for this particular project. In this snapshot of the data, the input from seven participants is presented. The total value for the project would be the total of the input from all who provided data.

Although this is an estimate, the approach has considerable accuracy and credibility. Four adjustments are effectively used to reflect a conservative approach:

1. The individuals who do not respond to the questionnaire or provide usable data on the questionnaire are assumed to have no improvements. This is probably an overstatement, since some individuals will have improvements but not report them on the questionnaire. This is Guiding Principle #6, discussed in the previous chapter.

2. Extreme data and incomplete, unrealistic, and unsupported claims are omitted from the analysis, although they may be included in the intangible benefits. This is Guiding Principle #8, discussed in the next chapter.

3. Since only annualized values are used, it is assumed that there are no benefits from the project after the first year of

Table 5-2
Sample of Input from Senior Managers Participating in a Business Intelligence Initiative

Participant Number	Annual Improvement Value	Basis for Value	Confidence	Isolation Factor	Adjusted Value
11	$36,000	*Improvement in efficiency of group. $3,000 month × 12 (Group Estimate)*	85%	50%	$15,300
42	$90,000	*Turnover reduction. Two turnover statistics per year. Base salary × 1.5 = 45,000*	90%	40%	$32,400
74	$24,000	*Improvement in customer response time. (8 hours to 6 hours.) Estimated value: $2,000/month*	60%	55%	$7,920
55	$2,000	*5% improvement in my effectiveness ($40,500 × 5%)*	75%	50%	$750
96	$10,000	*Error reduction. (50 errors per year × $200)*	85%	75%	$6,375
117	$8,090	*Team project completed 10 days ahead of schedule. Annual salaries $210,500 = $809 per day × 10 days.*	90%	45%	$3,279
118	$159,000	*Under budget for the year by this amount.*	100%	30%	$47,700

implementation. In reality, a business intelligence initiative or any strategic IT project should be expected to add value for many years after the system is deployed. This is Guiding Principle #9, discussed in the next chapter.

4. The confidence level, expressed as a percentage, is multiplied by the improvement value to reduce the amount of the improvement by the potential error. This is Guiding Principle #4, discussed earlier.

When presented to senior management, the results of this impact study were perceived to be an understatement of the project's success. The data and the process were considered credible and accurate.

Collecting an adequate amount of quality data from the series of impact questions is the critical challenge with this process. Participants must be primed to provide data, which can be accomplished in several ways.

1. Participants should know in advance that they are expected to provide this type of data along with an explanation of why this is needed and how it will be used.
2. Ideally, participants should see a copy of this questionnaire and discuss it while they are involved in the IT project. If possible, a verbal commitment to provide the data should be obtained at that time.
3. Participants could be reminded of the requirement prior to the time of data collection. The reminder should come from others involved in the process—even the immediate manager.
4. Participants could be provided with examples of how the questionnaire can be completed, using most-likely scenarios and typical data.
5. The immediate manager could coach participants through the process.
6. The immediate manager could review and approve the data.

These steps help keep the data collection process, with its chain of impact questions, from being a surprise. It will also accomplish three critical tasks:

1. *The response rate will increase.* Because participants commit to provide data during the session, a greater percentage will respond.

2. *The quantity of data will improve.* Participants will understand the chain of impact and understand how data will be used. They will complete more questions.
3. *The quality of the data is enhanced.* With up-front expectations, there is greater understanding of the type of data needed and improved confidence in the data provided. Perhaps subconsciously, participants begin to think through consequences of IT investments and specific impact measures. The result: improved quality of input.

Participant estimation is a critical technique to isolate the effect of IT investments. However, the process has some disadvantages. It is only an estimate and, therefore, does not have the accuracy desired by some IT managers. Also, the input data may be unreliable because some participants are incapable of providing these types of estimates. They might not be aware of exactly which factors contributed to the results, or they may be reluctant to provide data. If the questions come as a surprise, the data will be scarce.

Several advantages make this strategy attractive. It is a simple process, easily understood by most participants and by others who review evaluation data. It is inexpensive, takes little time and analysis, and therefore results in an efficient addition to the evaluation process. Estimates originate from a credible source: the individuals who actually produced the improvement.

The advantages seem to offset the disadvantages. Isolating the effects of IT will never be precise, and this estimate may be accurate enough for most clients and management groups. The process is appropriate when the participants are managers, supervisors, team leaders, business analysts, consultants, system engineers, and other professional and technical employees.

This technique is the fallback isolation strategy for many types of projects. If nothing else works, this method is used. A fallback approach is needed if the effect of the IT project is always isolated. The reluctance to use the process often rests with project managers, IT managers, consultants, and performance improvement specialists. They are reluctant to use a technique that is not proven. Estimates are typically avoided. However, the primary audience for the data (the sponsor or senior manager) will readily accept this approach. Living in an ambiguous world, they understand that estimates may be the only way to approach this issue. They understand the challenge and appreciate the conservative approach, often commenting that the actual value is probably greater than the value presented.

When organizations begin to use this routinely, it sometimes becomes the method of choice for isolation. Because of this, approximately 50 percent of the first 100 published studies on the ROI Methodology use this as a technique to isolate the effects of IT.

Supervisor Estimate of IT's Impact

In lieu of (or in addition to) participant estimates, the participants' supervisor may be asked to provide the extent of IT's role in producing performance improvement within the organization. In some settings, participants' supervisors may be more familiar with the other factors influencing performance. Therefore, they may be better equipped to provide estimates of impact. The following are recommended questions to ask supervisors after describing the improvement caused by the participants:

1. In addition to IT, what other factors could have contributed to this success?
2. What percent of the improvement in performance measures of the participant resulted from the IT project (0–100 percent)?
3. What is the basis for this estimate?
4. What is your confidence in this estimate, expressed as a percentage (0% = no confidence; 100% = complete confidence)?
5. What other individuals or groups would know about this improvement and could estimate this percentage?

These questions are similar to those in the participants' questionnaire. Supervisor estimates should be analyzed in the same manner as participant estimates. To be more conservative, estimates may be adjusted by the confidence percentage. If feasible, it is recommended that inputs be obtained from both participants and supervisors. When participants' estimates have been collected, the decision of which estimate to use becomes an issue. If there is some compelling reason to think that one estimate is more credible than another, the more credible estimate should be used. The most conservative approach is to use the lowest value and include an appropriate explanation. Another potential option is to recognize that each source has its own unique perspective and that an average of the two is appropriate, placing an equal weight on each input.

An example illustrates how manager input can closely parallel participants' input. Table 5-3 shows the comparison of participant input to manager input for an IT project for technicians involved

Table 5-3
Comparison of Participants and Managers

Factor	Participants	Managers
ISDN knowledge, skills, or experience *before* they participated in the IT project	13%	14%
ISDN knowledge, skills, or experience graduates gained *from* the project	37%	36%
ISDN knowledge, skills, or experience graduates acquired on their own *after* the project	16%	12%
ISDN reference material or job aids such as bulletins, methods and procedure documentation	7%	9%
Coaching or feedback from peers	18%	18%
Coaching or feedback from graduates' managers	2%	5%
Observation of others	7%	6%

with ISDN lines in a telecommunications company. Both the participants and the managers were asked to allocate the various factors that contributed to the overall improvement. In this case, both participants and managers gave almost the same allocation, bringing increased credibility to the participants' estimate. In this situation, the managers were familiar and involved with the various factors that contribute to improved performance. They understood the factors enough to provide credible input. This may not always be the case. Managers removed from a particular job by distance or function are unable to make this type of allocation.

This approach has the same disadvantages as participant estimates. It is subjective and may be viewed with skepticism by senior management. Also, supervisors may be reluctant to participate or be incapable of providing accurate impact estimates. In some cases they may not know about other factors that contributed to the improvement.

The advantages of this approach are similar to the advantages of participant estimation. It is simple and inexpensive and enjoys an acceptable degree of credibility because it comes directly from the supervisors of those individuals who received benefits from the IT upgrades. When combined with participant estimation, the credibility is enhanced considerably. Also, when factored by the level of confidence, its value further increases.

Management Estimate of IT's Impact

In some cases, upper management may estimate the percent of improvement that should be attributed to the IT project. This method is not necessarily recommended because of its subjective nature. Senior managers may not understand all the factors or have an indication of the relative difference of the factors that could have affected the business measure driven by IT. Therefore, the use of this method should be avoided or used only when it is necessary to secure buy-in from the senior management team.

In some situations, the IT impact will be large, providing a high ROI. Top managers may feel more comfortable making an adjustment in the actual data. In essence, they are applying their discount factor for an unknown factor, although attempts have been made to identify each factor. Although there is no scientific basis for this technique, it provides some assurance that the data are appropriately discounted.

Customer Input of IT's Impact

One helpful approach in some narrowly focused situations is to solicit input on the impact of IT directly from customers. In these situations, customers are asked why they chose a particular product or service or to explain how individuals applying skills and abilities have influenced their reaction to the product or service learned as part of a technology initiative. This strategy focuses directly on what the IT project is often designed to improve. For example, after a teller-focused IT project was conducted following a bank merger, market research data showed that the percentage of customers who were dissatisfied with teller systems efficiency was reduced by 5 percent when compared to market survey data before the teller automation upgrade. Since only the IT project increased teller efficiency, the 5 percent reduction of dissatisfied customers was directly attributable to the IT project.

In another example, a large real estate company provided a comprehensive IT project for agents, focusing on tangible real estate search technology. As customers listed their homes with an agent, they received an electronic survey that explored the reasons for deciding to list their home with the company. Among the reasons listed were the technology tools leveraged by the real estate company to show real-time comparisons of related properties through its Web-based search application. Responses on this question and related questions provided evidence of the percentage of new listings attributed to the IT project.

This approach can be used only in situations where customer input can be obtained. Even then, customers may not be able to provide accurate data. Because customer input is critical, however, the approach is useful in those situations where it can be utilized.

EXPERT ESTIMATION OF IT'S IMPACT

External or internal experts can sometimes estimate the portion of results that can be attributed to IT. When using this strategy, experts must be carefully selected based on their knowledge of the process, project, and situation. For example, an expert in quality might be able to provide estimates of how much change in a quality measure can be attributed to IT and how much can be attributed to other factors in the implementation of a TQM project.

This approach would most likely be used in a scenario involving the success of a project developed by an external supplier. In a detailed evaluation of previous studies, a certain amount of the results have been attributed to IT. This figure from the supplier is used to extrapolate it to the current situation. This approach should be pursued cautiously because the situation may be different. However, if it is a project application with many similarities, this value may be a rough estimate—a *very* rough estimate. Because of these concerns, this approach should be used with explanations. Also, it is important to check the actual studies that have been conducted to ensure that a credible, objective process was used in data collection and analysis.

This technique has an advantage in that its credibility often reflects the reputation of the expert or independent consultant. It is a quick source of input from a reputable expert or independent consultant. Sometimes top management will place more confidence in external experts than its own internal staff.

CALCULATING THE IMPACT OF OTHER FACTORS

Although not appropriate in all cases, there are some situations where it may be feasible to calculate the impact of factors (other than IT) that influenced the improvement and then conclude that IT is credited with the remaining portion. In this approach, IT takes credit for improvement that cannot be attributed to other factors.

An example will help explain the approach. In a consumer-lending automation project for a large bank, a significant increase in consumer loan volume was generated after Web-based applications were deployed to allow customers to apply online. Part of the increase was attributed to the IT initiative, and the remainder was due to the influence of other factors operating during the same time period. Two other factors were identified by the evaluator: A loan officer's production improved with time and falling interest rates stimulated an increase in consumer loans.

In regard to the first factor, loan officers' confidence improved as they closed more loans. They used consumer lending policy manuals and gained knowledge and expertise through trial and error. The amount of this factor was estimated by using input from several internal experts in the marketing department.

For the second factor, industry sources were used to estimate the relationship between increased consumer loan volume and falling interest rates. These two estimates accounted for a certain percent of increased consumer loan volume. The remaining improvement was attributed to the IT project.

This method is appropriate when the other factors are easily identified and the appropriate mechanisms are in place to calculate their impact on the improvement. In some cases it is just as difficult to estimate the impact of other factors as it is for the impact of the IT project, leaving this approach less advantageous. This process can be credible if the method used to isolate the impact of other factors is credible.

USING THE TECHNIQUES

With several techniques available to isolate the impact of strategic IT initiatives, selecting the most appropriate techniques for the specific project can be difficult. Some techniques are simple and inexpensive, and others are more time consuming and costly. When attempting to make the selection decision, several factors should be considered:

- Feasibility of the technique
- Accuracy provided with the technique when compared to the accuracy needed
- Credibility of the technique with the target audience

- Specific cost to implement the technique
- The amount of disruption in normal work activities as the technique is implemented
- Participant, staff, and management time needed with the particular technique

Multiple techniques or sources for data input should be considered, since two sources are usually better than one. When multiple sources are used, a conservative method is recommended to combine the inputs. A conservative approach builds acceptance. The target audience should always be provided with explanations of the process and the various subjective factors involved. Multiple sources allow an organization to experiment with different techniques and build confidence with a particular technique. For example, if management is concerned about the accuracy of participants' estimates, a combination of a control group arrangement and participants' estimates could be attempted to check the accuracy of the estimation process.

It is not unusual for the ROI of IT projects or technology development initiatives to be extremely large. Even when a portion of the improvement is allocated to other factors, the numbers are still impressive in many situations. The audience should understand that although every effort was made to isolate the impact, it is still a figure that is not precise and may contain error. It represents the best estimate of the impact given the constraints, conditions, and resources available. Chances are it is more accurate than other types of analysis regularly used in other functions within the organization.

Final Thoughts

This chapter presented a variety of techniques that isolate the effects of IT investments. The techniques represent the most effective approaches to tackle this issue and are used by some of the most progressive organizations. Too often, results are reported and linked to IT without any attempt to isolate the portion of results that can be attributed to the specific IT project. It is impossible to link IT to business impact if this issue is ignored. If the IT and Technology Development function is to continue to improve its professional image as well as meet its responsibility for obtaining results, this issue must be addressed early in the process.

References

Armstrong, J.S. (Ed.). *Principles of Forecasting: A Handbook for Researchers and Practitioners*, Boston, MA: Kluwer Academic Publishers, 2001.

Kaufman, R. "Resolving the (Often-Deserved) Attacks on Training." *Performances Impermanency*, July 2002, vol 41, no 6.

Salkind, N.J. *Statistics for People Who (Think They) Hate Statistics.* Thousand Oaks, CA: Sage Publications, Inc., 2000.

Wang, G. "Control Group Methods for HPT Project Evaluation and Measurement," *Performance Improvement Quarterly*, 15(2), 2002, pp. 32–46.

CHAPTER 6

Exposing the Value of Strategic Technology Projects

Traditionally, most ROI evaluations stop with a tabulation of business results, which is a Level 4 evaluation. In those situations, the project is considered successful if it produced improvements such as productivity increases, user interface enhancements, system error reductions, or customer satisfaction improvements. Although these results are important, converting the data to monetary values and showing the total impact of the improvement may be more insightful. The monetary value is also needed to compare the costs of the project to develop the ROI. This evaluation is the ultimate level of the five-level evaluation framework presented in Chapter 1. This chapter shows how leading organizations are moving beyond tabulating business results and are adding the step of converting data to monetary values. Chapter 4 outlined the methods used to collect data, and Chapter 5 described a variety of techniques used to isolate the effects of strategic IT projects. This chapter outlines the techniques to convert the data to monetary values.

PRELIMINARY ISSUES

Hard and Soft Data

After collecting impact data, many organizations find dividing data into hard and soft categories helpful. *Hard data* are the traditional measures of organizational performance. They are objective, easy to measure, and easy to convert to monetary values. Hard data are often common measures, achieve high credibility with management, and are available in every type of organization. They are destined to be converted to monetary values and included in the ROI formula.

Hard data represent the output, quality, cost, and time of work-related processes. Table 6-1 shows a sampling of typical hard data under these four categories. Almost every department or unit will have hard-data performance measures. For example, a government office that has implemented automation technology to aid in approving applications for work visas in a foreign country will have these four measures among its overall performance measurements:

Table 6-1
Examples of Hard Data

Output	Time
Units produced	System downtime
Items assembled	Overtime
Items sold	On-time shipments
Forms processed	Time to project completion
Loans approved	Processing time
Inventory turnover	Cycle time
Patients visited	Meeting schedules
Applications processed	Repair time
Productivity	Efficiency
Work backlog	Work stoppages
Shipments	Order response time
New accounts opened	Late reporting
	Lost time days

Costs	Quality
Budget variances	Scrap
Unit costs	Rejects
Cost by account	Error rates
Variable costs	Rework
Fixed costs	Shortages
Overhead costs	Deviation from standard
Operating costs	Product failures
Number of cost Reductions	Inventory adjustments
Accident costs	Percent of Tasks completed
Sales expense	Number of accidents

1. Number of applications processed (output)
2. Cost per application processed (cost)
3. Number of input or system errors made processing applications (quality)
4. Time taken to process and approve an application (time)

Ideally, IT projects for employees in this unit should be linked to one or more hard data measures.

Because many IT projects are designed to enhance the soft and hard skills of the end users, soft data are needed in the evaluation. *Soft data* are usually subjective, sometimes difficult to measure, almost always difficult to convert to monetary values, and are behaviorally oriented. When compared to hard data, soft data are usually less credible. Soft data measures may or may not be converted to monetary values.

Soft data items can be grouped into several categories. Table 6-2 shows one grouping. Measures such as employee turnover, absenteeism, and grievances appear as soft data items, not because they are difficult to measure but because accurately converting them to monetary values is difficult.

General Steps to Convert Data

Before describing the techniques to convert either hard or soft data to monetary values, the general steps used to convert data in each strategy are briefly summarized. These steps should be followed for each data conversion.

Focus on a unit of measure. First, identify a unit of improvement. For output data, the unit of measure is the item produced, service provided, or sale consummated. Time measures are varied and include items such as the time to complete a project, cycle time, system response time, or customer response time. The unit is usually expressed as seconds, minutes, hours, or days. Quality is a common measure, and the unit may be one error, reject, defect, or rework item. Soft data measures are varied, and the unit of improvement may include items such as a grievance, an absence, an employee turnover statistic, or a change of one point in the customer satisfaction index.

Determine a value of each unit. Place a value (V) on the unit identified in the first step. For measures of production, quality, cost, and time, the process is relatively easy. Most organizations have records or reports reflecting the value of items, such as one unit of

Table 6-2
Examples of Soft Data

Work Habits	Customer Satisfaction
Absenteeism	Churn rate
Tardiness	Number of satisfied customers
Visits to the dispensary	Customer satisfaction index
First-Aid treatments	Customer loyalty
Violations of safety rules	Customer complaints
Excessive breaks	

Work Climate	Development/Advancement
Number of grievances	Number of promotions
Number of discrimination	Number of Pay increases
Charges	Number of training Programs attended
Employee complaints	Requests for transfer
Job satisfaction	Performance appraisal ratings
Employee turnover	Increases in job effectiveness
Litigation	

Job Attitudes	Initiative
Job satisfaction	Implementation of new ideas
Organizational commitment	Successful completion of projects
Perceptions of job responsibilities	Number of suggestions implemented
Employee loyalty	Number of goals
Increased confidence	

production or the cost of a system-driven defect. Soft data are more difficult to convert to monetary values, as the cost of one absence, one grievance, or a change of one point on an employee attitude survey is often difficult to pinpoint. The techniques in this chapter provide an array of possibilities to support this conversion. When more than one value is available, either the most credible or the lowest value is used.

Calculate the change in performance data. The change in output data is developed after the effects of a specific IT project have been isolated from other influences. The change (Δ) is the performance improvement, measured as hard or soft data, that is directly attributable to the IT project. The value may represent the performance improvement for an individual, a team, a group, or several groups of participants.

Determine an annual amount for the change. Annualize the ΔP value to develop a total change in the performance data for one year. This timeframe has become a standard approach with many organizations wishing to capture the total benefits of an IT project. Although the benefits may not be realized at the same level for an entire year, some projects will continue to produce benefits beyond one year. In some cases, the stream of benefits may involve several years. However, using one year of benefits is considered a conservative approach. This leads to Guiding Principle 9:

Guiding Principle 9

Only the first year of benefits (annual) should be used in the ROI analysis of short-term projects/initiatives.

Calculate the total value of the improvement. Develop the total value of the improvement by multiplying the annual performance change (ΔP) by the unit value (V) for the complete group in question. For example, if one group of participants for a project is being evaluated, the total value will include complete improvement for all group participants. This value for annual project benefits is then compared to the cost of the project, usually through the ROI formula presented in Chapter 1.

Techniques for Converting Data to Monetary Values

An example taken from a team-building project at a silicon chip manufacturing facility describes the five-step process of converting data to monetary values. This project was developed and implemented after a needs assessment revealed that a lack of teamwork was causing an excessive number of system manufacturing errors. Therefore, the actual number of system-related manufacturing errors resolved at Step 2 in the quality assurance process was selected as an output measure. Table 6-3 shows the steps taken to assign monetary values to the data arrived at a total project impact of $546,000.

Table 6-3
Converting Data to Monetary Values

Setting: Technology in a Silicon Chip Manufacturing Facility	

Step 1   Focus on a unit of improvement.

One error reaching Step 2 in the four-step quality assurance/testing process.

Step 2   Determine a value of each unit.

Using internal experts, the quality assurance staff, the cost of an average system related manufacturing error was estimated to be $6,500 when considering time and direct costs. (V = $6,500)

Step 3   Calculate the change (Δ) in performance data.

Six months after the project was completed, total system-related manufacturing errors per month reaching Step 2 declined by 10. Seven of the 10 error reductions were related to the program as determined by supervisors (isolating the effects of IT projects).

Step 4   Determine an annual amount for the change.

Using the six-month value, 7 per month yields an annual improvement of 84 ($\Delta P = 84$) for the first year.

Step 5   Calculate the annual value of the improvement.

$$\text{Annual value} = \Delta P \times V$$
$$= 84 \times \$6,500$$
$$= \$546,000$$

Several techniques are available to convert data to monetary values. Some techniques are appropriate for a specific type of data or data category, and others can be used with virtually any type of data. The IT staff's challenge is to select the particular strategy that best matches the type of data and the situation. Each method is presented here, beginning with the most credible approach.

CONVERTING OUTPUT DATA TO CONTRIBUTION

When an IT project has produced a change in output, the value of the increased output can often be determined from the organization's accounting or operating records. For organizations operating on a profit basis, this value is usually the marginal profit contribution of an additional unit of production or unit of service provided. For example, a production team in a major appliance manufacturer boosts production of small refrigerators with a series of comprehensive IT process automation projects. The unit of improvement, therefore, is the profit margin of one refrigerator. In organizations that are performance-driven rather than profit-driven, this value is usually reflected in the savings accumulated when an additional unit of output is realized for the same input requirements. For example, in a visa section of a government office, an additional visa application is processed at no additional cost. Therefore, an increase in output translates into a cost savings equal to the unit cost of processing a visa.

The formulas and calculations used to measure this contribution depend on the organization and its records. Most organizations have this type of data readily available for performance monitoring and goal setting. Managers often use marginal cost statements and sensitivity analyses to pinpoint the value associated with changes in output (Boulton, Libert, & Samek, 2000). If the data are not available, the IT staff must initiate or coordinate the development of appropriate values.

In one case involving a commercial bank, a customer relationship management system was implemented. It resulted in additional consumer loan volume (output). To measure the ROI for the CRM project, it was necessary to calculate the value (profit contribution) of one additional consumer loan. This was a relatively easy item to calculate from the bank's records (Phillips, 2000). As shown in Table 6-4, several components went into this calculation.

The first step was to determine the yield, which was available from bank records. Next, the average spread between the cost of funds and the yield received on the loan was calculated. For example, the

Table 6-4
Loan Profitability Analysis

Profit Component	Unit Value
Average loan size	$15,500
Average loan yield	9.75%
Average cost of funds (including branch costs)	5.50%
Direct costs for consumer lending	0.82%
Corporate overhead	1.61%
Net Profit Per Loan	**1.82%**

bank could obtain funds from depositors at 5.5 percent on average, including the cost of operating the branches. The direct costs of making the loan, such as salaries of employees directly involved in consumer lending and advertising costs for consumer loans, had to be subtracted from this difference. Historically, these direct costs amounted to 0.82 percent of the loan value. To cover overhead costs for other corporate functions, an additional 1.61 percent was subtracted from the value. The remaining 1.82 percent of the average loan value represented the bank's profit margin on a loan.

The good news about this technique is that standard values are available for many of the measures. The challenge is to quickly find the appropriate and most credible value. As the previous example illustrates, the value had already been developed for other purposes. This value was then used in the evaluation of the IT project. Table 6-5

Table 6-5
Common Measures and the Methods to Convert Output to Monetary Values

Output Measures	Example	Technique	Comments
Production unit	One unit assembled	Standard value	Available in almost every manufacturing unit
Service unit	Packages delivered on time	Standard value	Developed for most service providers when it is a typical service delivery unit
Sales	Monetary increase in revenue	Standard value (profit margin)	The profit from one additional dollar of sales is a standard item
Market share	10% increase in market share in one year	Standard value	Margin of increased sales
Productivity measure	10% change in productivity index	Standard value	This measure is very specific to the type of production or productivity measured. It may include per unit of time.

provides additional detail on the common measures of output data, showing how they are typically developed and some of the comments concerning them. As the table illustrates, standard values are almost always available in most organizations. However, if no value has been developed for a particular measure, one of the other techniques discussed in this chapter can be used to determine the value.

Calculating the Cost of Quality

Ensuring quality is a critical concern, and its cost is an important measure within the IT function for most manufacturing and service firms. Since many IT projects are designed to improve quality, the IT staff must place a value on the improvement in certain quality measures. For some quality measures, the task is easy. For example, if quality is measured with a defect rate, the value of the improvement is the cost to repair or replace the defective product. The most obvious cost of poor quality is the scrap or waste generated by mistakes. Defective products, spoiled raw materials, and discarded paperwork are all results of poor quality. This scrap and waste translates directly into monetary values. For example, in a production environment, the cost of a defective product is the total cost incurred to the point the mistake is identified minus the salvage value.

Employee mistakes and errors can cause expensive rework. The most costly rework occurs when a product is delivered to a customer and must be returned for correction. The cost of rework includes both labor and direct costs. In some organizations, the cost of rework can be as much as 35 percent of operating costs (Campanella, 1999). In one example of a project involving a customer service and service route optimization system for dispatchers in an oil company, a measure of rework was the number of pullouts. A pullout occurs when a delivery truck cannot fill an order for fuel at a service station. The truck must return to the terminal for an adjustment to the order. Tabulating the cost of a sample of actual pullouts developed the average cost of the pullout. The cost elements included driver time involved, the cost of the truck, the cost of terminal use, and an estimate of administrative costs.

In another example involving couriers with DHL Worldwide Express (Spain), a global tracking system project was implemented for couriers. Several measures were involved in the payoff of the project. One of those was a quality measure known as repackaging error. This occurs when a parcel is damaged due to mishandling and must be repackaged before it can be delivered to the customer. The time and repackaging costs are small, but when spread over several parcels, couriers, and several locations, the value can be significant. The company had already developed a cost for this error, and the standard value was used in the ROI study. The study involved enhanced use of the routing technology designed to expedite packages falling behind in the standard shipping process as a result of damage and repackaging.

Perhaps the costliest element of poor quality is customer and client dissatisfaction. In some cases, serious mistakes can result in lost business. Customer dissatisfaction is difficult to quantify, and attempts to arrive at a monetary value may be impossible using direct methods. Usually, the judgment and expertise of sales, marketing, or quality managers may be the best technique to measure the impact of dissatisfaction. A growing number of quality experts are now measuring customer and client dissatisfaction with automated market surveys (Johnson & Gustafsson, 2000). However, other strategies discussed in this chapter may be more appropriate to quantify the cost of customer dissatisfaction.

The good news about quality measures is that much has been done to develop the value for improving the particular measure. This is due in part to total quality management, continuous process improvement, and Six Sigma. All these processes have focused on individual quality measures and the cost of quality. Specific standard values have been developed. If standard values are not available for any of the quality measures, one of the other techniques in this chapter can be used to develop the value.

CONVERTING EMPLOYEE TIME

Reduction in employee time needed to complete a specific process or systems-related task is a common objective for IT and technology development projects. In a team environment, a project could enable the team to perform tasks in a shorter timeframe or with fewer people. On an individual basis, computer skills workshops are designed to help professional, sales, supervisory, and managerial employees save time in performing daily systems-related tasks. The value of the time saved is an important measure of the project's success, and this conversion is a relatively easy process.

The most obvious time savings are from labor-reduction costs in performing work. The monetary savings are found by multiplying the hours saved by the labor cost per hour. For example, after using an advanced online order entry system, participants estimated that each saves an average of 74 minutes per day, worth $31.25 per day or $7,500 per year. These time savings were based on the average salary plus benefits for the typical participant.

The average wage, with a percent added for employee benefits, will suffice for most calculations. However, employee time may be worth more. For example, additional costs in maintaining an employee (office space, furniture, telephone, utilities, computers, secretarial support, and other overhead expenses) could be included in the average labor cost. Therefore, the average wage rate may quickly escalate to a large number. The conservative approach, however, is to use the salary plus employee benefits.

In addition to the labor cost per hour, other benefits can result from time savings. These include improved service, avoidance of penalties for late projects, and the creation of additional opportunities for profit. These values can be estimated using other methods discussed in this chapter.

Use caution when the time savings are developed. Time savings are only realized when the amount of time saved translates into an additional contribution. If an IT project resulted in saving manager time, a monetary value is realized only if the manager used the additional time in a productive way. If a team-based project generated a new process that eliminated several hours of work each day, the actual savings would be realized only if cost savings resulted from a reduction in employees, a reduction in overtime pay, or increased productivity. Therefore, an important preliminary step in developing time savings is to determine if a "true" savings will be realized (Harbour, 1996).

USING HISTORICAL COSTS

Sometimes, historical records contain the value of a measure and reflect the cost (or value) of a unit of improvement. This method involves identifying the appropriate records and tabulating the actual cost components for the item in question. For example, a large construction firm implemented an IT project to improve tracking of safety, compliance, and reporting. The project improved several safety-related performance measures, ranging from OSHA fines to total workers' compensation costs. Examining the company's records using one year of data, the IT staff calculated the average cost for each systems-related safety measure.

In another example, a large city initiated an absenteeism-reduction project for its city bus drivers. The city implemented a biometric (thumb scan) employee time and attendance system. There was a significant issue with drivers clocking each other in and out of their outdated timecard system. The IT vice president was interested in showing the ROI for the project. To show the impact of the absenteeism reduction, the cost of one absence was needed. As part of the study, the external consulting firm developed a detailed cost of an absence considering the full costs of a driver pool maintained to cover an unexpected absence. All the costs were calculated in a fully loaded profile to present the cost of an absence. As this impact study revealed, the time to develop historical costs is sometimes expensive, leaving researchers looking for an easier way. Using historical cost data may not be the technique of choice because of the time and effort involved. In those situations, one or more of the techniques described in the remainder of this chapter can be used.

Using Internal and External Experts' Input

When faced with converting soft data items for which historical records are not available, obtaining input from experts may be a solution. With this approach, internal experts provide the cost (or value) of one unit of improvement. The individuals who have knowledge of the situation and the respect of the management group are often the best prospects for expert input. These experts must understand the processes and be willing to provide estimates as well as the assumptions used in arriving at the estimate. When requesting input from experts, the full scope of what is needed should be explained with as many specifics as possible. Most experts have their own method to develop this value.

An example will help clarify this approach. In one silicon chip manufacturing plant, a technology project was designed to reduce the number of system-related manufacturing errors discovered at Step 2 of the quality assurance process (see Table 6-3). This is the step in which the error is recorded in writing and becomes a measurable soft data item. Except for the actual cost of silicon chip rework and direct external costs, the company had no records of the total costs of manufacturing errors (i.e., there were no data for the time required to resolve an error). Therefore, an estimate was needed from an expert. The manager of quality assurance and testing, who had credibility with senior management and thorough knowledge of the manufacturing process, provided an estimate of the cost. He based his estimate on the average rework when a manufacturing error was discovered; the direct costs related to the error (rework, material costs, quality review, error documentation); the estimated amount of supervisory, staff, and employee time associated with the error; and a factor for reduced morale and other "soft" consequences. This internal estimate, although not a precise figure, was appropriate for this analysis and had adequate credibility with management.

When internal experts are not available, external experts are sought. External experts must be selected based on their experience with the unit of measure. Fortunately, many experts are available who work directly with important measures such as creativity, innovation, employee attitudes, customer satisfaction, productivity, employee turnover, and absenteeism. They are often willing to provide estimates of the cost (or value) of these items. Because the credibility of the value is directly related to the expert's reputation, their credibility and reputation are critical.

Using Values from External Databases

For some soft data items, it may be appropriate to use databases to locate the cost (or value) of one unit based on the research of others. This technique taps external databases that contain studies and research projects focusing on the cost of data items. Fortunately, many databases are available that report cost studies of a variety of data items related to IT projects. Data are available on the costs of software bugs, application rework, error rates, system modifications, and even customer self-service. The difficulty lies in finding a database with studies or research efforts for a situation similar to the project under evaluation. Ideally, the data would come from a similar setting in the same industry, but that is not always possible. Sometimes, data on all industries or organizations would be sufficient, perhaps with an adjustment to fit the industry under consideration. There are a number of online technical articles and blogs, with these types of comparison data that should be well researched to find the best overall fit for your project.

Using Estimates from Participants

In some situations, project participants estimate the value of a soft data improvement. This strategy is appropriate when participants are capable of providing estimates of the cost (or value) of the unit of measure improved by applying the skills learned in the project. When using this approach, participants should be provided with clear instructions, along with examples of the type of information needed. The advantage of this approach is that the individuals closest to the improvement are often capable of providing the most reliable estimates of its value.

An example illustrates this process. A group of supervisors attended a group training session for the rollout of the e-commerce module of a new Enterprise Resource Planning (ERP) system that a direct sales and marketing company was ready to deploy. A successful deployment of this module should reduce internal order entry time because more customers will be driven through the e-commerce process on the company's website instead of having to speak with a call center representative. To calculate the ROI for the project, it was necessary to determine the average value of one automated order process for the company. As is the case with most organizations, historical records for the cost of order processing were not available. Experts were not available, and external studies were sparse for this particular industry. Therefore, supervisors (project participants) were asked to estimate the cost of the manual order process.

In a group-interview format, each participant was asked to walk through the current system-related steps for order processing. After reflecting on what must be done to manually get an order into the system, each supervisor was asked to provide an estimate of the average cost of an order in the company. Although some supervisors are reluctant to provide estimates, with prodding and encouragement they will usually provide a value. The values are averaged for the group, and the result is the cost of an order manually entered into the system to be used in evaluating the project. Although this is an estimate, it is probably more accurate than data from external studies, calculations using internal records, or estimates from experts. And because it comes from supervisors who deal with the issue daily, it will usually have credibility with senior management.

USING ESTIMATES FROM SUPERVISORS AND MANAGERS

In some situations, participants may be incapable of placing a value on the improvement. Their work may be so far removed from the output of the process that they cannot reliably provide estimates. In these cases, the team leaders, supervisors, or managers of participants may be capable of providing estimates. They may be asked to provide a value for a unit of improvement linked to the project. For example, a Web-based customer self-service project for customer service representatives was designed to reduce customer complaints and empower customers to find solutions to their issues online without having to contact a representative by phone. Applying the project resulted in a reduction in complaints, but the value of a single customer complaint was needed to determine the value of improvement. Although customer service representatives had knowledge of some issues surrounding customer complaints, they were not well versed in the full impact, so their supervisors were asked to provide a value.

In other situations, supervisors are asked to review and approve participants' estimates. After the project is completed, participants estimated the value of their improvements that were directly related to their participation in the project. Their immediate managers are then asked to review the estimates and the process used by the participants to arrive at the estimates. Supervisors could confirm, adjust, or discard the values provided by the participants.

In some situations, senior management provides estimates of the data value. With this technique, senior managers who are interested in the process or project are asked to place a value on the improvement, based on their perception of its worth. This approach is used in situations in which it is difficult to calculate the value or when other sources of estimation are unavailable or unreliable. An example will illustrate this strategy. A hospital chain was attempting to improve customer satisfaction with a help desk and workflow routing system for all employees. The project was designed to improve customer service and therefore improve the external customer satisfaction index. To determine the value of the project, a value for a unit of improvement (one point on the index) was needed. Because senior management was interested in improving the index, it was asked to provide input on the value of one unit. In a regular executive staff meeting, each senior manager and hospital administrator was asked to describe what it means for a hospital when the index increases. After some discussion, each individual was asked to provide an estimate of the monetary value gained when the index moves one point. Although initially reluctant to provide the information, with some encouragement, monetary values were provided, totaled, and averaged. The result was an estimate of the worth of one unit of improvement, which was used as a basis of calculating the benefit of the project. Although this process is subjective, it does have the benefit of ownership from senior executives, the same executives who approved the project budget.

Linking with Other Measures

When standard values, records, experts, and external studies are unavailable, a feasible method might be developing a relationship between the measure in question and some other measure that may be easily converted to a monetary value. This approach involves identifying, if possible, existing relationships showing a strong correlation between one measure and another with a standard value.

For example, the classic relationship depicted in Figure 6-1 shows a correlation between system adoption and error rate. In a consulting project designed to improve system adoption, a value is needed for changes in the system adoption index. A predetermined relationship showing the correlation between improvements in system adoption and reductions in error rate can directly link the changes to entry errors in the system. Using standard data or external studies, the cost of error rates can easily be developed, as described earlier. Therefore, a change in system adoption is converted to a monetary value, or at least an approximate value. It is not always exact because of the potential for error and other factors, but the estimate is sufficient for converting the data to monetary values.

In some situations, a chain of relationships may be established to show the connection between two or more variables. In this approach,

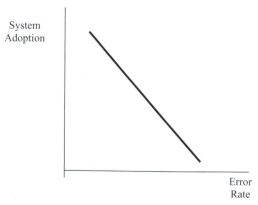

*Figure 6-1. Relationship Between System Adoption
and Error Rate*

a measure that may be difficult to convert to a monetary value is linked to other measures that, in turn, are linked to measures on which a value can be placed. Ultimately, these measures are traced to a monetary value that is often based on profits. Figure 6-2 shows the model used by Sears, one of the largest retail chains (Ulrich, 1998). The model connects job attitudes (collected directly from the employees) with customer service, which is directly related to revenue growth. The rectangles in the chart represent survey information, and the ovals represent hard data. The shaded measurements are collected and distributed in the form of Sears's total performance indicators.

As the model shows, a five-point improvement in employee attitudes will drive a 1.3-point improvement is customer satisfaction. This, in turn, drives a 0.5 percent increase in revenue growth. Therefore, if employee attitudes at a local store improved by five points, and previous revenue growth was 5 percent, the new revenue growth would be 5.5 percent. These links between measures, often called the *service-profit chain*, create a promising way to place monetary values on hard-to-quantify measures.

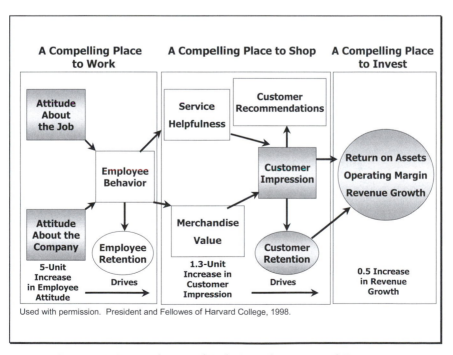

Figure 6-2. Linkage of Job Satisfaction and Revenue

Using IT Staff Estimates

The final technique for converting data to monetary values is to use IT staff estimates. Using all the available information and experience, the staff members most familiar with the situation provide estimates of the value. For example, an international electronics retailer created a route optimization application for its mobile installation technicians. The IT staff estimated the cost of one missed service call to be $250. This value was then used in calculating the savings for the reduction of missed service calls following the implementation of the route optimization system. Although the staff may be capable of providing accurate estimates, this approach may be perceived as being biased, since the IT staff wanted it to be large (a motive). It should be used only when other approaches are not available.

Selecting the Appropriate Technique

With so many techniques available, the challenge is to select one or more techniques appropriate to the situation. The following guidelines can help determine the proper selection:

Use the technique appropriate for the type of data. Some techniques are designed specifically for hard data, whereas others are more appropriate for soft data. Therefore, the type of data will often dictate the strategy. Hard data, although always preferred, are not always available. Soft data are often required and must be addressed with the techniques appropriate for soft data.

Move from most accurate to least accurate techniques. The ten techniques are presented in order of accuracy and credibility, beginning with the most credible. Standard, accepted values are most credible. IT staff estimates are least credible. Working down the list, each technique should be considered for its feasibility in the situation. The technique with the most accuracy and credibility is recommended.

Consider availability and convenience when selecting the technique. Sometimes the availability of a particular source of data will drive the selection. In other situations, the convenience of a technique may be an important factor in its selection.

When estimates are sought, use the source who has the broadest perspective on the issue. To improve the accuracy of an estimate, the broadest perspective on the issue is needed. The individual providing an estimate must be knowledgeable of all the processes and the issues surrounding the value of the data item.

Use multiple techniques when feasible. Sometimes it is helpful to have more than one technique for obtaining a value for the data. When multiple sources are available, more than one source should be used to serve as a comparison or to provide another perspective. When multiple sources are used, the data must be integrated using a convenient decision rule, such as the lowest value, a preferred approach because of the conservative nature of the lowest value.

This leads to a guiding principle:

> ### Guiding Principle 4
> When analyzing data, choose the most conservative among all the alternatives.

By *most conservative*, we mean the approach that yields the lowest ROI. Therefore, if the benefits are in consideration (numerator), it is the lowest value that yields that lowest ROI.

Minimize the amount of time required to select and implement the appropriate technique. As with other processes, it is important to keep the time invested as low as possible so the total time and effort for the ROI do not become excessive. Some strategies can be implemented with less time than others. This block in the ROI model can quickly absorb more time than the remainder of all the steps. Spending too much time on this step can dampen an otherwise enthusiastic attitude about the process.

Accuracy and Credibility of Data

The Credibility Problem

The techniques presented in this chapter assume that each data item collected and linked with strategic IT projects can be converted to a monetary value. Although estimates can be developed using one or more of these techniques, the process of converting data to monetary values may lose credibility with the target audience, who may doubt its use in analysis. Subjective data, such as a change in employee satisfaction with a new system or a reduction in the number of employee complaints about a system or process, are difficult to convert to monetary values. The key question for this determination is "Could these results be presented to senior management with confidence?" If the process does not meet this credibility test, the data should not be converted to monetary values and should be instead listed as an intangible benefit. Other data, particularly hard data items, could be used in the ROI calculation, leaving the subjective data as intangible improvements.

When converting data to monetary value, it is important to be consistent in the approach. Specific rules for making conversions will ensure this consistency and, ultimately, enhance the reliability of the study. When it is questionable if a data item should be converted, a four-part test is suggested starting with the question is "Is there a standard value?" If the answer is yes, it is used. If not, the next part of the test is considered. The next question is "Is there a method available to convert data to monetary value?" If this answer is no, the item is listed as an intangible. If it can be converted using one of the methods in this chapter, the next step is considered. The next question is "Can the conversion be accomplished with minimum resources?" If the answer is no, the item should be considered an intangible. If yes, the final step is considered. The last question is "Can the conversion process be described to an executive audience and obtain a buy-in in two minutes?" If yes, the value can be placed in the ROI calculation. If no, it is listed as an intangible. These guidelines are very critical in converting data consistently. The four-part test is also described in Table 9-4. The important point is to be consistent and methodical when converting data.

The accuracy of data and the credibility of the conversion process are important concerns. Technology professionals sometimes avoid converting data because of these issues. They are more comfortable in reporting that a CRM project resulted in increasing contact rates from 60 to 65 percent without attempting to place a value on the improvement. They assume that each person who receives the information will place a value on the increased contact rate. Unfortunately, the target audience may know little about the value of a customer contact rate and will usually underestimate the actual value of the improvement. Therefore, there should be some attempt to include this conversion in the ROI analysis.

How the Credibility of Data Is Influenced

When ROI data is presented to selected target audiences, its credibility will be an issue. The degree to which the target audience will believe the data will be influenced by the following factors.

Reputation of the Source of Data

The actual source of the data represents the first credibility issue. How credible is the individual or group providing the data? Do they understand the issues? Are they knowledgeable of all the processes? The target audience will often place more credibility on data obtained from those who are closest to the source of the actual improvement or change.

Reputation of the Source of the Study

The target audience scrutinizes the reputation of the individual, group, or organization presenting the data. Do they have a history of providing accurate reports? Are they unbiased with their analyses? Are they fair in their presentation? Answers to these and other questions will form an impression about the reputation.

Audience Bias

The audience may have a bias—either positive or negative—to a particular study or the data presented from the study. Some executives have a positive feeling about a particular project and will need less data to convince them of its value. Other executives may have negative bias toward the project and will need more data to make this comparison. The potential bias of the audience should be understood so the data can be presented to counter any attitude.

Motives of the Evaluators

The audience will look for motives of the person(s) conducting the study. Do the individuals presenting the data have a hidden agenda? Do they have a personal interest in creating a favorable or unfavorable result? Are the stakes high if the study is unfavorable? These, and other issues, will cause the target audience to examine motives.

Methodology of the Study

The audience will want to know specifically how the research was conducted. How were the calculations made? What steps were followed? What processes were used? A lack of information on the methodology will cause the audience to become wary and suspicious of the results. They will substitute their own perception of the methodology.

Assumptions Made in the Analysis

The audience will try to understand the assumptions made in the analysis. What are the assumptions in the study? Are they standard? How do they compare with other assumptions in other studies? When assumptions are omitted, the audience will substitute their own, often unfavorable assumptions. In ROI studies, conservative guiding principles influence calculations and conclusions.

Realism of the Outcome Data

Impressive ROI values could cause problems. When outcomes appear to be unrealistic, the target audience may have difficulty believing them. Huge claims often fall on deaf ears, causing reports to be thrown away before they are reviewed.

Types of Data

The target audience will usually have a preference for hard data. They are seeking business performance data tied to output, quality, costs, and time. These measures are usually easily understood and closely related to organizational IT performance. Conversely, soft data are sometimes viewed suspiciously from the outset, as many senior executives are concerned about their soft nature and limitations on the analysis.

Scope of Analysis

The smaller the scope, the more credible the data. Is the scope of the analysis narrow? Does it involve just one group or all the employees in the organization? Limiting the study to a small group, or series of groups, makes the process more accurate and believable.

Collectively, these factors will influence the credibility of an ROI impact study and provide a framework from which to develop the ROI report. Therefore, when considering each of the issues, the following key points are suggested for developing an ROI impact study and presenting it to the management group:

- Use the most credible and reliable source for estimates.
- Present the material in an unbiased, objective way.
- Be prepared for the potential bias of the audience.
- Fully explain the methodology used throughout the process, preferably on a step-by-step basis.
- Define the assumptions made in the analysis, and compare them to assumptions made in other similar studies.
- Consider factoring or adjusting output values when they appear to be unrealistic.
- Use hard data whenever possible and combine with soft data if available.
- Keep the scope of the analysis narrow. Conduct the impact with one or more groups of participants in the project, instead of all the participants or all the employees.

Making Adjustments

Two potential adjustments should be considered before finalizing the monetary value. In some organizations where soft data are used and values are derived with imprecise methods, senior management is sometimes offered the opportunity to review and approve the data. Because of the subjective nature of this process, management may factor (reduce) the data so that the final results are more credible.

The other adjustment concerns the time value of money. Since an investment in a project is made at one time period and the return is realized in a later time period, a few organizations adjust the project benefits to reflect the time value of money, using discounted cash flow techniques. The actual monetary benefits of the project are adjusted for this time period. The amount of this adjustment, however, is usually small compared with the typical benefits realized from IT and Technology Development projects.

FINAL THOUGHTS

In conclusion, organizations are attempting to be more aggressive when defining the monetary benefits of IT and Technology Development projects. Progressive IT managers are no longer satisfied with reporting business performance results from IT. Instead, they are taking additional steps to convert business results data to monetary values and compare them with the project's cost to develop the ultimate level of evaluation, the return on investment. This chapter presented ten specific techniques to convert business results to monetary values, offering an array of possibilities to fit any situation and project.

Case Study: Staggering ROI Results for a Successful Customer Relationship Management (CRM) Implementation

This case study is a beautiful example of the ROI that can be achieved when the right technology investments are made to address a well-defined business need. Salesforce.com is the market leader in hosted Customer Relationship Management (CRM) solutions, and DecisionOne is a leading supplier of technology support services to commercial enterprises, government agencies, and resellers across the country. With industry statistics, which claim that 70 percent of CRM implementations fail and that 55 percent of CRM projects fail to meet customers' expectations, this ROI case study becomes even more compelling.

Need for Collaboration and Forecasting Prompts CRM Search

With more than 4,000 employees, an extensive and geographically distributed network of service locations, DecisionOne provides the coverage, availability, and response to satisfy the technology support needs of its clients' employees and their customers.

In 2002, the company implemented a new customer engagement model designed to deliver higher customer value and service through the creation of virtual account teams. For optimal success, the distributed teams would need to work effectively together in a common customer system. The old process involved using legacy systems and other nonintegrated, manual tools such as Excel, making it challenging and time consuming to get accurate and up-to-date revenue forecasts and other critical metrics.

DecisionOne decided it needed a single, centralized CRM solution that its sales, marketing, and sales support teams could use to maintain and share customer and prospect information in real time. The company also valued accessibility and ease of use to ensure that its virtual account teams could easily collaborate to provide top-notch service.

"We needed an online CRM solution that delivered immediate benefit to our sales team without the barriers characteristic of traditional CRM products—such as high costs, long implementations, and unnecessarily complex designs," explains Frank Tait, vice president of marketing for DecisionOne.

Customized and Deployed in Under a Month

After considering solutions from leading CRM providers, DecisionOne selected Salesforce.com's Enterprise Edition for its rapid, cost-effective deployment and mobile accessibility. The company standardized its North American sales operations on Salesforce, with 120 active users. Virtual account teams could work collaboratively in Salesforce anywhere they have an Internet connection—in the office, at home, or on the road.

In less than a month, the system was tailored to match DecisionOne's opportunity and account management processes and deployed across North America, meeting the company's aggressive implementation timeline. A customized, online training curriculum enabled management and the sales team to get up to speed quickly.

DecisionOne now has a singular, company-wide view of its sales process, empowering its new virtual account teams to access information, collaborate, and respond to customer needs, all in real time. The ROI related highlights from this project as reported by DecisionOne's leadership:

- Investment recouped in four months
- First-year ROI of 1,150 percent
- 73 percent increase in the value of add-on deals
- 68 percent increase in new deal win rate

The ability to drive real-time data throughout its operations generated immediate benefits for DecisionOne. The sales team increased its efficiency, and senior management had much greater insight into its customers and sales data, as well as a more accurate revenue forecast. Tait reported that management could track high-level, real-time customer information and then drill down to explore more granular data, such as baseline revenue by account or renewals by account.

Even more amazing were DecisionOne's ROI calculations for CRM. The company calculated its first-year ROI with salesforce.com to be a whopping 1,150 percent. "It's incredible—Salesforce has seen bottom-line profitable in the order of hundreds of thousands of dollars every month, and we recouped our initial investment in just four months," said Tait.

References

Boulton, R.E.S., B.D. Libert, and S.M. Samek. *Cracking the Value Code: How Successful Businesses Are Creating Wealth in the New Economy*. New York: Harper Business, 2000.

Campanella, Jack (Ed.). *Principles of Quality Costs*, 3rd ed. Milwaukee, WI: American Society for Quality, 1999.

Harbour, J.L. *Cycle Time Reduction: Designing and Streamlining Work for High Performance*. New York: Quality Resources, 1996.

Johnson, M.D. and A. Gustafsson. *Improving Customer Satisfaction, Loyalty, and Profit: An Integrated Measurement and Management System*. San Francisco, CA: Jossey-Bass, 2000.

Phillips, J.J. *The Consultant's Scorecard: Tracking Results and Bottom-Line Impact of Consulting Projects*. New York: McGraw-Hill, 2000.

Ulrich, D. (Ed.). *Delivering Results*. Boston, MA: Harvard Business School, 1998.

CHAPTER 7

Tabulating Project Costs

The cost of implementing successful IT and technology development projects is increasing, putting more pressure on IT managers to figure out how and why the money is spent. The total cost of strategic IT initiatives is required, which means that the cost profile includes all direct and indirect costs. Fully loaded cost information is used to manage resources, develop standards, measure efficiencies, and examine alternative delivery processes.

Tabulating project costs is an essential step in developing the ROI calculation, and these costs are used as the denominator in the ROI formula. It is just as important to focus on costs as it is on benefits. In practice, however, costs are often more easily captured than benefits. This chapter explores the costs accumulation and tabulation steps, outlines the specific costs that should be captured, and presents economical ways to develop costs.

COST STRATEGIES

Importance of Costs

Many factors have contributed to the increased attention now given to monitoring IT costs accurately and thoroughly. Every organization should know approximately how much money it spends on IT and technology development. Many organizations calculate this expenditure and make comparisons with that of other organizations, although comparisons are difficult to make because of the different bases for cost calculations. Some organizations calculate IT and technology development costs as a percentage of payroll costs and set targets for increased investment. In the United States, the range based on industry vertical is between 2 and 8 percent. A consulting firm whose primary resource is human capital would be an example of the low end of the scale. A software development company whose focus is technology and technology-related products would be at the high end of the range. In a company like Microsoft, which is continually making multibillion-dollar R&D investments to keep up with ever-mounting competition, the percentages would be even higher.

An effective system of cost monitoring enables an organization to calculate the magnitude of total IT expenditures. Collecting this information also helps top management answer two important questions:

1. How much *do* we spend on IT compared with other organizations?
2. How much *should* we spend on IT?

The IT and technology development staff should know the relative cost effectiveness of projects and their components. Monitoring costs by project allows the staff to evaluate the relative contribution of a project and to determine how those costs are changing. If a project's cost rises, it might be appropriate to reevaluate the project's impact and overall success. It may be useful to compare specific components of costs with those of other projects or organizations. For example, the cost per milestone for one project could be compared with the cost per milestone for a similar project. Huge differences may signal a problem. Also, costs associated with design, development, or delivery could be compared with those of other projects within the organization and used to develop cost standards.

Accurate costs are necessary to predict future costs. Historical costs for a project provide the basis for predicting future costs of a similar project or budgeting for a project. Sophisticated cost models make it possible to estimate or predict costs with reasonable accuracy.

When a return on investment or cost-benefit analysis is needed for a specific project, costs must be developed. One of the most significant reasons for collecting costs is to obtain data for use in a cost-benefit analysis. In this comparison, cost data are equally as important as the project's economic benefits.

To improve the efficiency of the IT and technology development function, controlling costs is necessary. Competitive pressures place increased attention on efficiencies. Most IT and technology development departments have monthly budgets with cost projections listed by various accounts and, in some cases, by project. Cost monitoring is an excellent tool for identifying problem areas and taking corrective action. In the practical and classical management sense, the accumulation of cost data is a necessity.

Capturing costs is challenging because the figures must be accurate, reliable, and realistic. Although most organizations develop costs with much more ease than developing the economic value of benefits, the true cost of IT is often an elusive figure, even in some of the best organizations. Since the total direct IT budget is usually a number that is easily developed, it is more difficult to determine the specific costs of a project, including the indirect costs related to it. To develop a realistic ROI, costs must be accurate and credible. Otherwise, the painstaking difficulty and attention given to the benefits will be wasted because of inadequate or inaccurate costs.

Disclosing All Costs

Today there is increased pressure to report *all* IT costs, or fully loaded costs. This takes the cost profile beyond the direct cost of hardware, software, and services and includes the time that participants are involved in technology-oriented project tasks, including their benefits and other overhead. For years, management has understood that there are many indirect costs of IT, and now they want an accounting of these costs. Perhaps this point is best illustrated in a situation that recently developed in state government where the management controls of a large state agency were being audited. A portion of the audit focused on IT and technology development costs. The following comments are taken from the auditor's report.

Costs tracked at the project level focus on direct or "hard" costs and largely ignore the cost of time spent implementing or supporting IT. The costs of a project team's time to scope and design a specific IT initiative are typically not tracked. For one series of projects, including these costs raised the total IT cost dramatically. The agency stated that the total two-year cost for the specific project was about $600,000. This figure generally includes only direct costs and, as such, is substantially below the costs of the time spent by staff in preparation and implementation of the project. When accounting for the business analysis, formal scope definition, documentation of the requirements, training, and rollout costs the figure totals $1.39 million. If the statewide average of 45.5 percent for fringe benefits is considered, the total indirect cost of staff time to prepare for and implement the project becomes $2 million. Finally, if the agency's direct costs of $600,000 are added to the $2 million total indirect cost just noted, the total becomes more than $2.6 million. Among other factors that would drive actual total costs higher are the following:

- Cost of travel, meals, and lodging for project participants
- Allocated salaries and fringe benefits of providing administrative and logistic support
- Opportunity costs of productivity lost by staff in doing prework and implementing IT

Numerous barriers exist to hamper agency efforts in determining "How much do we spend on IT?"

- Cost systems tend to hide administrative, support, internal, and other indirect or "soft" costs.
- Costs generally are monitored at the department level rather than at the level of individual projects or activities.
- Cost information required by activity-based cost systems is not being generated.

As this case vividly demonstrates, the cost of organizational IT is much more than direct expenditures, and the IT and technology development departments are expected to report fully loaded costs in its reports.

Fully Loaded Costs

The conservative approach to calculating the ROI has a direct connection to cost accumulation. A guiding principle focuses directly on this issue.

> **Guiding Principle 10**
> Project costs should be fully loaded for
> ROI analysis.

With this approach, all costs that can be identified and linked to a particular project are included. The philosophy is simple: When in doubt, in the denominator, put it in (i.e., if it is questionable whether a cost should be included, it is recommended that it be included, even if the cost guidelines for the organization do not require it). This parallels a rule for the numerator, which states, "When in doubt, leave it out" (i.e., if it is questionable whether a benefit should be included in the numerator, it should be omitted from the analysis). When an ROI is calculated and reported to target audiences, the process should withstand even the closest scrutiny in terms of its accuracy and credibility. The only way to meet this test is to ensure that all costs are included. Of course, from a realistic viewpoint, if the controller or chief financial officer insists on not using certain costs, then it is best to leave them out.

The Danger of Costs Without Benefits

It is dangerous to communicate the costs of IT and technology development without presenting benefits. Unfortunately, many organizations have fallen into this trap for years. Costs are presented to management in all types of ingenious ways, such as cost of the project, cost per employee, and cost per development hour. Although these may be helpful for efficiency comparisons, it may be troublesome to present them without benefits. When most executives review IT costs, a logical question comes to mind: What benefit was received from the project? This is a typical management reaction, particularly when costs are perceived to be high. Because of this, some organizations have developed a policy of not communicating IT cost data for a specific project unless the benefits can be captured and presented along with the costs. Even if the benefit data is subjective and intangible, it is included with the cost data. This helps to keep a balance with the two issues.

Policies and Guidelines

It may be helpful to detail the philosophy and policy on costs in guidelines for the IT project managers, staff, and others who monitor and report costs. Cost guidelines detail specifically what costs are included with technology projects and how cost data are captured, analyzed, and reported. Cost guidelines can range from a one-page document to a 50-page manual in a large, complex organization. The simpler approach is better. When fully developed, they should be reviewed by the finance and accounting staff. The final document serves as the guiding force in collecting, monitoring, and reporting costs. When an ROI is calculated and reported, costs are included in a summary form, and the cost guidelines are referenced in a foot-note or attached as an appendix.

Cost Tracking Issues

Sources of Costs

It can be helpful to first consider the sources of IT and technology development cost. There are three major categories of sources, as illustrated in Table 7-1. The IT staff expenses usually represent the greatest segment of costs and are sometimes transferred directly to the client or project sponsor. The second major cost category con-sists of participant expenses, both direct and indirect. These costs are not identified in many IT and technology development projects, but they reflect a significant amount. The third cost source is the payments made to external vendors. These include payments directly to hardware, software, and service providers prescribed in the project. As Table 7-1 shows, some of these cost categories are understated. The finance and accounting records should be able to track and reflect the costs from these three different sources. The process presented in this chapter has the capability of tracking these costs, as well.

Table 7-1
Sources of Costs

Source of Costs	Cost Reporting Issues	
1. IT and technology development staff expenses	A.	Costs are usually accurate.
	B.	Variable expenses may be underestimated.
2. Participant expenses (direct and indirect)	A.	Direct expenses are usually not fully loaded.
	B.	Indirect expenses are rarely included in costs.
3. External expenses (hardware, software, and services)	A.	Sometimes understated.
	B.	May lack accountability.

IT Process Steps and Costs

Another important way to consider IT and technology development costs is in the characteristics of how the project unfolds. Figure 7-1 shows the typical IT and development cycle, beginning with the initial analysis and assessment, and progressing to the evaluation and reporting of the results. These functional process steps represent the typical flow of work. As a performance problem is addressed, a solution is developed or acquired and implemented in the organization. Implementation is often grouped with delivery. The entire process is routinely reported to the client or sponsor, and evaluation is undertaken to show the project's success. There are also a group of costs to support the process: administrative support and overhead costs. To fully understand costs, the project should be analyzed in these different categories, as described later in this chapter.

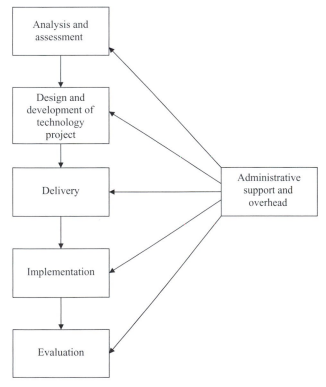

Figure 7-1. IT Project Steps and Cost Categories

Prorated versus Direct Costs

Usually all costs related to a project are captured and expensed to that project. However, three categories are usually prorated over several sessions of the same project. Needs assessment, design and development, and implementation are all significant costs that should be prorated over the shelf life of the project. Using a conservative approach, the shelf life should be short. Some organizations will consider one year of operation for the project, and others may consider two or three years. If there is some dispute about the specific time period to be used in the prorating formula, the shorter period should be used. If possible, the finance and accounting staff should be consulted.

A brief example will illustrate prorating for development costs. In a large technology company, an e-learning project was developed for $98,000. It was anticipated that it would have a three-year life cycle before it would require updating. The revision costs at the end of the three years were estimated to be about one-half of the original development costs, or $49,000. It was estimated that 400 participants would take the project in a three-year period, with an ROI calculation planned for 20 participants. Since the project will have one-half of its residual value at the end of three years, one-half of the cost should be written off for this three-year period. Therefore, the $49,000, representing half of the development costs, would be spread over the 400 participants as a prorated development cost, or $122.50 per participant. An ROI for 20 participants would therefore have a development cost of $2,450 included in the cost profile.

Employee Benefits Factor

When presenting salaries for participants and IT staff associated with projects, the benefits factor should be included. This number is usually well known in the organization and used in other cost applications. It represents the cost of all employee benefits expressed as a percent of base salaries. In some organizations this value is as high as 50 to 60 percent. In others, it may be as low as 25 to 30 percent. The average in the United States is approximately 30 percent (Bureau of Labor Statistics, 2006).

MAJOR COST CATEGORIES

The most important task is to define which specific costs are included in a tabulation of the project costs. This task involves

Table 7-2
Technology Project Cost Categories

Cost Item	Prorated	Expensed
Needs assessment	✓	
Business analysis	✓	
Functional requirements	✓	
System design	✓	
Development/Acquisition	✓	
Delivery/implementation		✓
• Salaries/benefits—project Managers		✓
• Salaries/benefits—Development staff		✓
• Materials, equipment, and services		✓
• Travel/lodging/meals		✓
• Project team Salaries/benefits		✓
• Travel time		✓
• Preparation time		✓
Evaluation		✓
Overhead	✓	

decisions that will be made by the IT staff and usually approved by management. If appropriate, the finance and accounting staff may need to approve the list. Table 7-2 shows the recommended cost categories for a fully loaded, conservative approach to estimating costs. Each category is described following.

Needs Assessment, Analysis, and Functional Requirements

One of the most often overlooked items is the cost of conducting a needs assessment. In some projects this cost is zero because the project is conducted without a needs assessment. As more organizations focus increased attention on needs assessment, however, this item will become a more significant cost in the future. All costs associated with the needs assessment should be captured to the fullest extent possible. These costs include the time of staff members conducting the assessment, direct fees and expenses for external consultants who conduct the needs assessment, and internal resources used in the analysis. The total costs are usually prorated over the life of the project. Depending on the type and nature of the project, the shelf life should be kept to a reasonable number in the one- to two-year timeframe. The exception would be expensive projects that are not expected to change significantly for several years.

Design, Development Costs and Acquisition

One of the most significant items is the cost of designing and developing the project. These costs include internal staff time in both design and development and the purchase of hardware, software, and services and other components directly related to the project. It would also include the use of consultants. As with needs assessment costs, design and development costs are usually prorated, perhaps using the same timeframe. One to two years is recommended unless the project is not expected to change for many years and the costs are significant.

When pilot projects are implemented, a prorating dilemma may surface. For expensive pilots, the complete design and development costs could be significant. In this situation, prorating may not be an issue because the pilot is completely at risk. If all of those costs are included in the ROI analysis, it may be difficult, if not impossible, for a project to produce a positive ROI. The following rules can help work through this dilemma.

1. If the pilot project is completely at risk, all the costs should be placed in the ROI evaluation decision, (i.e., if the pilot does not have a positive ROI with all the costs included, it will not be implemented). In this scenario, it is best to keep the design and development costs to a minimum. Perhaps the project could be implemented without all of the "bells and whistles." Perhaps nonenterprise or trial versions of the hardware and software or other expensive development tools may be delayed until the use of system or automated processes are proven. This approach can often be a challenge.

2. If project implementation is not at risk, the cost of the development should be prorated over the anticipated life cycle. This is the approach taken in most situations. It is plausible to have a significant investment in the design and development of a pilot when it is initiated, with the understanding that if it is not adding value, it can be adjusted, changed, or modified to add value. In these cases, a prorated development cost would be appropriate.

Regardless of the approach taken, these should be discussed before the evaluation begins. A dispute over prorating should not occur at the time the results are being tabulated. This discussion should also involve the sponsor of the project and a representative from finance and accounting.

In lieu of development costs, many organizations purchase off-the-shelf technology to use directly or in a modified format. The acquisition costs for these applications include the purchase price for the licensing agreements, system enhancement costs, training, and other costs associated with the right to deliver the application to the enterprise. These acquisition costs should be prorated using the preceding rationale; one to two years should be sufficient. If modification of the packaged application is needed or some additional development is required, these costs should be included as development costs. In practice, many projects have both acquisition costs and development costs.

Delivery and Implementation Costs

Usually the largest segment of IT costs would be those associated with delivery. Five major categories are included.

Salaries of Project Managers and Development Stage

The salaries of project managers and development stage should be included. If a project manager is involved in more than one project, the time should be allocated to the specific project under review. If external consultants or trainers are used, all charges should be included for the session. The important issue is to capture all of the direct time of internal employees or external consultants who work directly with the project. The benefits factor should be included each time direct labor costs are involved. This factor is a widely accepted value, usually generated by the finance and accounting staff and in the 25 to 50 percent range.

Project Materials, Equipment, Services, and Fees

Specific project materials such as hardware user guides, system manuals, CD ROMs, exercises, and other participant materials should be included in the delivery costs, along with license fees, user fees, and royalty payments. Personal copies of software are also included in this category.

Travel, Lodging, and Meals

Direct travel for the project team, project managers, or cross departmental participants are included. Lodging and meals are included for participants during travel, as well as meals during the stay for the project. Refreshments should also be included.

Facilities

The direct cost of the facilities should be included. If the project is conducted in-house, the conference room or "war room" represents a cost for the organization, then the cost should be estimated and included even if it is not the practice to include facilities' cost in other reports. The cost of internal facilities can easily be estimated by obtaining a room rental rate of the same size room at a local hotel. Sometimes, this figure is available on a square-foot basis from the finance and accounting staff (e.g., the value per square foot, per day). In other situations, the cost of commercial real estate, on a square-foot basis, could be determined locally from commercial real estate agents or the newspaper. The important point is to quickly come to a credible estimate for the value of the cost of the room.

This is an important issue that is often overlooked. With encouragement from the finance and accounting staff, some IT staff members do not charge an amount for the use of internal facilities. The argument is that the room would be used regardless. However, the complete cost of IT should include the item because the room would probably not exist unless there were routine IT projects taking place. In the total cost picture, this is a minor charge. It might have more value from the gesture than influencing the ROI calculation.

Participants' Salaries and Benefits

The salaries plus employee benefits of participants represent an expense that should be included. For situations where the project has been conducted, these costs can be estimated using average or midpoint values for salaries in typical job classifications. When a project is targeted for an ROI calculation, participants can provide their salaries directly and in a confidential manner.

For major IT and technology development projects, there may be a separate category for implementation. If the project involves meetings, follow-ups, system reinforcement training, and a variety of other activities beyond the specific IT project, an additional category for implementation may be appropriate. In some extreme examples, on-site resources are available to provide assistance and support for the project as it is implemented throughout the region, branch, or division. The total expense of these individuals is implementation expenses that should be included. The specific cost categories for implementation are often mirrored in the delivery categories. However, in most situations, the implementation is considered part of the delivery and is placed in that category. The remainder of this book presents them as a combined category.

Evaluation

Usually the total evaluation cost is included in the project costs to compute the fully loaded cost. ROI costs include the cost of developing the evaluation strategy, designing instruments, collecting data, data analysis, and report preparation and distribution. Cost categories include time, purchased evaluation instruments, or surveys. A case can be made to prorate the evaluation costs over several projects instead of charging the total amount as an expense. For example, if five training sessions are conducted for the rollout on an Enterprise Resource Planning system and one of the training groups is selected for an ROI calculation, then the ROI costs could logically be prorated over the five training groups, since the results of the ROI analysis would reflect the success for the overall project and will perhaps result in changes that will enhance the ERP project's outcome.

Overhead

A final charge is the cost of overhead, the additional costs in the IT function not directly related to a particular project. The overhead category represents any IT department cost not considered in the preceding calculations. Typical items include the cost of administrative support, the departmental office expenses, salaries of IT managers, and other fixed costs. Some organizations obtain an estimate for allocation by dividing the total overhead by the number of IT project days or hours for the year. This becomes a standard value to use in calculations.

An example illustrates the simplicity of this approach. An organization with 50 technology projects tabulates all of the expenditures in the budget not allocated directly to a particular project ($548,061 in this example). This part of the budget is then viewed as total overhead, unallocated to specific IT and technology development projects. The hours approach may be helpful if there are a significant number of resources who are involved in projects an hour at a time. The allocation of days may be appropriate in others. Next, this number is divided by the total number of participant days or hours (e.g., five-day projects are implemented approximately ten times a year, 50 days should be put in the total days category, or 400 hours for an eight-hour day). In this example, the total days were approximately 7,400. The total unallocated overhead of $548,061 is divided by 7,400 days to arrive at $74. Therefore, an overhead amount of $74 is charged for overhead for each day of IT project work. A three-day minor system upgrade would be charged $222 for overhead. The amount is usually small and will have little impact on the ROI calculation. The gesture of including the number as part of a fully loaded cost profile builds credibility with the sponsor and senior executives.

Cost Reporting

An example, using an actual case study, shows how the total costs are presented. Table 7-3 shows the cost for the design of an expert system for an executive management team in the high-tech industry. This was an extensive system project involving four

Table 7-3
Expert System Project Costs

Program Costs	
Analysis/Design/Development	
External functional experts	$525,330
IT department	28,785
Management committee	26,542
Delivery	
Conference facilities (Hotel)	142,554
Consultants and experts	812,110
IT department salaries and benefits (for direct work with the program)	15,283
IT department travel expenses	37,500
Management committee (time)	75,470
Direct IT project costs ($25,000 × 4)	100,000
Participant salaries and benefits (facilitated sessions) (Average daily salary × benefits factor × number of program days)	84,564
Participant salaries and benefits (project work)	117,353
Travel and lodging for participants	100,938
Cost of materials (software, purchased materials)	6,872
Research and Implementation	
Research	110,750
Implementation	125,875
Total Costs	**$2,309,926**

one-week off-site sessions with the executive management team and various functional experts to capture the business requirements and design specifications for this expert system. Working in teams, participants tackled this critical project that was important to top executives. Each team reported the results to management. The project teams could hire consultants, as well. These costs are listed as project costs. The costs for the first group, involving 22 participants, are detailed in the table.

The issue of prorating costs was an important consideration. In this case, it was reasonably certain that a second group would be conducted. The analysis, design, and development expenses of $580,657 could, therefore, be prorated over two sessions. Therefore, in the actual ROI calculation, half of this number was used to arrive at the total value ($290,328). This left a total project cost of $2,019,598 to include in the analysis ($2,309,926 – $290,328). On a participant basis, this was $91,800, or $22,950 for each week of formal sessions. Although this project was expensive, it was still close to a rough benchmark of weekly costs of several senior executive focused IT projects.

COST ACCUMULATION AND ESTIMATION

There are two basic ways to accumulate costs. One is by a description of the expenditure such as labor, hardware, software, services, travel, and so forth. These are expense account classifications. The other is by categories in the IT process or methodology such as project design, development, and implementation. An effective system monitors costs by account categories, according to the description of those accounts, but also includes a method for accumulating costs by the IT process/functional category. Many systems stop short of this second step. Although the first grouping sufficiently gives the total project cost, it does not allow for a useful comparison with other projects or indicate areas where costs might be excessive by relative comparisons.

Cost Classification Matrix

Costs are accumulated under both of the preceding classifications. The two classifications are obviously related, and the relationship depends on the organization. For instance, the specific costs that comprise the analysis part of a project may vary substantially within the organization. An important part of the classification process is to define the kinds of costs in the account classification system that normally apply to the major process/functional categories. Table 7-4 is a matrix that represents the categories for accumulating all IT-related costs in the organization. Those costs, which normally are a part of a process/functional category, are checked in the matrix. Each member of the IT staff should know how to charge expenses properly. For example, equipment is leased or purchased to use in the development and delivery of a project. Should all or part of the cost be charged to development? Or should it be charged to delivery? More than likely, the cost will be allocated in proportion to the extent in which the item was used for each category.

Cost Accumulation

With expense account classifications clearly defined and the process/functional categories determined, it is easy to track costs on individual projects. This is accomplished by using special account numbers and project numbers. An example illustrates the use of these numbers.

A project number is a three-digit number representing a specific IT project, such as the following:

CRM implementation	112
Accounting system version upgrade	215
Ecommerce design	418
Clustering e-mail System	791

Numbers are assigned to the process/functional breakdowns. Using the example presented earlier, the following numbers are assigned:

Design	1
Development	2
Implementation	3
Evaluation	4

Using the two-digit numbers assigned to account classifications in Table 7-4, an accounting system is complete. For example, if outside consultants are used during the design phase to verify the technical architecture for the Cluster E-mail System for a high-availability project, the appropriate charge number for that reproduction is 08-1-791. The first two digits denote the account classification, the next digit represents the process/functional category, and the last three digits are the project number. This system enables rapid accumulation and monitoring of IT costs. Total costs can be presented by the following:

Table 7-4
Cost Classification Matrix

Expense Account Classification	Process / Functional Categories			
	Design	Development	Implementation	Evaluation
00 Salaries and benefits—IT staff	X	X	X	X
01 Salaries and benefits—other staff		X	X	
02 Salaries and benefits—participants			X	X
03 Meals, travel, and incidental expenses—IT staff	X	X	X	X
04 Meals, travel, and accommodations—participants			X	
05 Office supplies and expenses	X	X		X
06 Program materials and supplies		X	X	
07 Printing and copying	X	X	X	X
08 Consulting services	X	X	X	X
09 Equipment expense allocation	X	X	X	X
10 Equipment—rental		X	X	
11 Equipment—maintenance			X	
12 License fees	X			
13 Facilities expense allocation			X	
14 Facilities rental			X	
15 General overhead allocation	X	X	X	X
16 Other miscellaneous expenses	X	X	X	X

- Project (Clustering e-mail system)
- Process/functional categories (design)
- Expense account classification (consulting services)

Cost Estimation

The previous sections covered procedures for classifying and monitoring costs related to IT projects. It is important to monitor and compare ongoing costs with the budget or with projected costs. However, a significant reason for tracking costs is to predict the cost of future projects. Usually, this goal is accomplished through a formal cost estimation method unique to the organization.

Some organizations use cost estimating worksheets to arrive at the total cost for a proposed project. Figure 7-2 shows an example of a

Design Costs		Total
Salaries and employee benefits—IT staff (Number of people × average salary × employee benefits factor × number of hours on project)		_____
Meals, travel, and incidental expenses		_____
Office supplies and expenses		_____
Printing and reproduction		_____
Consulting services		_____
Equipment expenses		_____
License fees		_____
General overhead allocation		_____
Other miscellaneous expenses		_____
Total Design Cost		_____
Development Costs		**Total**
Salaries and employee benefits (Number of people × avg. salary × employee benefits factor × number of hours on project)		_____
Meals, travel, and incidental expenses		_____
Office supplies and expenses		_____
Program materials and supplies		_____
Software	_____	
Media	_____	
User guides	_____	
Other	_____	
Printing and reproduction		_____
Outside services		_____
Equipment expense		_____
General overhead allocation		_____
Other miscellaneous expense		_____
Total Development Costs		_____

Figure 7-2. Cost Estimating Worksheet

Implementation Costs	Total	
Participant costs (A)*		
Salaries and employee benefits (Number of participants × avg. salary × employee benefits factor × Hrs. or days of training time)		
Meals, travel, and accommodations (Number of participants × avg. daily expenses × days of training)		
Program materials and supplies		
Participant replacement costs (if applicable) (B)*		
Lost production (Explain basis) (C)*		
Project management costs		
Salaries and benefits		
Meals, travel, and incidental expense		
Outside consultants		
Facility costs		
Facilities rental		
Facilities expense allocation		
Equipment expense		
General overhead allocation		
Other miscellaneous expense		
Total delivery costs		

*Use A, B, or C – Not a combination

Evaluation Costs	Total
Salaries and employee benefits—IT staff (Number of people × avg. salary × employee benefits factor × number or hours on project)	
Meals, travel, and incidental expense	
Participant costs	
Office supplies and expense	
Printing and reproduction	
Outside services	
Equipment expense	
General overhead allocation	
Other miscellaneous expenses	
Total Evaluation Costs	
TOTAL PROGRAM COSTS	

Figure 7-2. Continued

cost estimating worksheet that calculates design, development, implementation, and evaluation costs. The worksheets contain a few formulas that make it easier to estimate the cost. In addition to these worksheets, current charge rates for services, supplies, and salaries are available. These data become outdated quickly and are usually prepared periodically as a supplement.

The most appropriate basis for predicting costs is to analyze the previous costs by tracking the actual costs incurred in all phases of a project—from design to evaluation. This way, it is possible to see how much is spent on projects and how much is being spent in the different categories. Until adequate cost data are available, it is necessary to use the detailed analysis in the worksheets for cost estimation.

FINAL THOUGHTS

Costs are important for a variety of uses and applications. They help the IT staff manage the resources carefully, consistently, and efficiently. They also allow for comparisons between different elements and cost categories. Cost categorization can take several different forms. The most common are presented in this chapter. Costs should be fully loaded for ROI calculation. From a practical standpoint, including certain cost items may be optional, based on the organization's guidelines and philosophy. However, because of the scrutiny involved in ROI calculations, it is recommended that all costs be included, even if it goes beyond the requirements of the company policy.

REFERENCES

Employer Costs for Employee Compensation Summary, *Bureau of Labor Statistics*, June 2006.

CHAPTER 8

Calculating the Return

The monetary values for project benefits, developed in Chapter 6, are combined with project cost data, developed in Chapter 7, to calculate the ROI. This chapter explores several approaches for developing the return on investment, describing the techniques, processes, and issues involved. Before presenting the formulas for calculating the ROI, a few basic issues are described. An adequate understanding of these issues is necessary to complete this major step in the ROI Methodology. The uses and abuses of ROI are fully explored.

Basic Issues

Definitions

The term *return on investment* is often misused, sometimes intentionally. In some situations, a broad definition for ROI includes any benefit from the project. In these situations, ROI is a vague concept in which even subjective data linked to a project are included. In this book, the return on investment is more precise and is meant to represent an actual value developed by comparing project costs to benefits. The two most common measures are the benefit-cost ratio and the ROI formula. Both are presented along with other approaches that calculate the return.

For many years, IT and technology development practitioners and consultants have sought to calculate the actual return on the investment for IT. Technology is considered an investment, not an expense, it is appropriate to place the IT and technology development investment in the same funding mechanism as other investments, such as the investment in machines and facilities. Although these other investments are different, management often views them in the same way. Therefore, it is critical to the success of the

IT and technology development function within a business to develop specific values that reflect the return on the investment.

Annualized Values

All of the formulas presented in this chapter use annualized values so that the first year impact of the project investment is developed. Using annual values is becoming a generally accepted practice for developing the ROI in many organizations. This approach is a conservative way to develop the ROI, since many short-term IT projects have added value in the second or third year. For long-term IT projects, annualized values are inappropriate and longer timeframes need to be used. For example, in an ROI analysis of a project to upgrade legacy manufacturing systems in a global operation, a London-based company used a four-year timeframe due to the enormity of the project. The project itself required two years and a three-year impact, with postproject data used to develop the ROI. However, for most projects lasting several weeks to several months, first year values are appropriate.

When selecting the approach to measure ROI, it is important to communicate to the target audience the formula used and the assumptions made to arrive at the decision to use it. This action can avoid misunderstandings and confusion surrounding how the ROI value was developed. Although several approaches are described in this chapter, two stand out as the preferred methods: the benefits/costs ratio and the basic ROI formula. These two approaches are described next, along with the interpretation of ROI and a brief coverage of the other approaches.

Benefits/Costs Ratio

One of the earliest methods for evaluating IT investments is the benefit-cost ratio. This method compares the benefits of the project to the costs in a ratio. In formula form, the ratio is

$$BCR = \frac{Project\ Benefits}{Project\ Costs}$$

In simple terms, the BCR compares the annual economic benefits of the project to the cost of the project. A BCR of 1 means that the benefits equal the costs. A BCR of two, usually written as 2:1, indicates that for each dollar spent on the project, two dollars were returned as benefits.

The following example illustrates the use of the benefit-cost ratio. A large metropolitan bus system introduced a biometric employee time and attendance system to reduce unscheduled absences. The increase in absences left the system facing many delays, and therefore a large pool of drivers to fill in for the absent drivers was created. The pool had become substantial, representing a significant expenditure. The project involved a change in policy, and a change in the selection process, coupled with meetings and communication. Significant improvements were generated. The benefits of the project were captured in a one-year follow-up and compared to the total cost of the project. The first-year payoff was $662,000, based on the two major issues: a no-fault policy and changes in the screening process. The total fully-loaded implementation cost was $67,400. Therefore, the benefit-cost ratio is

$$BCR = \frac{\$662,000}{\$67,400} = 9.82$$

For every dollar invested in this project, almost $10 in benefits was generated.

The principal advantage of using this approach is that it avoids traditional financial measures so there is no confusion when comparing technology investments with other investments in the company. Investments in plants, equipment, or subsidiaries, for example, are not usually evaluated with the cost-benefit analysis. Some IT and technology development executives prefer not to use the same method to compare the return on IT investments with the return on other investments. The ROI for IT stands alone as a unique type of evaluation.

Unfortunately, there are no standards for what constitutes an acceptable benefit-cost ratio. A standard should be established within an organization, perhaps even for a specific type of project. However, a 1 : 1 ratio is unacceptable for most projects, and in some organizations, a 1.25 : 1 ratio is required, where 1.25 times the cost of the project is the benefit.

ROI Formula

Perhaps the most appropriate formula for evaluating IT investments is net project benefits divided by cost. The ratio is usually expressed as a percentage when the fractional values are multiplied by 100. In formula form, the ROI is

$$\text{ROI}\,(\%) = \frac{\text{Net Project Benefits}}{\text{Project Costs}} \times 100$$

Net benefits are project benefits minus project costs. The ROI value is related to the BCR by a factor of one. For example, a BCR of 2.45 is the same as an ROI value of 145 percent. This formula is essentially the same as ROI in other types of investments. For example, when a firm builds a new plant, the ROI is found by dividing annual earnings by the investment. The annual earnings are comparable to net benefits (annual benefits, minus the cost). The investment is comparable to project costs, which represent the investment in the project.

An ROI on an IT investment of 50 percent means that the costs are recovered and an additional 50 percent of the costs are reported as "earnings." An IT investment of 150 percent indicates that the costs have been recovered and an additional 1.5, multiplied by the costs, is captured as "earnings." An example illustrates the ROI calculation. Hewlett-Packard took a unique approach to enhancing telephone-based sales. Leveraging technology and an innovative, multistep sales skills intervention, tremendous improvement was driven in sales skills. The actual sales improvement, when translated into increased profit, yielded impressive results. The monetary benefit was $3,296,977, the total fully loaded cost was $1,116,291, and when the net benefits were calculated, a value of $2,180,616 was yielded.

$$\text{ROI}\,\% = \frac{\$2,180,686}{\$1,116,291} \times 100 = 195\%$$

Therefore, after the cost of the project had been recovered, Hewlett-Packard received almost $2 for each dollar invested.

Using the ROI formula essentially places IT investments on a level playing field with other investments, using the same formula and similar concepts. The ROI calculation is easily understood by key management and financial executives who regularly use ROI with other investments.

ROI INTERPRETATION

Choosing the Right Formula

What quantitative measure best represents top management goals? Many managers are preoccupied with the measures of sales, profits (net income), and profit percentages (the ratio of profits to dollar sales). However, the ultimate test of profitability is not the absolute amount of profit or the relationship of profit to sales. The critical test is the relationship of profit to invested capital. The most popular way of expressing this relationship is by the a rate of return on investment (Anthony & Reece, 1983).

Profits can be generated through increased sales or cost savings. In practice, there are more opportunities for cost savings than profit. Cost savings can be generated when there is improvement in productivity, quality, efficiency, cycle time, or actual cost reduction. When reviewing almost 500 studies with the author's involvement, the vast majority of the studies were based on cost savings. Approximately 85 percent of the studies had a payoff based on output, quality, efficiency, time, or cost reduction. The other had a payoff based on sales increases, where the earnings are derived from the profit margin. This situation is important for nonprofits and public sector organizations where the profit opportunity is often unavailable. Most IT and technology development initiatives will be connected directly to cost savings portion. ROIs can still be developed in those settings.

In the finance and accounting literature, return on investment is defined as net income (earnings), divided by investment. In the context of IT and technology development, net income is equivalent to net monetary benefits (project benefits, minus project costs). Investment is equivalent to project costs. The term investment is used in three different senses in financial analysis, giving three different ROI ratios: return on assets (ROA), return on owners' equity (ROE), and return on capital employed (ROCE).

Financial executives have used the ROI approach for centuries. Still, this technique did not become widespread in industry for judging operating performance until the early 1960s. Conceptually, ROI has innate appeal because it blends all the major ingredients of profitability in one number. The ROI statistic by itself can be compared with opportunities elsewhere (both inside or outside). Practically, however, ROI is an imperfect measurement that should be used in conjunction with other performance measurements (Horngren, 1982).

It is important for the preceding formula to be utilized in the organization. Deviations from (or misuse of) the formula can create confusion not only among users but also among the finance and accounting staff. The chief financial officer (CFO) and the finance and accounting staff should become partners in the implementation of the ROI Methodology. Without their support, involvement, and

Table 8-1
Misuse of Financial Terms

Term	Misuse	CFO Definition
ROI	Return of Information or Return of Intelligence	Return on Investment
ROE	Return on Expectation	Return on Equity
ROA	Return on Anticipation	Return on Assets
ROCE	Return on Client Expectation	Return on Capital Employed
ROW	Return on Web	??
ROR	Return on Resources	??
ROT	Return on Technology	??

commitment, it is difficult for ROI to be used on a large-scale basis. Because of this relationship, it is important that the same financial terms be used as those experienced and expected by the CFO.

Table 8-1 shows some misuse of financial terms that appear in the literature. Terms such as *return on intelligence* (or information), abbreviated as ROI, do nothing but confuse the CFO, who believes that ROI is the actual return on investment just described. Sometimes *return on expectations* (ROE), *return on anticipation* (ROA), or *return on client expectations* (ROCE) are used, confusing the CFO, who is thinking *return on equity, return on assets*, and *return on capital employed*, respectively. Use of these terms in the calculation of a payback of an IT and technology development project will do nothing but confuse, and perhaps lose the support of, the finance and accounting staff. Other terms such as *return on people, return on resources, return on IT*, and *return on Web* are often used with almost no consistent financial calculations. The bottom line is, don't confuse the CFO! Consider this individual to be an ally, and use the same terminology, processes, and concepts when applying financial returns for projects.

ROI Objectives: The Ultimate Challenge

When reviewing the specific ROI calculation and formula, it is helpful to position the ROI calculation in the context of all the data. The ROI calculation is only one measure generated with the ROI Methodology. Six types of data are developed, five of which are the five levels of evaluation. The data in each level of evaluation are driven by a specific objective, as was described earlier. In terms of

ROI, specific objectives are often set, creating the expectations of an acceptable ROI calculation.

ROI Targets

Specific expectations for ROI should be developed before an evaluation study is undertaken. Although there are no generally accepted standards, four strategies have been used to establish a minimum expected requirement, or hurdle rate, for ROI on an IT or technology development project. The first approach is to set the ROI using the same values as when investing in capital expenditures, such as equipment, facilities, and new companies. For North America, Western Europe, most of the Asian Pacific area, including Australia and New Zealand, the cost of capital is low, and this internal hurdle rate for ROI is usually in the 15 to 20 percent range. Therefore, using this strategy, organizations would set the expected ROI the same as the value expected from other investments.

A second strategy is to use an ROI minimum that represents a higher standard than the value required for other investments. This target value is above the percentage required for other types of investments. The rationale is that the ROI process for IT and technology development is still relatively new and often involves subjective input, including estimations. Because of that, a higher standard is required or suggested. For most areas in North America, Western Europe, and the Asia Pacific area, this value is usually set at 25 percent.

A third strategy is to set the ROI value at a break-even point. A 0 percent ROI represents break-even. This is equivalent to a costs/benefits ratio of 1. The rationale for this approach is an eagerness to recapture the cost of IT and technology development only. This is the ROI objective for many public sector organizations. If the funds expended for projects can be captured, there is still value and benefit from the project through the intangible measures, which are not converted to monetary values and the behavior change that is evident in the application and implementation data. Some organizations will use a break-even under the philosophy that they are not attempting to make a profit from IT and technology development investments.

Finally, a fourth, and sometimes recommended, strategy is to let the client or project sponsor set the minimum acceptable ROI value. In this scenario, the individual who initiates, approves, sponsors, or supports the project, establishes the acceptable ROI. Almost every project has a major sponsor, and that person may be willing to offer the acceptable value. This links the expectations, or financial return, directly to the expectations of the individual sponsoring the project.

ROI Can Be Very Large

As the examples in this book have demonstrated, the actual ROI value can be quite large—far exceeding what might be expected from other types of investments in plant, equipment, and companies. It is not unusual for projects involved in process automation, customer relationship management, sales force automation, enterprise resource planning, and business intelligence to generate ROIs in the 100 to 700 percent range. This does not mean that all ROI studies are positive; many are, infact, negative. However, the impact of the IT and technology development can be impressive. It is helpful to remember what constitutes the ROI value. Consider, for example, the investment in process automation for a team leader. If the leader's productivity changes as he or she works directly with the team, a chain of impact can produce a measurable change in performance from the team. This measure now represents the team's measure. That behavior change, translated into a measurement improvement for the entire year, can be significant. When the monetary value of the team's improvement is considered for an entire year and compared to the relatively small amount of investment in the automation of key processes for one team leader, it is easy to see why this number can be large.

More specific, as Figure 8-1 shows, there are some important factors that contribute to high ROI values. The impact can be large when a specific need has been identified and a performance gap exists. A new requirement is introduced and the solution is implemented at the right time for the right people at a reasonable cost. The solution is applied and supported in the work setting, and there is a linkage to one or more business measures. When these conditions are met, high ROI values can be recognized.

It is important to understand that a high ROI value can be developed that does not necessarily relate directly to the health of the rest of the organization. For example, a high impact ROI can be generated in an organization that is losing money (or in bankruptcy) because the impact is restricted to those individuals involved in the IT and technology development project, and the monetary value of improvement is connected to that project. At the same time, there

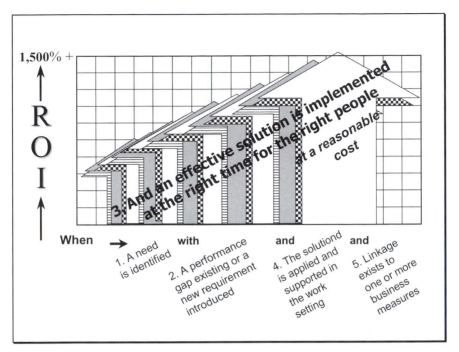

Figure 8-1. The Factors that Contribute to High ROI Values

can be some disastrous projects generating a negative ROI in a company that is profitable. This is a microlevel activity that evaluates the success of a particular project within a particular timeframe.

What Happens When the ROI Is Negative?

Perhaps one of the greatest fears of using ROI is the possibility of having a negative ROI. This strikes terror in the hearts of not only the project sponsor or owner but also those who are involved in the design, development, and delivery of the project. Few individuals want to be involved in a process that exposes a failure. They are concerned that the failure may reflect unfavorably on them. On the positive side, a negative ROI study provides the best opportunity for learning. The ROI Methodology reveals problems and barriers. As data are collected through the chain of impact, the reasons for failure become clear. Data on barriers and enablers to the transfer of IT knowledge captured at Level 3 (Application) usually reveal why the project did not work. Although a negative ROI study is the ultimate learning situation, no one wants to invite the opportunity to his or her back door. The preference would be to learn from others.

Sometimes the damage created by a negative ROI is the sense of expectations that are not managed properly up front and the fear of the consequences of the negative ROI.

The following steps can help minimize or avoid this dilemma:

1. *Raise the question about the feasibility of the impact study.* Is it appropriate to use the ROI Methodology for this particular project? Sometimes, a project may appear to be a failure, at least in terms of ROI.

2. *Make sure there is a clear understanding of the consequences of a negative ROI.* This issue should be addressed early and often. The ROI Methodology is a process improvement tool and not a performance evaluation tool. The individuals involved should not necessarily be penalized or have their performance evaluated unfavorably because of the negative ROI.

3. *Look for warning signs early in the process—they are usually everywhere.* Level 1 data can often send strong signals that an evaluation may result in a negative ROI. Signals of a negative ROI study may be if project timelines begin to extend, the packaged software is not meeting expectations, consulting costs begin to soar, project scope ("scope creep") is dramatically affecting the project, or cross-departmental users are reacting negatively to the project.

4. *Manage expectations.* It is best to lower expectations around ROI. Anticipating a high ROI and communicating that to the client or other stakeholders may create a false expectation that will not materialize. Keep the expectations low and the delivery performance high.

5. *Using the negative data, reposition the story.* Instead of communicating that great results have been achieved with this effective project, the story now becomes "We have some great information that tells how to change the project to obtain better results." This is more than a play on words, it underscores the importance of learning what went wrong and what can be done in the future.

6. *Use the information to drive change.* Sometimes the negative ROI can be transformed into a positive ROI with some minor alterations of the project. Implementation issues may need to be addressed in terms of support and use of knowledge and skills in the workplace. In other situations, a complete redesign of the project may be necessary. In a few isolated cases, dis-

continuing the project may be the only option. Whatever the option, use the data to drive action so that the overall value of conducting the study has been realized.

These strategies can help minimize the unfavorable, and sometimes disastrous, perceptions of a negative ROI.

ROI Is Not for Every Project

The ROI Methodology should not be applied to every project. It takes time and resources to create a valid and credible ROI study. Although this issue is addressed in Chapter 12, it is appropriate now to underscore the types of projects where this technique is best suited. ROI is appropriate for the following types of projects:

- *Projects that have a long life cycle*. At some point in the life of the project, this level of accountability should be applied to the project.
- *Projects that are important to the organization in meeting its operating goals*. These projects are designed to add value. ROI may be helpful to show that value.
- *Projects that are closely linked to the organization's strategic initiatives*. Anything this important needs a high level of accountability.
- *Projects that are very expensive to implement*. An expensive project should be subjected to this level of accountability.
- *Projects that are highly visible and sometimes controversial*. These projects often require this level of accountability to satisfy the critics.
- *Projects that have a large target audience*. If a project is designed for all employees, it may be a candidate for ROI.
- *Projects that command the interest of a top executive group*. If top executives are interested in knowing the impact, the ROI Methodology should be applied.

These are only guidelines and should be considered in the context of the organization. Other criteria may also be appropriate. These criteria can be used in a scheme to sort out those projects most appropriate for this level of accountability.

It is also helpful to consider the projects where the ROI Methodology is not appropriate. ROI is seldom appropriate for the following types of projects:

- *Projects that are short in duration, such as code fixes or minor upgrades.* It is difficult to demonstrate increased value in such a short timeframe.
- *Projects that are legislated or required by regulation.* It would be difficult to change anything as a result of this evaluation.
- *Projects that are required by senior management.* It may be that these projects will continue, regardless of the findings.
- *Projects that are small in scope.*
- Projects that are inexpensive.

This is not meant to imply that the ROI Methodology cannot be implemented for these types of projects. However, when considering the limited resources for measurement and evaluation, careful use of these resources and time will result in evaluating more strategic types of projects. It is also helpful to think about the projects that are appropriate for the first one or two ROI evaluations. Initially, the use of this process will be met with some anxiety and tentativeness. The projects initially undertaken should not only meet the preceding requirements but should also meet other requirements:

1. Be as simple as possible. Reserve the complex projects for later.
2. Be a known commodity. This helps ensure that the first study is not negative.
3. Be void of hidden agendas and political sensitivity. The first study should not necessarily be wrapped up in the organization politics.

Deciding the level at which to allocate resources to this process, which projects to pursue for ROI, and the number of projects to pursue in any given timeframe are important issues detailed in Chapter 12.

CASE APPLICATION

Background Information

Wall Department Store (WDS), a large national chain located in most major markets in the United States, attempted to boost sales by conducting a salesforce automation project for sales associates. The project, developed and delivered by an outside consulting firm, was a response to a clearly defined need to increase the level of interaction between the sales associate and the customer. After implementing the salesforce automation application, the rollout consisted of two days of hands-on system training, followed by three weeks of on-the-job application of the system. The final component of the project was designed for user follow-up and to identify any remaining process or technology gaps. Three groups representing the electronics departments of three stores were initially selected for a pilot implementation. A total of 48 participated.

ROI Analysis

Post-project data collection was accomplished using three methods. First, the average weekly sales of each associate was monitored (business performance monitoring of output data). Second, a follow-up electronic questionnaire was e-mailed to the participants three months after the implementation was completed to determine Level 3 success (actual application of the skills on the job). Third, Level 3 data were solicited in a follow-up session. In this session, participants disclosed their success (or lack of success) with the new salesforce automation application. They also discussed techniques to overcome the barriers to project implementation.

The method used to isolate the effects of this strategic IT initiative was a control group arrangement. Three store locations were identified (control group) and compared with the three groups in the pilot (experimental group). The variables of previous store performance, store size, store location, and customer traffic levels were used to match the two groups so that they could be as similar as possible. The method to convert data to monetary values was a direct profit contribution of the increased output. The actual profit obtained from one additional dollar of sales (profit margin) was readily available and used in the calculation.

BCR and ROI Calculations

Although the project was evaluated at all five levels, the emphasis of this study was on Levels 4 and 5. Levels 1, 2, and 3 data either met or exceeded expectations. Table 8-2 shows the Level 4 data,

Table 8-2
Level 4 Data: Average Weekly Sales

Weeks After Implemented	Post Implementation Data SFA Groups	Control Groups
1	$9,723	$9,698
2	9,978	9,720
3	10,424	9,812
13	13,690	11,572
14	11,491	9,683
15	11,044	10,092
Average for Weeks 13, 14, 15	$12,075	$10,449

Table 8-3
Salesforce Automation (SFA) Annualized Program Benefits

46 participants were still in job after 3 months.

Average Weekly Sales SFA Groups	$12,075	
Average Weekly Sales Non-SFA Groups	10,449	
Increase	1,626	
Profit Contribution (2% of sales)	32.50	
Total Weekly Improvement (32.50 × 46)	1,495	
Total Annual Benefits ($1,495 × 48 Weeks)		**$71,760**

which are the average weekly sales of both groups after the system rollout to the control group. For convenience and at the request of management, a three-month follow-up period was used. Management wanted to make the decision to implement the project at other locations if it appeared to be successful in this first three months of operation. Three months may be premature to determine the total impact of the project, but it often becomes a convenient time period for evaluation. Data for the first three weeks after rollout are shown in Table 8-3 along with the last three weeks of the evaluation period (weeks 13, 14, and 15). The data show what appears to be a significant difference in the two values.

Two steps were required to move from the Level 4 data to Level 5. First, Level 4 data had to be converted to monetary values. Second, the cost of the project had to be tabulated. Table 8-3 shows the annualized project benefits. The total benefit was $71,760. Since only 46 participants were still in their current job after three months, to be conservative, the other two participants' potential improvements were removed from the calculation. The profit contribution at the store level, obtained directly from the accounting department, was 2 percent of sales. For every dollar of additional sales attributed to the project, only two cents would be considered to be the added value. At the corporate level, the number was even smaller: about 1.2 percent. First-year values are used to reflect the total impact of the project. Ideally, if new skills are acquired, as indicated in the Level 3 evaluation, there should be some value for the use of those skills in year two or, perhaps, year three. However, for short-term IT projects, only first-year values are used, requiring the investment to have an acceptable return in a one-year time period.

> ### Guiding Principle 9
> Only the first year of benefits (annual) should be used in the ROI analysis of short-term solutions.

The total benefit was $71,760.

Table 8-4 shows the cost summary for this project. Costs are fully loaded, including data for all 48 participants. Since an IT supplier conducts the project, there are no direct development costs. The consulting fee covered the prorated development costs, as well as prorated system use. The participants' salaries for the time away from work, (plus a 35 percent factor for employee benefits) were included in the costs.

Facilities costs were included, although the company does not normally capture the costs when internal facilities are used, as was

Table 8-4
Cost Summary

48 participants in the Pilot Project	
Consulting fees/system use	$11,250
Program Materials: 48 @ $35/participant	1,680
Meals/Refreshments: 3 days @ $28/participant	4,032
Facilities: 9 days @ $120	1,080
Participant Salaries Plus Benefits (35% of salaries)	12,442
Coordination/Evaluation	2,500
Total Costs	**$32,984**

the case with this project. The estimated cost for the coordination and evaluation was also included. The total cost was $32,984. Therefore, the benefit-cost ratio was

$$\text{BCR} = \frac{\$71,760}{\$32,984} = 2.2:1$$

and the ROI was

$$\text{ROI}(\%) = \frac{\$71,760 - \$32,984}{\$32,984} \times 100 = 118\%$$

The acceptable ROI, defined by the client, was 25 percent. Therefore, the project has an excellent return on investment in its initial trial run after three months of on-the-job application of the new system.

The decision to implement the salesforce automation application throughout the other store locations becomes much easier. Six types of data are collected to show the full range of success, including the actual ROI. This represents an excellent use of the ROI Methodology, where the payoff is developed on the new pilot project. Historically, the decision to go from pilot to full implementation is often based on the reaction data alone. Sometimes, learning and, in limited cases, application data are used. Using the preceding approach, those types of data are collected, but more important, business impact, ROI, and intangibles add to the rich database from which to make this critical decision. It is a much less risky process when a full implementation is recommended from the pilot.

OTHER ROI MEASURES

In addition to the traditional ROI formula discussed previously, several other measures are occasionally used under the general term of *return on investment*. These measures are designed primarily for evaluating other types of financial measures, but they sometimes work their way into IT evaluations.

Payback Period

The payback period is a common method for evaluating capital expenditures. With this approach, the annual cash proceeds (savings) produced by an investment are equated to the original cash outlay required by the investment to arrive at some multiple of cash proceeds equal to the original investment. Measurement is usually in terms of years and months. For example, if the cost savings generated from an IT project are constant each year, the payback period is determined by dividing the total original cash investment (development costs, outside project purchases, etc.) by the amount of the expected annual or actual savings. The savings represent the net savings after the project expenses are subtracted. To illustrate this calculation, assume that an initial project cost is $100,000 with a three-year useful life. The annual net savings from the project is expected to be $40,000. Therefore, the payback period becomes

$$\text{Payback Period} = \frac{\text{Total Investment}}{\text{Annual Savings}} = \frac{\$100,000}{\$40,000} = 2.5 \text{ years}$$

The project will "pay back" the original investment in 2.5 years.

The payback period is simple to use, but it has the limitation of ignoring the time value of money. It has not enjoyed widespread use in evaluating IT investments.

Discounted Cash Flow

Discounted cash flow is a method of evaluating investment opportunities in which certain values are assigned to the timing of the proceeds from the investment. The assumption, based on interest rates, is that money earned today is more valuable than money earned a year from now.

There are several ways of using the discounted cash flow concept to evaluate capital expenditures. The most popular is probably the net present value of an investment. This approach compares the savings, year by year, with the outflow of cash required by the investment. The expected savings received each year is discounted by selected interest rates. The outflow of cash is also discounted by the same interest rate. If the present value of the savings should exceed the present value of the outlays after discounting at a common interest rate, the investment is usually acceptable in the eyes of management. The discounted cash flow method has the advantage of ranking investments, but it becomes difficult to calculate.

Internal Rate of Return

The internal rate of return (IRR) method determines the interest rate required to make the present value of the cash flow equal to zero. It represents the maximum rate of interest that could be paid if all project funds were borrowed and the organization had to break even on the projects. The IRR considers the time value of money and is unaffected by the scale of the project. It can be used to rank alternatives and can be used to make accept/reject decisions when a minimum rate of return is specified. A major weakness of the IRR method is that it assumes all returns are reinvested at the same internal rate of return. This can make an investment alternative with a high rate of return look even better than it really is and a project with a low rate of return look even worse. In practice, the IRR is rarely used to evaluate IT investments.

CONSEQUENCES OF NOT INVESTING IN IT

For some organizations, the consequences of not making strategic technology investments can be serious. A company's inability to perform adequately might mean that it is unable to take on additional business or that it may lose existing business because of a workforce that lacks proper technology automation. This method of calculating the return on IT investments has received recent attention and involves the following steps:

- Recognize that there is a potential problem, loss, or negative consequence if the status quo is maintained.
- Isolate the potential problem linked to lack of systems automation, identified by too many repetitive processes performed by employees.
- Identify the specific measure that reflects the potential problem.
- Pinpoint the anticipated level of the measure if the status quo is maintained (industry average, benchmarking data, etc.).
- Calculate the difference in the measure from current levels desired and the potential problem level of the measure. This becomes the change that could occur if the project is not implemented.
- Develop the unit value of the measure using standard values, expert input, or external databases.
- Develop an estimate of the potential value. This becomes the total value of benefits derived from implementing the project.

- Estimate the total cost of IT using the techniques outlined in Chapter 7.
- Compare benefits with costs.

ROI, THE PROFIT CENTER, AND EVA

With the increased interest in converting the IT function to the profit center concept, it is helpful to distinguish between the ROI Methodology and the profit center strategy. The ROI process described in this book shows the payoff of a specific project, or a group of projects, with highly integrated objectives. It is a micro-level process that shows the economic value derived from these projects. The profit center concept usually applies to the entire IT function. Under this concept, the IT department operates as a privately owned business, with profit showing the true measure of economic success. Its customers, usually the key managers in the organization, have complete autonomy to use the internal services of the IT function or to purchase those services externally. When the services are purchased internally, competitive prices are usually charged and transferred from the operating department to IT. This serves as revenue to the IT department. The department's expenses include salaries, office space, materials, fees, and services. Therefore, the IT department operates as a wholly owned subsidiary of the organization and with revenues for all the services and expenses representing the total expenses of the IT staff. If the department realizes a profit, it means that the value received from the transfer of funds exceeds the costs. This approach holds much interest, particularly for senior executives who are seeking to bring complete accountability to this function. Also, this is a true test of the perceived value if managers have complete autonomy for using or not using the processes.

The profit center concept can be perceived to be a high level of evaluation, as depicted in Figure 8-2, which shows the progression of evaluation levels to include the profit center. The figure illustrates the relative progression of these different levels of measurement. Level 1 has been used for many years and represents the most common and accepted evaluation data. Level 2 followed, as did Levels 3, 4, and now 5. The profit center concept is actually a higher level of accountability if it can be achieved. In essence, this is placing the value on the entire technology function and can show the economic value added (EVA) to the organization. This is particularly important because of the recent emphasis on the EVA concept (Young

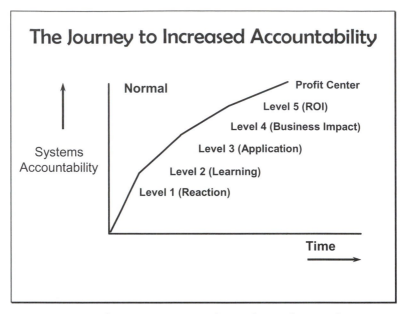

Figure 8-2. The Progression of Levels to the Profit Center

& O'Byrne, 2001). This concept can be applied to departments that generate revenue to offset expenses.

Figure 8-2 also underscores the fact that the previous levels of evaluation need to be in place before the next level will work. It is difficult for the profit center to be effective if Level 4 and 5 evaluations have not become routine parts of the measurement scheme. Some of the organizations that have failed in the move to the profit center concept used their success with Level 1 and 2 evaluation, skipping Levels 3, 4, and 5. Because participants reacted positively or developed skills, the IT staff perceived that the project was adding value. Operating managers, on the other hand, were unable to see the value from this level of evaluation and were reluctant to purchase the projects when given the option. They were not convinced of the added value because they have not seen any data previously that showed the impact of the projects in their operating departments.

The profit center and EVA are excellent concepts for evaluating the impact of the entire IT and technology development function. They are the goals of many technology executives and managers. In reality, there are many barriers to making the process operational. Not every project should be optional. Some projects and initiatives need to be consistent, and the quality must be controlled in some way. Having managers opt out of projects and purchasing their own may develop a wide variety of projects that are not necessarily adding value. Also, some projects are necessary and should not be optional. Still, many IT managers have this as a goal.

ROI ISSUES

Cautions When Using ROI

Because of the sensitivity of the ROI process, caution is needed when developing, calculating, and communicating the return on investment. The implementation of the ROI process is an important issue and a goal of many IT and technology development departments. In addition to the guiding principles, a few issues should be addressed to keep the process from going astray. The following cautions are offered when using ROI.

Take a conservative approach when developing both benefits and costs. Conservatism in ROI analysis builds accuracy and credibility. What matters most is how the target audience perceives the value of the data. A conservative approach is always recommended for both the numerator of the ROI formula (benefits) and the denominator (project costs). The conservative approach is the basis for the guiding principles.

Use caution when comparing the ROI in IT and technology development with other financial returns. There are many ways to calculate the return on funds invested or assets employed. The ROI is just one of them. Although the calculation for ROI in IT and technology development uses the same basic formula as in other investment evaluations, it may not be fully understood by the target group. Its calculation method and its meaning should be clearly communicated. More important, it should be an item accepted by management as an appropriate measure for IT project evaluation.

Involve management in developing the return. Management ultimately makes the decision if an ROI value is acceptable. To the extent possible, management should be involved in setting the parameters for calculations and establishing targets by which projects are considered acceptable within the organization.

Fully disclose the assumptions and methodology. When discussing the ROI methodology and communicating data, it is important to fully disclose the process, steps, and assumptions used in the process. Strengths should be clearly communicated as well as weaknesses and shortcomings.

Approach sensitive and controversial issues with caution. Occasionally, sensitive and controversial issues will be generated when discussing an ROI value. It is best to avoid debates over what is measurable and what is not measurable unless there is clear evidence of the issue in question. Also, some projects are so fundamental to the survival of the organization that any attempt to measure it is unnecessary. For example, a project designed to improve customer service through customer relationship management technology in a customer-focused organization may escape the scrutiny of an ROI evaluation, on the assumption that if the project is well designed, it will improve customer service.

Teach others the methods for calculating the return. Each time an ROI is calculated, the IT and technology development manager should use this opportunity to educate other managers and colleagues in the organization. Even if it is not in their area of responsibility, these individuals will be able to see the value of this approach to IT evaluation. Also, when possible, each project should serve as a case study to educate the IT staff on specific techniques and methods.

Recognize that not everyone will buy into ROI. Not every audience member will understand, appreciate, or accept the ROI calculation. For a variety of reasons, one or more individuals may not agree with the values. These individuals may be highly emotional about the concept of showing accountability for IT. Attempts to persuade them may be beyond the scope of the task at hand.

Do not boast about a high return. It is not unusual to generate what appears to be a very high return on investment for an IT project. Several examples in this book have illustrated the possibilities. An IT manager who boasts about a high rate of return will be open to potential criticism from others, unless there are indisputable facts on which the calculation is based.

Choose the place for the debates. The time to debate the ROI Methodology is not *during* a presentation (unless it cannot be avoided). There are constructive times to debate the ROI process: in a special forum, among the IT staff, in an educational session, in professional literature, on panel discussions, or even during the development of an ROI impact study. The time and place for debate should be carefully selected so as not to detract from the quality and quantity of information presented.

Do not try to use ROI on every project. As discussed earlier, some projects are difficult to quantify, and an ROI calculation may not be feasible. Other methods of presenting the benefits may be more appropriate. As discussed in Chapter 11, IT executives are encouraged to set targets for the percent of projects in which the ROI is developed. Also, specific criteria should be established that select projects for ROI analysis, as briefly described.

ROI Myths

Although most practitioners recognize the ROI Methodology as an important addition to measurement and evaluation, they often struggle with how to address the issue. Many professionals see the ROI Methodology as a ticket to increased funding and prosperity for IT. They believe that without it, they may be lost in the shuffle, and with it, they may gain the respect they need to continue moving the function forward. Regardless of their motivation for pursuing ROI evaluation, the key question is "Is it a feasible process that can be implemented with reasonable resources, and will it provide the benefits necessary to make it a useful, routine tool?" The answer to this question may lead to debate, even controversy.

The controversy surrounding the ROI Methodology stems from misunderstandings about what the process can and cannot do and how it can or should be implemented in an organization. As a conclusion to the chapter, these misunderstandings are summarized as 15 myths about the ROI Methodology. The myths are based on years of experience with ROI analysis and the perceptions discovered during hundreds of consulting projects and workshops. Each myth is presented here, with an appropriate explanation.

ROI is too complex for most users. This issue has been a problem because of a few highly complex models that have been presented publicly. Unfortunately, these models have done little to help users and have caused confusion about the ROI process. The ROI Methodology is a basic financial formula for accountability that is simple and understandable: Earnings are divided by investment; earnings equate to net benefits from the IT project, and the investment equals the actual cost of the project. Straying from this basic formula can add confusion and create tremendous misunderstanding. The ROI model is simplified with a step-by-step, systematic process. Each step is taken separately and issues addressed for a particular topic; the decisions are made incrementally all the way through the process. This helps to reduce a complex process to a more simplified and manageable effort.

ROI is expensive, consuming too many critical resources. The ROI process can become expensive if it is not carefully organized, controlled, and properly implemented. Although the cost of an external ROI impact study can be significant, there are many actions that can be taken to keep costs down. Cost savings approaches to ROI evaluation are presented in Chapter 12.

If senior management does not require ROI, there is no need to pursue it. This myth captures the most innocent bystanders. It is easy to be lulled into providing evaluation and measurement that simply meets the status quo, believing that no pressure or requests means no requirement. The truth is that if senior executives have only seen Level 1 reaction data, they may not be asking for higher level data because they think it is not available. In some cases, IT and technology development leaders have convinced top management that projects cannot be evaluated at the ROI level or that the specific impact of a project cannot be determined. Given these conditions, it comes as no surprise that some top managers are not asking for Level 5 (ROI) data.

There is another problem with this thinking. Paradigms are shifting—not only within the IT context but within senior management teams, as well. Senior managers are beginning to request this type of data. Changes in corporate leadership sometimes initiate important paradigm shifts. New leadership often requires proof of accountability. The process of integrating ROI into an organization takes time—about 12 to 18 months for many organizations. It is not a quick fix, and when senior executives suddenly ask the corporate IT function to produce this kind of data, they may expect the results to be produced quickly.

Because of this, IT and technology development departments should initiate the ROI process and develop ROI impact studies long before senior management begins asking for ROI data.

ROI is a passing fad. Unfortunately, this comment does apply to many of the processes being introduced to organizations today. Accountability for expenditures will always be present, and the ROI provides the ultimate level of accountability. As a tool, ROI has been used for years. Previously, ROI has been used to measure the investment of equipment and new plants. Now it is being used in many other areas, including IT, training, and learning solutions. With its rich history, ROI will continue to be used as an important tool in measurement and evaluation.

ROI is only one type of data. This is a common misunderstanding. The ROI calculation represents one type of data that shows the costs versus benefit for the project. However, six types of data are generated, representing both qualitative and quantitative data and often involves data from different sources, making the ROI Methodology a rich source for a variety of data.

ROI is not future-oriented; it only reflects past performance. Unfortunately, many evaluation processes are past-oriented and reflect only what has happened with a project. This is the only way to have an accurate assessment of impact. However, the ROI Methodology can easily be adapted to forecast the ROI, as described in Chapter 10.

ROI is rarely used by organizations. This myth is easily dispelled when the evidence is fully examined. More than 3,000 organizations use the ROI Methodology, and there are at least 400 case studies published about the ROI Methodology. Leading organizations throughout the world, including businesses of all sizes and sectors, use the ROI Methodology to increase accountability and improve projects. This process is also being used in the nonprofit, educational, and government sectors. There is no doubt that it is a widely used process that is growing in use.

The ROI methodology cannot be easily replicated. This is an understandable concern. In theory, any process worthy of implementation is one that can be replicated from one study to another. For example, if two different people conducted an ROI impact study on the same project, would they obtain the same results? Fortunately, the ROI Methodology is a systematic process with certain standards and guiding principles. The likelihood of two different evaluators obtaining the same results is high. Because it is a process that involves step-by-step procedures, it can also be replicated from one project to another.

ROI is not a credible process; it is too subjective. This myth has evolved because some ROI studies involving estimates have been publicized and promoted in literature and conferences. Many ROI studies have been conducted without the use of estimates. The problem with estimates often surfaces when attempting to isolate the effects of other factors. Using estimates from the participants is only one of several techniques used to isolate the effects of a project. Other techniques involve analytical approaches such as use of control groups and trend line analysis. Sometimes estimating is used in other steps of the process, such as converting data to monetary values or estimating output in the data collection phase. In each of these situations, other options are often available, but for convenience or economics, estimation is often used. Although estimations often represent the worst-case scenario in ROI, they can be extremely reliable when they are obtained carefully, adjusted for error, and reported appropriately. The accounting and engineering fields routinely require the use of estimates—often without question or concern.

ROI is not possible for soft skills projects, only for production and sales. ROI often is most effective in soft skills projects. The soft skills developed around the implementation of a specific technology solution often drive hard data items such as output, quality, cost, or time. Case after case shows successful application of the ROI Methodology to projects such as workflow automation and enterprise collaboration. Any type of project or process can be evaluated at the ROI level. The issue surfaces when ROI is used for projects that should not be evaluated at this level. The ROI Methodology should be reserved for projects that are expensive, address operational problems and issues related to strategic objectives, or attract the interest of management in terms of increased accountability.

ROI is for manufacturing and service organizations only. Although initial studies appeared in the manufacturing sector, the service sector quickly picked up the process as a useful tool. Then, it migrated to the nonprofit sector as hospitals and health-care firms began endorsing and using the process. Next, ROI moved through government sectors around the world, and now, educational institutions are beginning to use the ROI Methodology. Several educational institutions use ROI to measure the impact of delivering online degree and certificate programs.

It is not always possible to isolate the influence of other factors. Isolating the effects of other factors is always achieved when using the ROI Methodology. There are at least nine ways to isolate the influence of other factors, and at least one method will work in any given situation. The challenge is to select an appropriate isolation method for the resources and accuracy needed in a particular situation. This myth probably stems from an unsuccessful attempt at using a control group arrangement—a classic way of isolating the effect of a process, project, or initiative. In practice, a control group does not work in a majority of situations, causing some researchers to abandon the issue of isolating other factors. In reality, many other techniques provide accurate, reliable, and valid methods for isolating the effects.

Since there is no control over what happens after the rollout of a new system, a process based on measuring on-the-job improvements should not be used. This myth is fading as organizations face the reality of implementing technology solutions. Although the IT staff does not have direct control of what happens in the workplace, it does have influence on the process. An IT or technology development project must be considered within the context of the workplace; the project is owned by the organization. Many individuals and groups are involved in IT with objectives that push expectations beyond the keyboard. Objectives focus on application and impact data used in the ROI analysis. Also, the partnership often needed between key managers produces objectives that drive the project. In effect, IT is a process with partnerships and a common framework to drive the results.

ROI is appropriate only for large organizations. Although it is true that large organizations with enormous IT budgets have the most interest in ROI, smaller organizations can also use the process, particularly when it is simplified and built into projects. Organizations with as few as 50 employees have successfully applied the ROI Methodology, using it as a tool to bring increased accountability and involvement to IT and technology development.

There are no standards for the ROI Methodology. An important problem facing measurement and evaluation is a lack of standardization or consistency. These questions often arise: "What is a good ROI?" or "What should be included in the cost so I can compare my data with other data?" or "When should specific data be included in the ROI value instead of as an intangible?" Although these questions are not easy to answer, some help is on the way. Standards for the ROI Methodology, using the guiding principles as a starting point, are under development. Also under development is a database that will share thousands of studies so that best practices, patterns, trends, and standards are readily available.

FINAL THOUGHTS

After the project benefits are collected and converted to monetary values and the project costs are developed in a fully loaded profile, the ROI calculation becomes an easy step. It is just a matter of plugging the values into the appropriate formula. This chapter has presented the two basic approaches for calculating the return: the ROI formula and the costs/benefits ratio. Each has its own advantages and disadvantages. Alternatives to ROI development were briefly discussed. Several examples were presented along with key issues that must be addressed in ROI calculations. Cautions and myths surrounding the ROI Methodology capped off the chapter.

In conclusion, the ROI Methodology is not for every organization or individual. The use of the ROI Methodology represents a tremendous paradigm shift as organizations attempt to bring more accountability and results to the entire IT and technology development process, from needs assessment to the development of an impact study. The ROI Methodology brings a results-based focus to learning issues. This process is client-focused, requiring much contact, communication, dialogue, and agreement with the client group.

REFERENCES

Anthony, R.N. and J.S. Reece. *Accounting: Text and Cases*, 7th ed. Homewood, IL: Irwin, 1983.

Horngren, C.T. *Cost Accounting*, 5th ed. Englewood Cliffs, NJ: Prentice-Hall, 1982.

Young, S.D. and S.F. O'Byrne. *EVA® and Value-Based Management: A Practical Guide to Implementation*. New York: McGraw-Hill, 2001.

CHAPTER 9

Identifying Intangible Measures

Intangible measures are the benefits or detriments directly linked to the IT project, which cannot or should not be converted to monetary values. These measures are often monitored after the IT project has been conducted, and, although not converted to monetary values, they are still important in the evaluation process. Although the range of intangible measures is almost limitless, this chapter describes a few common measures, listed in Table 9-1, often linked with strategic IT initiatives.

Key Issues

Importance

Not all measures are in the tangible category. By design, some measures are captured and reported as intangible measures. Although they may not be perceived as valuable as the measures converted to monetary values, intangible measures are critical to the overall success of the organization (Oxman, 2002). In some projects, such as a workforce automation implementation, schedule adherence, efficiency, and enhanced collaboration, the intangible benefits can be more important than tangible measures. Therefore, these measures should be monitored and reported as part of the overall evaluation. In practice, every project or initiative, regardless of its nature, scope, and content, will have intangible measures associated with it (Fitz-enz, 2001). The challenge is to efficiently identify and report them.

Perhaps the first step to understanding intangibles is to clearly define the difference between tangible and intangible assets in a business organization. As presented in Table 9-2, tangible assets are

Table 9-1
Typical Intangible Variables Linked with IT Projects

■ User adoption	■ Corporate image
■ Productivity	■ Customer satisfaction
■ Increased cooperation	■ Customer complaints
■ Corporate communication	■ Customer retention
■ Cross-departmental Collaboration	■ Customer response time
	■ Teamwork
■ Attitude	■ Decisiveness
■ Improved morale	■ Skill competencies
■ Corporate culture	■ Leadership
■ Employee adherence	■ Innovation and creativity

Table 9-2
Comparison of Tangible and Intangible Assets

Tangible Assets Required for Business Operations	Intangible Assets Key to Competitive Advantage
■ Readily visible	■ Invisible
■ Rigorously quantified	■ Difficult to quantify
■ Part of the balance sheet	■ Not tracked through accounting practices
■ Investment produces known returns	■ Assessment based on assumptions
■ Can be easily duplicated	■ Cannot be bought or imitated
■ Depreciates with use	■ Appreciates with purposeful use
■ Has finite application	■ Multi-application without reducing value
■ Best managed with "scarcity" mentality	■ Best managed with "abundance" mentality
■ Best leveraged through control	■ Best leveraged through alignment
■ Can be accumulated	■ Dynamic: short shelf life when not in use

required for business operations and are readily visible, rigorously quantified, and are represented as a line item on a balance sheet (Saint-Onge, 2000). The intangible assets are key to competitive advantage in the knowledge era and are invisible, difficult to quantify, and not tracked through traditional accounting practices. With

Table 9-3
Comparison of Hard Data and Soft Data

Hard Data	Soft Data
▪ Objectively based	▪ Subjectively based in many cases
▪ Easy to measure and quantify	▪ Difficult to measure and quantify, directly
▪ Relatively easy to assign monetary values	▪ Difficult to assign monetary values
▪ Common measures of organizational performance	▪ Less credible as a performance measure
▪ Very credible with management	▪ Usually behaviorally oriented

this distinction, it is easier to understand why intangible measures are difficult to convert to monetary values.

Another distinction between tangible and intangible is the concept of hard data versus soft data. This concept, discussed earlier, is perhaps more familiar to IT and technology development managers. Table 9-3 shows the difference between hard and soft data, used earlier in this book. The most significant part of the definition is the difficulty in converting the data to monetary value. It is from this point that the definition of intangible data is derived.

> **Intangible measures** are defined as measures that are purposely not converted to monetary values.

Using this simple definition avoids confusion about whether a data item should be classified as hard data or soft data. It is considered soft data if a credible, economically feasible process is unavailable for conversion. The ROI Methodology discussed throughout this book will use this definition of *intangibles*.

Identification of Measures

Intangible measures can be identified from different sources representing different time frames, as illustrated in Figure 9-1. First, they can be uncovered early in the process, during the needs assessment.

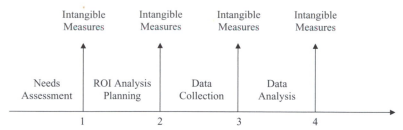

Figure 9-1. Identification of Intangible Measures:
Timing and Source

Once identified, the intangible data is planned for collection as part of the overall data collection strategy. For example, a SalesForce Automation project has multiple hard data measures linked to the project. An intangible measure, such as sales rep satisfaction, is identified and monitored with no plans to convert it to a monetary value. Therefore, from the beginning, this measure is destined to be a nonmonetary benefit reported along with the ROI results.

A second time an intangible benefit is identified is during discussions with clients or sponsors about the impact of an IT initiative. Clients can usually identify intangible measures that are expected to be influenced by the project. For example, an Enterprise Resource Planning (ERP) implementation in a large multinational company was conducted, and an ROI analysis was planned. During the ROI planning session, project managers, consultants, a sample of participants' managers, and a senior executive identified potential intangible measures that were perceived to be influenced by the project. These measures are included on the ROI analysis planning document.

A third time an intangible measure is identified is during a follow-up evaluation. Although the measure was not expected or anticipated in the initial project design, the measure surfaces on an electronic survey, in an interview, or during a post-implementation debriefing. Questions are often asked about other improvements linked to the IT project. Several intangible measures are usually provided, and there are no planned attempts to place a value on the actual measure. For example, in a Customer Relationship Management (CRM) project, participants were asked specifically what had improved in their work as a result of the project. The participants provided several intangible measures, which managers perceived to be linked to the project.

The fourth time an intangible measure is identified is during an attempt to convert the data to monetary values. If the process loses credibility, the measure should be reported as an intangible benefit. For example, in a Web-based customer self-service project, customer satisfaction is identified early in the process as one of the measures of IT success. A conversion of the data to monetary values was attempted. However, the process of assigning a value to the data lost credibility. Therefore, customer satisfaction was reported as an intangible benefit.

Is It Measurable?

Sometimes, debate will erupt over whether a particular item that is perceived as intangible (soft) can actually be measured. In reality, anything that can influence the outcome of the IT project can be measured. (The measure may have to be a perception of the issue taken from a particular stakeholder involved in the process, but it is still a measure.) The ROI Methodology rests on the assumption that anything can be measured. In the mind of the sponsor or senior executive, if an intangible (soft) item cannot be measured, why bother? The state of that situation or issue will never be known. Therefore, on a practical basis, any intangible can be measured— some more precisely than others. For example, tracking customer complaints is a measure that can be captured and categorized precisely. Every complaint received is recorded, and the types of complaints are placed in categories. However, to place a value on having less complaints may cause the data item to be intangible if there is not a credible, economically feasible way to convert it to monetary value.

Chapter 6 focuses on different ways to convert data to monetary values. The philosophy taken is that any data item can be converted to monetary value (i.e., there is no measure that can be presented to which a monetary value cannot be assigned). The key issue is credibility. Is it a believable value? Is the process to convert it to monetary value credible? Does it cost too much to convert it? Is that value stable over time? These are critical issues that will be explored mentally by senior executives when they examine the conversion of data to monetary value. For tangible data conversion, the issue is of little concern. Tangible data items are easily converted, such as increased output, reduction in rejects, and time savings. However, the soft measures (morale, communication, and attitudes) often lose credibility in the process. Table 9-4 shows a four-part test for converting intangibles to monetary values. The test was described on an operational basis in Chapter 6. It is repeated here because this is the test

Table 9-4
The Four-Part Test for Converting Intangibles to Monetary Values

Tangible versus Intangible

1. Does an acceptable, standard monetary value exist for the measure? If yes, use it; if not, go to the next step.
2. Is there a method that *can* be used to convert the measure to money? If not, list it as an intangible; if yes, go to the next step.
3. Can the conversion be accomplished with minimum resources? If not, list it as an intangible; if yes, go to the next step.
4. Can the conversion process be described to an executive audience *and* secure their buy-in in two minutes? If yes, use it in the ROI calculation; if not, list it as an intangible.

that often leads to the classification of data as intangible. The ultimate test is number 4. If the converted value cannot be communicated to the management group, securing their buy-in immediately, the data should be listed as intangible. This is a practical test that protects the credibility of the impact study and also allows for consistency from one study to another. It would be unreliable if only one evaluator converted a particular data item to monetary value. This is an important part of building the standards necessary for the ROI Methodology.

Intangible Measures versus Intellectual Capital

With the attention given to the concept of intellectual capital in recent years and the value of intangible assets in organizations, it is helpful to distinguish between the intangible measures from an IT or technology development project and those that might appear in a variety of measures in intellectual capital. Figure 9-2 shows the categories of intangible benefits and their relationship to intellectual capital. Intellectual capital typically involves customer capital, human capital, and structural capital (Saint-Onge, 2000). Most of the IT projects are driving measures in the structural and human capital area, which includes the capability of individuals to provide solutions to customers through the use of technology. More specifically, Table 9-5 offers the common human capital measures tracked by organizations as part of their human capital monitoring processes (Phillips, 2002). Many of these measures are driven by the IT and technology development projects and are often considered intangible. Some of these will be described in this chapter.

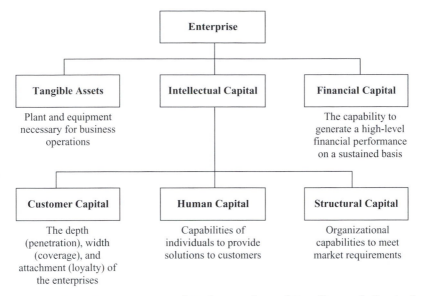

Figure 9-2. Categories and Relationship of Intellectual Capital

Table 9-5
Common Human Capital Measures

Human Capital Measures	
■ Innovation	■ Learning
■ Job satisfaction	■ Competencies
■ Organizational commitment	■ Educational level
■ Turnover	■ HR investment
■ Tenure	■ Leadership
■ Experience	■ Productivity

Analysis

For most intangible data, no specific analysis is planned. Previous attempts to convert intangible data to monetary units results in aborting the process, and, therefore, no further data analysis is conducted. In some cases, there may be attempts to isolate the effects of an IT project using one or more of the methods outlined in Chapter 5. This step is necessary when there is a need to know the specific amount of change in the intangible measure that is linked to the project. In many cases, however, the intangible data reflect evidence of improvement. Neither the precise amount of the improvement nor the amount of improvement related directly to the IT project is needed. Since the value of this data is not placed in the ROI calculation, intangible measures are not normally used to justify additional IT investments or the continuation of existing IT projects. Therefore, a detailed analysis is not justified. Intangible benefits are viewed as supporting evidence of the project's success and are presented as qualitative data.

Typical Intangible Measures

Most of the remainder of the chapter focuses on typical intangible measures. These measures are often presented as intangibles in impact studies. For each individual measure, there may be exceptions where organizations *can* convert the data to monetary value. Recent developments in the measurement of customer satisfaction include ways to convert these critical measures to monetary value. Customer satisfaction (and others) is described in more detail in this section.

Job Satisfaction

Employee satisfaction is perhaps one of the most important intangible measures. Some IT projects are designed to improve job satisfaction by reducing manual processes and making them more efficient. Attitude surveys are conducted to measure the extent to which employees are satisfied with the organization, their jobs, their supervisor, coworkers, and a host of other job-related factors. Attitude survey data is usually linked to IT results when specific issues on the survey are related to technology initiatives. For example, in an infrastructure hardware upgrade initiative at a large direct sales organization, the annual attitude survey contained five questions directly tied to perceptions and attitudes influenced by the IT project.

Because attitude surveys are usually taken annually, survey results may not be in sync with the timing of the specific IT project. When job satisfaction is one of the project objectives, and it is a critical outcome, some organizations conduct surveys at a prescribed timeframe after the completion of the project. They design the survey instrument around issues related to the IT initiative. This approach, however, is expensive.

While job satisfaction has always been an important issue in employee relations, in recent years it has taken on new importance because of the key relationships of job satisfaction to other measures. A classical relationship with job satisfaction is in the area of employee recruitment and retention. Firms with excellent job satisfaction ratings are often attractive to potential employees. It becomes a subtle but important recruiting tool. "Employers of Choice" and "Best Places to Work," for example, often have high levels of job satisfaction ratings that attract employees. There is also a relationship between job satisfaction and employee turnover. This relationship has taken on a new meaning as turnover and retention have become critical issues in the last decade and are projected to continue to be critical in the future. Today, these relationships are often easily developed as many of the human resource information systems have modules to calculate the correlation between the turnover rates and the job satisfaction scores for the various job groups, divisions, departments, and so on.

Job satisfaction has taken on new meanings in connection with customer service. Hundreds of applied research projects are beginning to show a high correlation between job satisfaction scores and customer satisfaction scores. Intuitively, this seems obvious: A more satisfied employee is likely to provide more productive, friendly, and appropriate customer service. Likewise, a disgruntled employee will provide poor service. These links, often referred to as a service-profit-chain, create a promising way to identify an important relationship between attitudes and profits in an organization.

Even with these developments, most organizations do not or cannot place credible values on job satisfaction data. The trend is definitely in that direction. But until that occurs, job satisfaction is usually listed as an intangible benefit in most impact studies.

Organizational Commitment

In recent years, organizational commitment (OC) measures have complemented or replaced job satisfaction measures. OC measures go beyond employee satisfaction and include the extent to which the employees identify with organizational goals, mission, philosophy, value, policies, and practices. The concept of involvement and becoming a part of the organization is the key issue. OC is a measure that more closely correlates with productivity and other performance improvement measures, whereas job satisfaction does not always correlate with improvements in productivity. As OC scores improve (taken on a standard index), there should be corresponding improvement in productivity. The OC is often measured the same way as attitude surveys, using a five- or seven-point scale taken directly from employees or groups of employees.

Organizational commitment is rarely converted to monetary value. Although some relationships have been developed to link it to more tangible data, this research is still in the developing stage. For most studies, organizational commitment would be listed as an intangible.

Climate Survey Data

Some organizations conduct climate surveys, which reflect work climate changes such as communication, openness, trust, and quality of feedback. Closely related to organizational commitment, climate surveys are more general and often focus on a range of workplace issues and environmental enablers and inhibitors. Climate surveys conducted before and after critical enterprise-wide IT initiatives may reflect the extent to which IT has changed these intangible measures.

Employee Retention

When job satisfaction deteriorates to the point where employees withdraw from work or the organization, either permanently or temporarily, the results can be disastrous. Perhaps the most critical employee withdrawal variable is employee turnover (or employee retention). An extremely costly variable, turnover can have devastating consequences on organizations when it is excessive. Few measures have attracted so much attention as employee turnover. Fueled in part by low unemployment rates in North America and industrialized countries, retention has become a strategic issue. The survival of some firms depends on low turnover rates for critical job groups. Not only is turnover compared to historical rates, but it is often compared to best-practice firms.

The good news is that many firms have made important strides in maintaining low turnover, even in high-turnover industries such as call center, retail, hotel, and restaurant. Turnover is defined as the number of employees leaving in a month divided by the average number of employees in the month. This is a standard turnover rate that includes all individuals leaving. A more appropriate measure would be to include only turnover considered to be avoidable, usually referring to employees who voluntarily leave or those whose departure could have been prevented. For example, if an employee is terminated for poor performance in the first six months of employment, something went wrong that could have been prevented. Avoidable turnover is an important issue.

It may be a surprise that many current technology automation initiatives have user adoption and satisfaction as critical components of IT success for the project. When surveying users in higher turnover environments, such as a call center, the users' perception of the quality of the organization is directly linked to the sophistication of the tools (enterprise systems, collaboration tools, personal computer, telephone, etc.) that are provided to the employee. Employers and IT organizations have become more sensitized to these issues as more of the technology-enabled generation enters the workforce. To more accurately quantify the costs related to employee satisfaction in the workplace, turnover is actually converted to monetary values using one of the methods described in Chapter 6. However, because of the multitude of costs and assumptions involved in developing the value, some organizations prefer not to convert turnover to a monetary value. In this case, turnover is reported as an intangible benefit, reflecting the success of the IT or technology development project.

Innovation and Creativity

For technology companies and other progressive organizations, innovation is a critical issue. A variety of technology-fueled innovation and creativity projects are implemented to make improvements in this critical area. Innovation is both easy and difficult to measure. It is easy to measure outcomes in areas such as copyright, patents, inventions, and employee suggestions. It is more difficult to measure the creative spirit of employees. Perhaps the most obvious measure is tracking the patents and trademarks that are not only used internally but are licensed for others to use through a patent and license exchange website.

An employee suggestion system, a longtime measure of the innovative and creative processes of an organization, still flourishes today in many firms. Employees are rewarded for their suggestions if they are approved and implemented. Tracking the suggestion rates and comparing them with other organizations is an important benchmarking item for innovation and creative capability. Other measures, such as the number of new projects, products, processes, and strategies, can be monitored and measured in some way. Subjectivity often enters the measurement process with these issues. Some organizations will actually measure the creative capability of employees using inventories and instruments. Comparing actual scores of groups of employees over time reflects the degree to which employees are improving innovativeness and creativity in the workplace. Having consistent and comparable measures is still a challenge. Because of the difficulty of converting data to monetary values, these measures are usually listed as intangibles.

Competencies

Organizations are interested in developing key competencies in particular areas such as the core mission, key product lines, and important processes. Core competencies are often identified and implemented in critical job groups. Competencies are measured with self-assessments from the individual employee, as well as assessments from the supervisor. In some cases, other inputs may be important or necessary to measure. That approach goes beyond just learning new skills, processes, or knowledge to using a combination of skills, knowledge, and behavior on the job to develop an acceptable level of competence to meet competitive challenges.

Leadership

Perhaps the most difficult measure is leadership, but leadership can make the difference in the success or failure of an organization. Without the appropriate leadership behaviors throughout the organization, the other resources can be misapplied or wasted. Measuring leadership can be done in many different ways.

One of the most common methods is known as a 360-degree feedback. Here, a prescribed set of leadership behaviors desired in an organization is assessed by different sources to provide a composite of the overall leadership capability. The sources often come from the immediate manager of the leader, a colleague in the same area, the employees under the direct influence of the leader, internal or external customers, and through a self-assessment. These assessments come from different directions, forming a 360-degree circle. The measure is basically an observation captured in a survey, often reported electronically. This 360-degree feedback has been growing rapidly in the United States, Europe, and Asia as an important way to capture overall leadership behavior change.

Customer Satisfaction

Because of the importance of building and improving customer service, a variety of measures are often monitored and reported as a payoff of specific customer-focused IT projects. A variety of technology-enabled customer service projects have a direct influence on these measures. One of the most important measures is survey data showing the degree to which customers are pleased with the products and services. These survey values, reported as absolute data or as an index, represent important data from which to compare the success of a customer service IT project.

As described earlier, customer satisfaction data is achieving a lot of interest. Its value is often connected with linkages to other measures such as revenue growth, market share, and profits. Several models are available to show what happens when customers are dissatisfied, along with the economic impact of those decisions. In the health-care arena, research shows linkages between patient satisfaction and customer retention. Still, others are showing relationships between customer satisfaction, innovation, product development, and other tangible measures. Techniques are available to convert survey data to monetary values. But in most situations, the conversion is rarely attempted. Therefore, customer satisfaction improvements at the present time are usually reported as intangible benefits.

Customer Complaints

Most organizations monitor customer complaints. Each complaint is recorded along with the disposition and the time required to resolve the complaint, as well as specific costs associated with the complaint resolution. Organizations sometimes design IT projects to reduce the number of customer complaints. The total cost and impact of a complaint has three components: the time it takes to resolve the complaint, the cost of making restitution to the customer, and the ultimate cost of ill-will generated by the dissatisfaction (lost future business). Because of the difficulty to assign an accurate monetary value to a customer complaint, the measure usually becomes a very important intangible benefit.

Customer Loyalty

Customer retention is a critical measure that is sometimes linked to sales, marketing, and customer service technology projects, especially in organizations whose products are technology focused. Long-term, efficient, and productive customer relationships are important to the success of an organization. Although the importance of customer retention is understood, it is not always converted to monetary value. Specific models have been developed to show the value of a customer and how to retain customers over a period of time. For example, the average tenure of a customer can translate directly into a bottom-line savings.

Tied very closely with customer loyalty is the rate at which customers leave the organization. The churn rate is a critical measure that can be costly, not only in lost business (profits from lost customers) but in the cost necessary to generate a new customer. Because of the difficulty of converting directly to a specific monetary value, customer loyalty is listed as an intangible benefit.

Customer Response Time

Providing prompt customer service is a critical issue in most organizations. Therefore, the time it takes to respond to specific customer service requests or problems is recorded and monitored. Response time reduction is sometimes an objective of IT projects, although the reduction is not usually converted to monetary values. Therefore, customer response time becomes an important intangible benefit.

Other Customer Responses

A variety of other types of customer responses can be tracked, such as creativity with customer response, responsiveness to cost and pricing issues, and other important issues customers may specify or require. Monitoring these variables can provide more evidence of the IT project's results when the project influences particular variables. And because of the difficulty of assigning values to the items, they are usually reported as intangible measures.

Teamwork

A variety of measures are often monitored to reflect how well teams are working. Although the output of teams and the quality of their work are often measured as hard data and converted to monetary values, other interpersonal measures may be monitored and reported separately. Sometimes, organizations survey team members before and after an IT project to determine if the level of teamwork has increased. Using a variable scale, team members provide a perception of improvement. The monetary value of increased teamwork is rarely developed, and therefore, it is reported as an intangible benefit.

Cooperation

The success of a team often depends on the cooperative spirit of team members. Some instruments measure the level of cooperation before and after specific technology-enabled, enterprise-wide collaboration initiatives, using a perception scale. Because of the difficulty of converting this measure to a monetary value, it is almost always reported as an intangible benefit.

Decisiveness

Teams make decisions, and the timing of the decision-making process often becomes an issue. Therefore, decisiveness is sometimes measured in terms of the speed at which decisions are made. Some IT projects such as Business Intelligence (BI) or the development of Key Performance Indicators (KPIs), or corporate dashboards, are expected to influence this process. Survey measures may reflect the perception of the team, or in some cases, they may monitor how quickly decisions are made. Although reductions in the timing of decisions can be converted to monetary values, improvements are usually reported as intangible benefits.

Communication

A variety of communication instruments reflect the quality and quantity of communication within a team. Improvement in communication effectiveness, or perceptions of effectiveness, driven by an IT project is not usually converted to monetary values and is reported as an intangible benefit.

FINAL THOUGHTS

A variety of available intangible measures reflect the success of an IT or Technology Development project. Although they may not be perceived to be as valuable as specific monetary measures, they are an important part of an overall evaluation. Intangible measures should be identified, explored, examined, monitored, and analyzed for changes when they are linked to the project. Collectively, they add a unique dimension to the overall project results since most, if not all, projects have intangible measures associated with them. Although some of the most common intangible measures were covered in this chapter, the coverage was not meant to be complete. The number of intangible measures is almost unlimited.

References

Fitz-enz, J. *The ROI of Human Capital: Measuring the Economic Value of Employee Performance.* New York: American Management Association, 2001.

Oxman, J.A. "The Hidden Leverage of Human Capital," *MIT Sloan Management Review,* Summer 2002.

Phillips, P.P. (Ed.). *In Action: Measuring Intellectual Capital.* Alexandria, VA: American Society for Training and Development, 2002.

Saint-Onge, H. "Shaping Human Resource Management within the Knowledge-Driven Enterprise." *Leading Knowledge Management and Learning,* edited by Dede Bonner. Alexandria, VA: American Society for Training and Development, 2002.

CHAPTER 10

ROI Forecasting

Sometimes there is confusion about when it is appropriate to develop the ROI. The traditional and recommended approach discussed in previous chapters is to base ROI calculations strictly on business impact data obtained after the project has been implemented. In the approach, business performance measures (Level 4) are easily converted to a monetary value, which is necessary for an ROI calculation. Sometimes these measures are not available, and it is usually assumed that an ROI calculation is out of the question. This chapter illustrates that ROI calculations are possible at a variety of time-frames using a variety of data. Preproject ROI forecasts are possible, as well as forecasts with reaction data (Level 1), learning data (Level 2), and application data (Level 3).

WHY FORECAST ROI?

The most accurate way to assess and develop an ROI calculation is based on post-project data. However, sometimes it is important to know the forecast *before* the final results are tabulated. Forecasting ROI during the project, or in some cases, before the project is pursued, is an important issue. Critical reasons drive the need for a forecasted ROI.

Reduce Uncertainty

Reducing uncertainty in a proposed project is sometimes critical. In a perfect world, the client or sponsor of a new project would like to know the expected payoff before any action is taken. Realistically, knowing the exact payoff may be impossible, and from a practical standpoint, it may not be feasible to obtain. However, there is still the desire to take the uncertainty out of the equation and act on the best data available. This sometimes requires pushing the project to a forecasted ROI before any resources are expended. Some managers will not budge without a pre-project forecast. They need some measure of expected success before allocating any resources to the project.

Lower Expenses

In some cases, even a pilot project is not practical until some analysis has been conducted to examine the potential ROI. For example, if the project involves a significant amount of work in design, development, and delivery, a client may not want to expend the resources, even for a pilot, unless there is some assurance of a positive ROI. Although there may be tradeoffs with a lower-profile and lower-cost pilot, the pre-project ROI, nevertheless, becomes an important issue, prompting some sponsors to stand firm until an ROI forecast is produced.

Compare with Postdata

Whenever there is a plan to collect data on the success of the application, impact, and ROI for a strategic technology investment, it is helpful to compare actual results to pre-project expectations. In an ideal world, a forecasted ROI should have a defined relationship with the actual ROI, or they should be similar. One important reason for forecasting ROI is to see how well the forecast is maintained following the scrutiny of post-project analysis.

Save Costs

There are several cost-saving issues prompting the use of ROI forecasting. First, developing the forecast itself is often an inexpensive process because it involves estimations and many different assumptions. Second, if the forecast becomes a reliable predictor of the post-project analysis, the forecasted ROI might substitute for the actual ROI, at least with some adjustments. This could save money on the post-project analysis. Finally, the forecasted ROI data might be used for comparisons in other areas, at least as a starting point for other types of projects. Therefore, there may be the potential to transfer the forecasted ROI to other specific projects.

Comply with Policy

More organizations are developing policy statements requiring a forecasted ROI before major projects are undertaken. For example, in one network engineering organization, any project exceeding $300,000 must have a forecasted ROI before it can be approved. In the United States, federal government units are required to show a pre-project benefits/costs analysis (ROI) for selecting new projects. In one country, an organization can receive partial payments for an IT project if the ROI forecast is positive and likely to enhance the organization. This formal policy and legal structure is becoming a more frequent reason for developing the ROI forecast.

Collectively, these five reasons are causing more organizations to examine ROI forecasts so that the client or sponsor will have some estimate of the expected payoff.

THE TRADEOFFS OF FORECASTING

ROI can be developed at different times using different levels of data. Unfortunately, the ease, convenience, and low cost involved in capturing a forecasted ROI create tradeoffs in accuracy and credibility. As shown in Figure 10-1, there are five distinct time intervals during the implementation of a project when the ROI can be developed. The relationship with credibility, accuracy, cost, and difficulty is also shown in this figure.

The time intervals are as follows:

1. A pre-project forecast can be developed using estimates of the impact of the IT or technology development project. This approach lacks credibility and accuracy, but it is also the least expensive and least difficult ROI to calculate. There is value in developing the ROI on a pre-project basis. This will be discussed in the next section.

2. Reaction and satisfaction data can be extended to develop an anticipated impact, including the ROI. In this case, participants anticipate the chain of impact as a project is applied, implemented, and influences specific business measures. Although

ROI with:	Data Collection Timing (Relative to Project Implementation)	Credibility	Accuracy	Cost to Develop	Difficulty
1. Preproject Data	Before Project	Not Very Credible	Not Very Accurate	Inexpensive	Not Difficult
2. Reaction and Perceived Value Data	During Project				
3. Learning and Confidence Data	During Project				
4. Application and Implementation Data	After Project				
5. Impact and Consequences Data	After Project	Very Credible	Very Accurate	Expensive	Very Difficult

Figure 10-1. ROI at Different Times and Levels

the accuracy and credibility are greater than for the pre-project forecast, this approach still lacks the credibility and accuracy desired in most situations.

3. Learning data in some projects can be used to forecast the actual ROI. This approach is applicable only when formal testing shows a relationship between acquiring certain skills or knowledge and subsequent business performance. When this correlation is available (it is usually developed to validate the test), test data can be used to forecast subsequent performance. The performance can then be converted to monetary impact and the ROI can be developed. This has less potential as an evaluation tool due to the lack of situations in which a predictive validation can be developed.

4. In some situations, when enhanced skills and processes for a technology deployment are critical, the application and implementation of those skills or knowledge can be converted to a value using employee compensation as a basis. This is particularly helpful in situations where competencies are being developed and values are placed on improving competencies, even if there is no immediate increase in pay.

5. Finally, the ROI can be developed from business impact data converted directly to monetary values and compared to the cost of the project. This post-project evaluation is the basis for the other ROI calculations in this book and has been the principal approach used in previous chapters. It is the preferred approach, but because of the pressures just outlined, it is critical to examine ROI calculations at other times and with data other than Level 4.

This chapter will discuss in detail pre-project evaluation and the ROI calculations based on reactions. To a lesser degree, the ROI calculations developed from learning and application data will be discussed.

Pre-project ROI Forecasting

Perhaps one of the most useful steps in convincing a sponsor that an IT investment is appropriate is to forecast the ROI for the project. The process is similar to the post-project analysis, except that the extent of the impact must be estimated along with the forecasted cost.

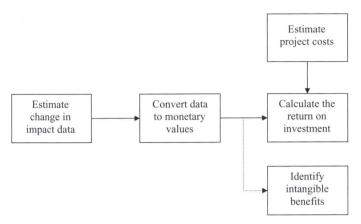

Figure 10-2. Pre-project ROI Forecast Model

Basic Model

Figure 10-2 demonstrates the basic model for capturing the necessary data for a pre-project forecast. This model is a modification of the post-project ROI model, except that data are projected instead of being collected during different timeframes. In place of the data collection is an estimation of the change in impact data expected to be influenced by the IT project. Isolating the effects of the initiative becomes a nonissue, as the estimation is focused on the IT project only, not considering other random factors.

The method to covert data to monetary values is the same as in post-project ROI because the data items examined in a pre- and post-project analysis should be the same. Estimating the project's cost should be an easy step, as costs can easily be anticipated based on previous projects using reasonable assumptions about the current project. The anticipated intangibles are merely speculation in forecasting but can be reliable indicators of which measures may be influenced in addition to those included in the ROI calculation. The formula used to calculate the ROI is the same as in the post-project analysis. The amount of monetary value from the data conversion is included as the numerator, and the estimated cost of the IT project is inserted as the denominator. The projected benefit-cost analysis can be developed along with the actual ROI. The steps to actually develop the process are detailed next.

Steps to Develop the ROI

The detailed steps to develop the pre-project ROI forecast are as follows:

1. Develop the Level 3 and 4 objectives with as many specifics as possible. Ideally, these should be developed from the initial needs analysis and assessment. They detail what will change in the work setting and identify which measures will be influenced. If these are not known, the entire forecasting process is in jeopardy. There must be some assessment of which measures will change as a result of the technology initiative, and someone must be able to provide the extent to which the measures will change.

2. Estimate or forecast the monthly improvement in the business impact data. This is considered to be the amount of change directly related to the intervention and is denoted by ΔP.

3. Convert the business impact data to monetary values using one or more of the methods described in Chapter 6. These are the same techniques, using the same processes as a post-project analysis. V denotes this value.

4. Develop the estimated annual impact for each measure. In essence, this is the first-year improvement from the IT project, showing the value for the change in the business impact measures directly related to the project. In formula form, this is $\Delta I = \Delta P \times V \times 12$.

5. Factor additional years into the analysis if a project will have a significant useful life beyond the first year. When this is the case, these values may be factored to reflect a diminished benefit in subsequent years. The sponsor or owner of the project should provide some indication as to the amount of the reduction and the values developed for years two, three, and so on. However, it is helpful to be conservative by using the smallest numbers possible.

6. Estimate the fully loaded cost of the project. Using all of the cost categories contained in Chapter 7, the fully loaded cost will be estimated and projected for the project. This is denoted as C. Again, all direct and indirect costs should be included in the calculation.

7. Calculate the forecasted ROI using the total projected benefits and the estimated cost in the standard ROI formula:

$$ROI(\%) = \frac{\Delta I - C}{C} \times 100$$

8. Use sensitivity analysis to develop several potential ROI values with different levels of improvement (ΔP). When more than

one measure is changing, that analysis would be performed using a spreadsheet showing different possible scenarios for output and the subsequent ROI.

9. Identify potential intangible benefits by getting input from those most knowledgeable of the situation. These are only anticipated and are based on assumptions from previous experience with this type of project implementation.

10. Communicate the ROI projection and anticipated intangibles with much care and caution. The target audience must clearly understand that this is based on several assumptions (clearly defined) and that the values are the best possible estimates. However, there is still room for error.

These ten steps enable an individual to forecast the ROI. The most difficult part of the process is the initial estimate of performance improvement. Several sources of data are available for this purpose, as described next.

FORECASTING/ESTIMATING PERFORMANCE IMPROVEMENT

Several sources of input are available when attempting to estimate the actual performance improvement that will be influenced by a define technology initiative. The following important considerations should be explored:

1. Experience in the organization with previous technology initiatives, or similar projects, can help form the basis of the estimate. Adapting that breadth of experience can be an important factor, since comparisons are rarely, if ever, exact.

2. Data sources may have experience with similar projects in other organizations or in other situations. Here, the experience of the designers, developers, and implementers involved in the project will be helpful as they reflect on their experiences with other organizations.

3. The input of external experts who have worked in the field or addressed similar projects in other organizations can be extremely valuable. These may be consultants, engineers, designers, or others who have earned a reputation as knowledgeable about this type of process in this type of situation.

4. Estimates can be obtained directly from a subject matter expert (SME) in the organization. This is an individual who is familiar with the internal processes being altered, modified or improved by the technology project. Internal SMEs are knowledgeable and sometimes the most favored source for obtaining conservative estimates.

5. Estimates can be obtained directly from the project sponsor. This is the individual who is ultimately making the purchasing decision and is providing data or input on the anticipated change in a measure linked to the IT project. This influential position makes this person a credible source.

6. Individuals who are directly involved in the project, often labeled participants, are sometimes in a position to know how much of a measure can be changed or improved with a particular type of project. These individuals understand the processes, procedures, and performance measurements being influenced. Their close proximity to the situation makes them highly credible and often the most accurate sources for estimating the amount of change.

Collectively, these sources provide an appropriate array of possibilities to help estimate the value of an improvement. This is the weakest link in the ROI forecasting process and deserves the most attention. It is important that the target audience understands where the estimates came from, as well as who provided them. Even more important, the target audience must view the source as credible. Otherwise, the forecasted ROI will have no credibility.

CASE EXAMPLE

It may be helpful to illustrate how a forecasted ROI can be developed using the processes explained here. A global financial services company was interested in deploying an integrated enterprise-wide Customer Relationship Management (CRM) system to enable its relationship managers to meet the needs of customers. According to the needs assessment and initial analysis, there was a need for the project. An enterprise CRM rollout would require detailed functional requirements, training on appropriate application specific skills, and implementing the skills and system-enhanced processes. However, before the project could be pursued, a forecasted ROI was needed. Following the steps outlined earlier in this chapter, it was determined that four business impact measures would be influenced by the implementation of this project:

1. Increase in sales to existing customers
2. Reduction in customer complaints due to missed deadlines, late responses, and failure to complete transactions
3. Reduction in the response time for customer inquiries and requests
4. Increase in customer satisfaction composite survey index

In examining the potential problem, several individuals provided input. With an integrated CRM solution deployed, relationship managers would benefit from enhanced customer communication tracking and a 360-degree view of the customer's interactions with the company. To determine the extent to which the measures would change, input was collected from four sources:

1. Internal developers with expertise in various enterprise CRM applications provided input on expected changes in each of the measures.
2. Relationship managers provided input on expected changes in the variables if the CRM application and revised sales processes were used properly.
3. The project sponsor provided input on what could be expected from the project.
4. Finally, a brief survey of internal project managers provided some input.

When input is based on estimates, the results may differ significantly. However, this project sponsor was interested in a forecast based on limited analysis but strengthened with the best expert opinions available. After some discussion of the availability of data and examining the techniques to convert data to monetary values, the following conclusions were reached:

• The increase in sales could easily be converted to a monetary value as the margin for this particular project is applied directly.
• The cost of a customer complaint could be based on a discounted internal value currently in use, therefore providing a generally accepted cost of a complaint.
• Customer response time was not tracked accurately nor was the value of this measure readily available. Therefore, it was anticipated that this would be an intangible benefit.
• There is no generally accepted value for increasing customer satisfaction, so customer satisfaction impact data would be listed as a potential intangible.

The forecasted ROI calculation was developed for a single division in the organization. After reviewing the possible scenarios, a range of possibilities was offered for increasing sales and reducing complaints. The sales increase should be in the range of 3 to 9 percent. Therefore, three scenarios were developed using 3, 6, and 9 percent as the increase in sales. Complaint reduction was expected to be in the range of 10 to 30 percent, so three scenarios were developed for the reduction in actual complaints, using 10, 20, and 30 percent in the ROI calculation. More detailed groupings could be developed, but three were considered appropriate.

The increase in sales was converted to monetary values using the margin rates, and the reduction in customer complaints was converted, using the discounted value for a customer complaint. The cost for the project was easily estimated, based on input from those who examined the situation. The total cost was developed to include business analysis, functional requirements, design, development, training, and implementation. This fully loaded projected cost, when compared to the benefits, yielded a range of expected ROI values. Table 10-1 shows a matrix of the nine possible scenarios using payoffs on the two measures. The ROI values range from a low of 60 percent to a high of 180 percent. With these values in hand, the decision to move forward was a relatively easy one, since even the worst-case scenarios were positive and the best case was approximately three times that amount. As this example illustrates, the process needs to be kept simple, using the most credible resources

Table 10-1
Expected ROI Values for Different Outputs

Potential Sales Increase (Existing Customers, %)	Potential Compliant Reduction (Monthly Reduction)	Expected ROI (%)
3	10	60
3	20	90
3	30	120
6	10	90
6	20	120
6	30	150
9	10	120
9	20	150
9	30	180

available to quickly arrive at estimates for the process. Recognizing this is an estimate, its advantage is simplicity and low cost—two factors that should be considered when developing the process.

FORECASTING WITH A PILOT PROJECT

Although the preceding steps provide a process for estimating the ROI when a pilot project is not conducted, the more favorable approach is to develop a small-scale pilot project and develop the ROI based on post-project data. This scenario involves the following five steps:

1. As in the previous process, develop Level 3 and 4 objectives.
2. Initiate the project on a small-scale sample as a pilot project, without all the bells and whistles. This keeps the cost extremely low without sacrificing the fundamentals of the project.
3. Fully implement the project with one or more of the typical groups of individuals who can benefit from the project.
4. Develop the ROI using the ROI model for post-project analysis. This is the ROI process used in the previous chapters.
5. Finally, decide whether to implement the project throughout the organization based on the results of the pilot project.

Post-project evaluation of a pilot project provides much more accurate information by which to base decisions regarding full implementation of the project. Using this scenario, data can be developed using all six types of measures outlined in this book.

FORECASTING ROI WITH REACTION DATA

When reaction data includes planned strategic technology applications, this important data can ultimately be used in forecasting ROI. Detailing how participants plan to use the enhanced system functionality they have learned and the results that they expect to achieve, more valuable evaluation information can be developed. The questions presented in Figure 10-3 illustrate how data are collected with an end-of-project questionnaire for a defined technology project. Participants are asked to state specifically how they plan to use the project material and the results they expect to achieve. They are asked to convert their accomplishments to an annual monetary value and show the basis for developing the values. Participants can moderate their responses with a confidence estimate to make the data

Planned Improvements

■ As a result of this technology initiative, what specific actions will you attempt as you apply what you have learned?

   1. _____
   2. _____
   3. _____

■ Please indicate what specific measures, outcomes, or projects will change as a result of your actions.

   1. _____
   2. _____
   3. _____

■ As a result of the anticipated changes in the preceding, please estimate (in monetary values) the benefits to your organization over a period of one year. _____

■ What is the basis of this estimate?

_____
_____

■ What confidence, expressed as a percentage, do you have in your estimate? (0% = No Confidence; 100% = Certainty) _____%

Figure 10-3. Important Questions for Feedback Questionnaires

more credible, while allowing participants to reflect their uncertainty with the process.

When tabulating data, the confidence level is multiplied by the annual monetary value, which yields a conservative estimate for use in the data analysis. For example, if a participant estimated that the monetary impact of the project will be $300,000 but is only 50 percent confident, a $250,000 value is used in the calculations.

To develop a summary of the expected benefits, several steps are taken. First, any data that are incomplete, unusable, extreme, or unrealistic are discarded.

> ## Guiding Principle 8
> Extreme data items and unsupported claims should not be used in ROI calculations.

Next, an adjustment is made for the confidence estimate as previously described. Individual data items are then totaled. Finally, as an optional exercise, the total value is adjusted again by a factor that reflects the subjectivity of the process and the possibility that participants will not achieve the results they anticipate. In many IT projects, the participants are enthusiastic about the results a specific project may garner and may be overly optimistic about expected returns. This figure adjusts for this overestimation and can be developed with input from management or established by the IT or Technology Development staff. In one organization, the benefits are multiplied by 50 percent to develop an even more conservative number to use in the ROI equation. Finally, the ROI is developed, using the net project benefits divided by the project costs. This value, in essence, becomes the expected return on investment, after the two adjustments for accuracy and subjectivity.

A word of caution is in order when using Level 1 ROI data. These calculations are highly subjective and do not reflect the extent to which participants actually apply what they have learned to achieve results. A variety of influences in the work environment can enhance or inhibit the participants' attainment of performance goals. Having high expectations at the end of the project is no guarantee that those expectations will be met. Disappointments are documented regularly in projects throughout the world and are reported in research findings.

Although this process is subjective and possibly unreliable, it does have some usefulness. First, if evaluation must stop at this level, this approach provides more insight into the value of the project than the data from typical reaction questionnaires. Managers will usually find this data more useful than a report stating, "Forty percent of system users rated the project above average." Unfortunately, a high percentage of evaluations stop at this first level. The majority of IT projects do not enjoy rigorous evaluations at Levels 3 and 4. Reporting Level 1 ROI data is a more useful indication of the potential impact of the project than the alternative of reporting attitudes and feelings about the project and facilitator.

Second, ROI forecast data can form a basis for comparison of different presentations of the same project. If one project forecasts an ROI of 300 percent, whereas another projects 30 percent, it appears that one project may be more effective than the other. The participants in the first project have more confidence in the planned application of the project material.

Third, collecting this type of data brings increased attention to project outcomes. Participants leave the project with an understanding that specific process automation enhancements are expected,

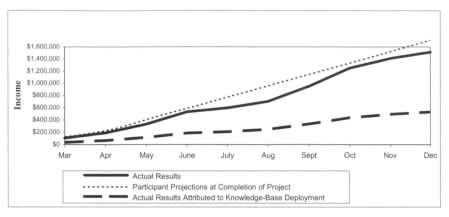

Figure 10-4. Results of Enterprise Knowledgebase Deployment

which produces results for the organization. This issue becomes clear to participants as they anticipate results and convert them to monetary values. Even if this projected improvement is ignored, the exercise is productive because of the important message sent to participants. It helps to change mindsets about the value, impact, and importance of IT.

Fourth, if a follow-up is planned to pinpoint post-project results, the data collected in the Level 1 evaluation can be helpful for comparison. This end of project data collection helps participants plan the implementation of what they have learned. For example, in an enterprise Knowledgebase initiative for a National Bank, the results after implementation are compared to the forecasted results. Figure 10-4 shows the results of the Knowledgebase deployment, the participant's projections at the end of project, and the results specifically attributed to the deployment. As the figure illustrates, the forecasts are slightly higher than the results attributed to the project. This comparison begins to build credibility in a forecasting method and, in this case, revealed that forecasting was actually more conservative than the actual results.

The use of Level 1 ROI is increasing, as more organizations base a larger part of ROI calculations on Level 1 data. Although it may be subjective, it does add value, particularly when it is included as part of a comprehensive evaluation system.

FORECASTING ROI WITH KNOWLEDGE DATA

Testing for changes in skills and knowledge in IT projects is becoming a common technique for learning evaluation (Level 2). In many situations, participants are required to demonstrate their knowledge or skills at the end of the project, and their performance is expressed as a numerical value. When this type of test is developed and used, it must be reliable and valid. A reliable test is one that is stable over time with consistent results. A valid test is one that measures what it purports to measure. Since a test should reflect the content and knowledge gained during the IT project, successful mastery of project content should be related to improved job performance. Therefore, there should be a relationship between test scores and subsequent on-the-job performance. Figure 10-5 illustrates a perfect correlation between test scores and job performance. This relationship, expressed as a correlation coefficient, is a measure of validity of the test.

This testing situation provides an excellent opportunity for an ROI calculation with Level 2 data using test results. When there is a statistically significant relationship between test scores and on-the-job performance, and the performance can be converted to monetary units, then it is possible to use test scores to estimate the ROI from the project, using the following steps:

- Ensure that the project content reflects desired on-the-job performance.
- Develop an end-of-project test that reflects project content and knowledge.
- Establish a statistical relationship between test data and output performance for participants.
- Predict performance levels of each participant with given test scores.
- Convert performance data to monetary value.
- Compare total predicted value of project with project costs.

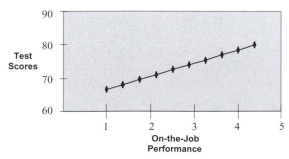

Figure 10-5. Relationship Between Test Scores and Performance

An example illustrates this approach. Consumer Products Marketing (CPM) is the marketing division of a large consumer products company. Sales representatives for CPM make frequent sales calls to large retail food and drug companies with the objective of increasing sales and market share of CPM products. Sales representatives must ensure that retailers understand the advantages of CPM products, provide adequate space for their products, and assist in promotional and advertising efforts.

CPM has developed a strong sales culture and recruits highly capable individuals for sales representative assignments. Newly recruited sales representatives rotate through different divisions of the company in a two-month assignment to learn where and how the products are made and their features and benefits, as well as specific product marketing strategies. During this process, new associates are trained on the company's SalesForce Automation (SFA) application, which is at the heart of the company's sales process strategy. The SFA training also focuses on sales techniques, marketing strategies, and customer service skills. At the end of the one-week training, participants complete a comprehensive exam that reflects the knowledge and skills taught in the project. As part of the exam, participants analyze specific customer service and sales situations and decide on specific actions. Also, the test covers product features, policies, and marketing practices.

To validate the test, CPM developed correlations between test scores and actual on-the-job performance measured by sales volumes, sales growth, and market shares for sales representatives six months after completing the project. The correlations were statistically significant with each variable. As a quick way of calculating the expected ROI for a project, CPM estimates output levels for each item using the test scores, converts them to monetary values, and calculates the ROI forecast.

As with the previous ROI estimate with end-of-project questionnaires, some cautions are in order. This is a forecast of the ROI and not the actual value. Although participants acquired the skills and knowledge from the project, there is no guarantee that they will apply the techniques and processes successfully and that the results will be achieved. This process assumes that the current group of participants has the same relationship to output performance as previous groups. It ignores a variety of environmental influences, which can alter the situation entirely. Finally, the process requires calculating the initial correlation coefficient that may be difficult to develop for most tests.

Although this approach develops an estimate, based on historical relationships, it can be useful in a comprehensive evaluation strategy and it has several advantages. First, if post-project evaluations (Level 4) are not planned, this process will yield more information about the projected value of the project than what would be obtained from the raw test scores. This process represents an expected return on investment based on the historical relationships involved. Second, by developing individual ROI measurements and communicating them to participants, the process has reinforcement potential. It communicates to participants that increased sales and market share are expected through the applications of what was learned in the project. Third, this process can have considerable credibility with management and can preclude expensive follow-ups and post-project monitoring. If these relationships are statistically sound, the estimate should have credibility with the target group.

FORECASTING ROI WITH SKILLS AND COMPETENCIES

In almost every IT project, participants are expected to change their on-the-job behaviors by applying the knowledge and skills learned during the project. On-the-job applications are critical to project success. Although the use of the skills on the job is no guarantee that results will follow, it is an underlying assumption for most projects that if the knowledge and skills are applied, then results will follow. Some of the most recognized IT organizations base their ultimate evaluation on this assumption. A few organizations attempt to take this process a step further and measure the value of on-the-job behavior change and calculate the ROI. In these situations, estimates are taken from individual participants, their supervisors, the management group, or experts in the field. This is a forecast of the impact, based on the change in behavior on the job immediately after the project. The following steps are used to develop the ROI:

1. Develop competencies for the target job.
2. Indicate percentage of job success that is covered in the IT project.
3. Determine monetary value of competencies using salaries and employee benefits of participants.
4. Compute the worth of pre- and post-project skill levels.
5. Subtract post-project values from pre-project values.
6. Compare the total added benefits with the project costs.

This analysis is usually described as utility analysis. It is attempting to place a value on the improvement of an individual. The concept ignores the consequence of this improvement but examines the behavior change and factors the monetary value relative to the salary of the individual. This is referred to as a Level 3 ROI forecast because it takes the change in behavior as a result of a strategic technology deployment and converts it to monetary value using salaries of participants as a base.

Although this process is subjective, it has several useful advantages. First, if there are no plans to track the actual impact of the project in terms of specific measurable business impact (Level 4), this approach represents a credible substitute. In many projects it may be difficult to identify tangible changes on the job. Therefore, alternative approaches to determine the worth of a project are needed. Second, this has been developed in the literature as utility analysis. Third, this approach results in data that are credible with the management group if they understand how it is developed and the assumptions behind it. An important point is that the data on the changes in competence level came from the managers who have rated their supervisors. In this specific project, the numbers were large enough to make the process statistically significant.

Forecasting Guidelines

With the four different timeframes for forecasting outlined in this chapter, a few guidelines may help drive the forecasting possibilities within an organization. These guidelines are based on experience in forecasting a variety of processes (Bowers, 1997).

1. *If you must forecast, forecast frequently.* Forecasting is a process that is both an art and a science, and it must be pursued regularly to build comfort, experience, and history with the process. Also, those who use the data need to see forecasting frequently, to further integrate it as part of the IT evaluation mix.

2. *Consider forecasting an essential part of the evaluation mix.* This chapter began with a listing of reasons why forecasting is essential. The concept is growing in use and is being demanded by many organizations. It can be an effective and useful tool when used properly and in conjunction with other types of evaluation data. Some organizations have targets for the use of forecasting (e.g., if a project exceeds a certain cost,

it will always require a pre-project forecast). Others will target a certain number of projects for a forecast based on reaction data and use that data in the manner described here. Others will have some low-level targets for forecasting at Levels 2 and 3. It is important to plan for the forecast and let it be a part of the evaluation mix, working it regularly.

3. *Forecast different types of data.* Although most of this chapter focuses on how to develop a forecasted ROI using the standard ROI formula, it is helpful to forecast the value of other data. A useable, helpful forecast will include predictions around reaction and satisfaction, the extent of learning, and the extent of application and implementation. These types of data are important in anticipating movements and shifts, based on the planned project. It is not only helpful in developing the overall forecast but is important in understanding the total anticipated impact of the project.

4. *Secure input from those who know the process best.* As forecasts are developed, it is essential to secure input from individuals who understand the dynamics of the workplace and the measures being influenced by the project. Sometimes the participants in strategic technology projects or the immediate managers are best. In other situations, it is the variety of analysts who are aware of the major influences in the workplace and the dynamics of those changes. It is important to go to the experts. This will increase not only the accuracy of the forecast but also the credibility of the final results.

5. *Long-term forecasts will usually be inaccurate.* Forecasting works much better in a short timeframe. For most short-term scenarios, it is possible to have a better grasp of the influences that might drive the measure. On a long-term basis, a variety of new influences, unforeseen now, could enter the process and drastically change the impact measures. If a long-term forecast is needed, it should be updated regularly to become a continuously improving process.

6. *Expect forecasts to be biased.* Forecasts will consist of data coming from those who have an interest in the issue. Some will want the forecast to be optimistic. Others will have a pessimistic view. Almost all input is biased in one way or another. Every attempt should be made to minimize the bias, adjust for the bias, or adjust for the uncertainty in the process. Still, the audience should recognize that it is a biased prediction.

7. *Serious forecasting is hard work.* The value of forecasting often depends on the amount of effort put into the process. High-stakes projects need to have a serious approach, collecting all possible data, examining different scenarios, and making the best prediction available. It is in these situations that mathematical tools can be most valuable.

8. *Review the success of forecasting routinely.* As forecasts are made, it is imperative to revisit the forecast with actual post-project data to check the success of the forecast. This can aid in the continuous improvement of the processes. Sources could prove to be more credible or less credible, specific inputs may be more biased or less biased, certain analyses may be more appropriate than others. It is important to constantly improve the ideal methods and approaches for forecasting within the organization.

9. *The assumptions is the most serious error in forecasting.* Of all the variables that can enter the process, the one possessing the greatest opportunity for error is the assumptions made by the individual providing the forecast. It is important for the assumptions to be clearly understood and communicated. When there are multiple inputs, each forecaster should use the same set of assumptions, if possible.

10. *Utility is the most important characteristic of forecasting.* The most important use of forecasting is the information and input for the decision maker. Forecasting is a tool for those attempting to make a decision about a specific IT or Technology Development investment. It is not a process that is trying to maximize the output or minimize any particular variable. It is not a process that is attempting to dramatically change the way in which the project is implemented. It is a process to provide data for decisions—the greatest utility of forecasting.

Final Thoughts

This chapter illustrated that ROI forecasts can be developed at different timeframes. Although most practitioners and researchers use application and impact data for ROI calculations, there are situations when Level 3 and Level 4 data are not available or evaluations at those levels are not attempted or planned. ROI forecasts, developed before the project is implemented, can be useful and helpful to management and the IT staff, while at the same time focusing attention on the potential economic impact of a strategic technology project. Forecasts are also possible with reaction and learning data. Be aware that using ROI forecasts may provide a false sense of accuracy. As would be expected, ROI forecasts on a preproject basis are the lowest in credibility and accuracy but have the advantage of being inexpensive and relatively easy to conduct. On the other hand, ROI forecasts using Level 3 data are highest in credibility and accuracy but are more expensive and difficult to develop.

Although ROI calculations with impact data (Level 4) are preferred, ROI forecasts at other times are an important part of a comprehensive and systematic evaluation process. This usually means that targets for evaluation should be established.

References

Bowers, D.A. *Forecasting for Control and Profit.* Menlo Park, CA: Crisp Publications, 1997.

CHAPTER 11

Communicating Results

Now that the data has been collected and analyzed, what do you do next? Should you use the data to modify the project, change the process, show the contribution, justify new projects, gain additional support, or build goodwill? How should the data be presented? Who should present the data? Where should the data be communicated? These and other questions are examined in this chapter. The worst course of action is to do nothing. Communicating results is as important as achieving them. Using many examples, this chapter provides useful information to help present evaluation data to the various audiences using both oral and written reporting methods.

THE IMPORTANCE OF COMMUNICATION

Communicating results is a critical issue in the ROI Methodology. Although it is important to communicate achieved results to interested stakeholders after the project is completed, constant communication at every step of the IT project is critical, as well. This ensures that information is flowing so adjustments can be made and all stakeholders are informed about the successes and issues surrounding the project. There are at least five key reasons to emphasize communicating results.

Measurement and Evaluation

Measuring success and collecting evaluation data mean nothing unless the findings are communicated promptly to the appropriate audiences. This allows awareness and prompts necessary actions. Communication allows a full loop to be made from the project results to actions based on those results.

Making Improvements

Because information is collected at different points during the process, the communication or feedback to the various groups who will take action is the only way adjustments can be made. Therefore, the quality and timeliness of communication become critical issues for making necessary adjustments or improvements. Even after the project is completed, communication is necessary to make sure the target audience fully understands the results achieved and how the results could either be enhanced in future projects or in the current project, if it is still operational. Communication is the key to making these important adjustments at all phases of the project.

Explaining Contributions

The contribution of a strategic technology project explained with six major types of measures is a confusing issue. The different target audiences will need a thorough explanation of the results. A communication strategy including techniques, media, and the overall process will determine the extent to which they understand the contribution. Communicating results, particularly with business impact and ROI, can quickly become confusing for even the most sophisticated target audiences. Communication must be planned and implemented with the goal of making sure the audiences understand the full contribution.

Communication and Diplomacy

Communication is one of those important issues that can cause major problems. Because the results of a project can be closely linked to the performance of others and the political issues in an organization, communication can upset some individuals and please others. If certain individuals do not receive the information or if it is delivered inconsistently from one group to another, problems can quickly surface. Not only is it an understanding issue, but it also involves fairness, quality, and political correctness. Always make sure that communication is properly constructed and effectively delivered to all key individuals.

Audiences

Because there are so many potential target audiences for receiving communication on the success of a project, the communication should be tailored to their needs. A varied audience will command varied needs. Planning and effort are necessary to make sure the audience receives all the pertinent information, in the proper format, and at the proper time. A single report for all audiences may not be appropriate. The scope, size, media, and even the actual information of different types and different levels will vary significantly from one group to another, making the target audience the key to determining the appropriate communication process.

Collectively, these reasons make communication a critical issue, although it is often overlooked or underestimated in strategic IT and technology development projects. This chapter builds on this important issue and shows a variety of techniques for accomplishing all types of communication for various target audiences.

Principles of Communicating Results

The skills required to communicate results effectively are almost as delicate and sophisticated as those needed to obtain results. The style is as important as the substance. Regardless of the message, audience, or medium, a few general principles apply and are explored next.

Use Timely Communication

Usually, results should be communicated as soon as they are known. From a practical standpoint, it may be best to delay the communication until a convenient time, such as the publication of the next corporate newsletter or the next senior management meeting. Timing issues must be addressed. Is the audience ready for the results in light of other things that may have happened? Is the audience expecting results? When is the best time for having the maximum effect on the audience? Are there circumstances that dictate a change in the timing of the communication?

Target Specific Audiences

Communication will be more effective if it is designed for a particular group. The message should be specifically tailored to the interests, needs, and expectations of the target audience.

The results described in this chapter reflect outcomes at all levels, including the six types of data developed in this book. Some of the data are developed earlier in the project and communicated during the project. Other data are collected after implementation and communicated in a follow-up study. Therefore, the results, in their broadest sense, may involve early feedback in qualitative terms to ROI values in varying quantitative terms.

Carefully Select Media

For particular groups, some media may be more effective than others. Face-to-face meetings may be better than special bulletins. A memo distributed exclusively to top management may be more effective than the company newsletter. Assuming the technology initiative results in a completed application and not just behind-the-scenes technical engineering, many times a demonstration of the application and its functionality provides the greatest return. The proper method of communication can help improve the effectiveness of the process.

Use Unbiased and Modest Communication

It is important to separate fact from fiction and accurate statements from opinions. Various audiences may accept communication from the IT staff with skepticism, anticipating biased opinions. Boastful statements sometimes annoy recipients, and most of the content can be lost. Observable, believable facts carry far more weight than extreme or sensational claims. Although such claims may get audience attention, they often detract from the importance of the results.

Make Communication Consistent

The timing and content of the communication should be consistent with previous practices. A special communication at an unusual time during the IT project may provoke suspicion. Also, if a particular group, such as top management, regularly receives communication on outcomes, it should continue receiving communication—even if the results are not positive. If some results are omitted, it might leave the impression that only positive results are reported.

Testimonials

Opinions are strongly influenced by others, particularly those who are respected and trusted. Testimonials about results, when solicited from individuals respected by others in the organization, can influence the effectiveness of the message. This respect may be related to leadership ability, position, special skills, or knowledge. A testimonial from an individual who commands little respect and is regarded as a substandard performer can have a negative impact on the message.

Audience Opinion

Opinions are difficult to change, and a negative opinion of the IT group may not change with the mere presentation of facts. However, the presentation of facts alone may strengthen the opinions held by those who already agree with the results. It helps reinforce their position and provides a defense in discussions with others. A technology department with a high level of credibility and respect may have a relatively easy time communicating results. Low credibility can create problems when trying to be persuasive. The reputation of the IT group is an important consideration in developing the overall strategy.

These general principles are important to the overall success of the communication effort. They should serve as a checklist for the IT team when disseminating project results.

ANALYZING THE NEED FOR COMMUNICATION

Because there are many reasons for communicating results, a list should be tailored to the situation and the project. The specific reasons depend on the project, the setting, and the unique needs of the sponsor:

- *To secure approval for the project and allocate resources of time and money.* The initial communication presents a proposal, projected ROI, or other data that are intended to secure the project approval. This communication may not have much data but anticipates what is to come.
- *To gain support for the project and its objectives.* It is important to have support from a variety of groups. This communication is intended to build the necessary support to make the project work successfully.
- *To secure agreement on the issues, solutions, and resources.* As the project begins, it is important for all those directly involved to have some agreement and understanding of the important elements and requirements surrounding the project.

- *To build credibility for the IT group, its techniques, and the finished products.* It is important early in the process to make sure that those involved understand the approach and reputation of the IT staff and, based on the approach taken, the commitments made by all parties.
- *To reinforce the processes.* It is important for key managers to support the project and reinforce the various processes used in design, development, and delivery. This communication is designed to enhance those processes.
- To *drive action for improvement in the project.* This early communication is designed as a process improvement tool to effect changes and improvements as the needs are uncovered and as various individuals make suggestions.
- *To prepare participants for the project.* It is necessary for those most directly involved in the project—the participants—to be prepared for learning, application, and responsibilities that will be required of them as they bring success to the project.
- *To enhance results throughout the project and the quality of future feedback.* This communication is designed to show the status of the project and to influence decisions, seek support, or communicate events and expectations to the key stakeholders. In addition, it will enhance both the quality and quantity of information as stakeholders see the feedback cycle in action.
- *To show the complete results of the IT project.* Perhaps the most important communication, this is where all the results involving all six types of measures are communicated to the appropriate individuals so they have a full understanding of the success or shortcomings of the project.
- *To underscore the importance of measuring results.* Some individuals need to understand the importance of measurement and evaluation and see the need for having important data on different measures.
- *To explain techniques used to measure results.* The project sponsor and support staff need to understand the techniques used in measuring results. In some cases, these techniques may be transferred internally to use with other projects. In short, these individuals need to understand the soundness and theoretical framework of the process used.
- *To stimulate desire in participants to be involved in the project.* Ideally, participants want to be involved in the project. This communication is designed to pique their interest in the project and inform them of its importance.

- *To stimulate interest in the IT function.* From an IT perspective, some communications are designed to create interest in all of their capabilities based on the results obtained by the current projects.
- *To demonstrate accountability for expenditures.* It is important for a broad group to understand the need for accountability and the approach of the IT staff. This ensures accountability for expenditures on the project.
- *To market future projects.* From an IT perspective, it is important to build a database of successful projects to use in convincing others that the IT and technology development function adds tremendous value.

Although this list is comprehensive, there may be other reasons for communicating results. The situation context should be considered when developing others.

PLANNING THE COMMUNICATION

Any successful activity must be carefully planned out if it is going to produce the maximum results. This is a critical part of communicating the results of major projects. The actual planning of the communications is important to ensure that each audience receives the proper information at the right time and that appropriate actions are taken. Three separate issues are important in planning the communication of results. These are presented next.

Communication Policy Issues

When examining the overall IT process, policy issues must be developed around the communication of results. These range from providing feedback during a project to communicating the ROI from an impact study. Seven different areas will need attention as the policies are developed:

1. *What will actually be communicated?* It is important to detail the types of information communicated throughout the project—not only the six types of data from the ROI model but the overall progress with the IT function of the organization may be a topic of communications as well.
2. *When will the data be communicated?* With communications, timing is critical. If adjustments in the project are required, the

information should be communicated quickly so that swift actions can be taken.

3. *How will the information be communicated?* This shows the preferences toward particular types of communication media. For example, some organizations prefer to have written documents sent out as reports, whereas others prefer face-to-face meetings, and still others want electronic communications used as much as possible.

4. *The location for communication.* Some prefer that the communication take place close to the sponsor. Others prefer to use the IT or technology development offices. The location can be an important issue in terms of convenience and perception.

5. *Who will communicate the information?* Will the IT staff, an independent consultant, or an individual from the sponsor's office communicate the information? The person communicating must have credibility so that the information is believable.

6. *The target audience.* Identify specific target audiences that should always receive information and others that will receive information only when appropriate.

7. *The specific actions that are required or desired.* When information is presented, in some cases no action is needed. In other cases, changes are desired and sometimes even required.

Collectively, these seven issues frame the policy around communication as a whole.

Communication and the Completed Project

When a major project is approved, the communication plan is usually created. This details how specific information is developed and communicated to various groups and the expected actions. In addition, the plan details how the overall results will be communicated, the timeframes for communication, and the appropriate groups who should receive information. The IT team and sponsor need to agree on the extent of detail in the plan. Additional information on this type of planning is provided later.

The Impact Study

A third issue is the plan aimed at presenting the results of an impact study. This occurs when a major project is completed and the detailed results are known. One of the major issues is who should receive the results and in what form. This is more specialized than the plan for the entire project because it involves the final study from the project. Table 11-1 shows the communication plan for a company that migrated from a legacy system to an industry leading Enterprise Resource Planning (ERP) system.

Five different communication pieces were developed for different audiences. The complete report was an ROI impact study, a 75-page report that served as the historical document for the project. It was distributed to the sponsor, the IT staff and the particular manager of each of the teams involved in the studies. An executive summary, a much smaller document, went to some of the higher-level executives. A general interest overview and summary without the ROI calculation went to the participants. A general-interest article was developed for company publications, and a brochure was developed to show the success of the project. That brochure was used in marketing the same process internally to other teams and served as additional marketing material for the IT staff. This detailed plan may be part of the overall plan for the assignment but may be fine-tuned

Table 11-1
Communication Plan for Project Results

Communication Document	Communication Target(s)	Distribution Method
Complete report with appendices (75 pages)	• Project sponsor • IT staff • Intact team manager	Distribute and discuss in a special meeting
Executive summary (eight pages)	• Senior management in the business units • Senior corporate management	Distribute and discuss in routine meeting
General interest overview and summary without the actual ROI calculation (10 pages)	• Participants	Detailed e-mail
General interest article (one page)	• All employees	Publish in company's electronic newsletter
Brochure highlighting project, objectives, and specific results	• Team leaders with an interest in the project • Prospective sponsors	Include with other marketing materials

during the actual process. These three issues and plans underscore the importance of organizing the communication strategy for a particular project or the overall IT process in an organization.

SELECTING THE AUDIENCE FOR COMMUNICATIONS

Preliminary Issues

When approaching a particular audience, the following questions should be asked about each potential group:

- Are they interested in the project?
- Do they want to receive the information?
- Has someone already made a commitment to them regarding communication?
- Is the timing right for this audience?
- Are they familiar with the project?
- How do they prefer to have results communicated?
- Do they know the team members?
- Are they likely to find the results threatening?
- Which medium will be most convincing to this group?

For each target audience, three actions are required:

1. To the greatest extent possible, the IT staff should know and understand the target audience.
2. The IT staff should find out what information is needed and why. Each group will have its own needs relative to the information desired. Some want detailed information, whereas others want brief information. Rely on the input from others to determine audience needs.
3. The IT staff should try to understand audience bias. Each will have a particular bias or opinion. Some will quickly support the results, whereas others may be against them or be neutral. The staff should be empathetic and try to understand differing views. With this understanding, communications can be tailored to each group. This is especially critical when the potential exists for the audience to react negatively to the results.

Basis for Selecting the Audience

The potential target audiences to receive information on results are varied in terms of job levels and responsibilities. Determining which groups will receive a particular communication piece deserves careful thought, as problems can arise when a particular group receives inappropriate information or when another is omitted altogether. A sound basis for proper audience selection is to analyze the reason for communication, as discussed in an earlier section. Table 11-2 shows common target audiences and the basis for selecting the audience.

Perhaps the most important audience is the sponsor, the individual, or the team that is supporting the ROI study. This group (or individual) initiates the project, reviews data, and weighs the final assessment of the effectiveness of the project. Another important target audience is the top management group. This group is responsible for allocating resources to the project and needs information to help justify expenditures and gauge the effectiveness of the efforts.

Table 11-2
Common Target Audiences

Reason for Communication	Primary Target Audiences
To secure approval for the project	Sponsor, top executives
To gain support for the project	Immediate managers, team leaders
To secure agreement with the issues	Participants, team leaders
To build credibility for IT	Top executives
To enhance reinforcement of the processes	Immediate managers
To drive action for improvement	Sponsor, IT staff
To prepare participants for the project	Team leaders
To enhance results and quality of future feedback	Participants
To show the complete results of the project	Sponsor
To underscore the importance of measuring results	Sponsor, IT staff
To explain techniques used to measure results	Sponsor, support staff
To create desire for a participant to be involved in the project	Team leaders
To stimulate interest in the IT staff	Top executives
To demonstrate accountability for expenditures	All employees
To market future projects	Prospective sponsors

Selected groups of managers (or all managers) are also important target audiences. Management's support and involvement in the process and the department's credibility are important to success. Effectively communicating project results to management can increase both support and credibility.

Communicating with the participants' team leaders or immediate managers is essential. In many cases, they must encourage participants to implement the project. Also, they often support and reinforce the objectives of the project. An appropriate ROI improves the commitment to IT and provides credibility for the entire technology staff.

Occasionally, results are communicated to encourage participation in the project. This is especially true for those projects offered on a volunteer basis. The potential participants are important targets for communicating results.

Participants need feedback on the overall success of the effort. Some individuals may not have been as successful as others in achieving the desired results. Communicating the results adds additional pressure to effectively implement the project and improve results for the future. For those achieving excellent results, the communication will serve as a reinforcement of the strategic technology initiative. Communicating results to participants is often overlooked, with the assumption that since the project is complete, they do not need to be informed of its success.

The IT staff must receive information about project results. Whether for small projects where the IT staff receives an update or for larger projects where a complete team is involved, those who design, develop, facilitate, and implement the project must be given information on the project's effectiveness. Evaluation information is necessary so adjustments can be made if the project is not as effective as it could be. The support staff should receive detailed information about the process to measure results. This group provides support services to the IT team, usually in the department.

Company employees and stockholders may be less likely targets. General-interest news stories may increase employee respect. Goodwill and positive attitudes toward the organization may also be by-products of communicating results. Stockholders, on the other hand, are more interested in the return on their investment.

Although Table 11-2 shows the most common target audiences, there may be others in certain organization. For instance, management or employees could be subdivided into different departments, divisions, or even subsidiaries of the organization. The number of audiences can be large in a complex organization. At a minimum, four target audiences are always recommended: a senior management group, the participants' immediate manager or team leader, the participants, and the IT staff.

Developing the Information: The Impact Study

The type of formal evaluation report depends on the extent of detailed information presented to the various target audiences. Brief summaries of results with appropriate charts may be sufficient for some communication efforts. In other situations, particularly with significant technology projects requiring extensive funding, the amount of detail in the evaluation report is more crucial. A complete and comprehensive impact study report may be necessary. This report can then be used as the basis of information for specific audiences and various media. The report may contain the following sections.

Executive Summary

The executive summary is a brief overview of the entire report, explaining the basis for the evaluation and the significant conclusions and recommendations. It is designed for individuals who are too busy to read a detailed report. It is usually written last but appears first in the report for easy access.

Background Information

The background information provides a general description of the project. If applicable, the needs assessment that led to the implementation of the project is summarized. The project is fully described, including the events that led to the intervention. Other specific items necessary to provide a full description of the project are included. The extent of detailed information depends on the amount of information the audience needs.

Objectives

The objectives for both the impact study and the actual IT or technology development project are outlined. Sometimes they are the same, but they may be different. The report details the particular objectives of the study itself so that the reader clearly understands the rationale for the study and how the data will be used. In addition, specific objectives of the IT project are detailed, as these are the objectives from which the different types or levels of data will be collected.

Evaluation Strategy/Methodology

The evaluation strategy outlines all the components that make up the total evaluation process. Several components of the results-based model and the ROI Methodology presented in this book are discussed in this section of the report. The specific purposes of evaluation are outlined, and the evaluation design and methodology are explained. The instruments used in data collection are also described and presented as exhibits. Any unusual issues in the evaluation design are discussed. Finally, other useful information related to the design, timing, and execution of the evaluation is included.

Data Collection and Analysis

This section explains the methods used to collect data as outlined in earlier chapters. The data collected are usually presented in the report in summary form. Next, the methods used to analyze data are presented with interpretations.

Project Costs

Project costs are presented in this section. A summary of the costs by category is included. For example, analysis, development, implementation, and evaluation costs are recommended categories for cost presentation. The assumptions made in developing and classifying costs are discussed in this section of the report.

Reaction and Satisfaction

This section details the data collected from key stakeholders, particularly the participants involved in the process, to measure reactions to the project and levels of satisfaction with various issues and parts of the process. Other input from the sponsor or managers may be included to show the levels of satisfaction.

Learning

This section shows a brief summary of the formal and informal methods for measuring learning. It explains how participants have learned new processes, skills, tasks, procedures, and practices.

Application and Implementation

This section shows how the project was actually implemented and the success with the application of new skills and knowledge. Implementation issues are addressed, including any major success and/or lack of success.

Business Impact

This section shows the actual business impact measures representing the business needs that initially drove the project. This shows the extent to which performance has changed during the implementation of the project.

Return on Investment

This section actually shows the ROI calculation along with the benefits/costs ratio. It compares the value to what was expected and provides an interpretation of the actual calculation.

Intangible Measures

This section shows the various intangible measures directly linked to the IT project. Intangibles are those measures not converted to monetary values or included in the actual ROI calculation.

Barriers and Enablers

The various problems and obstacles that might affect the success of the project are detailed and presented as barriers to implementation. Also, those factors or influences that had a positive effect on the project are included as enablers. Together, they provide tremendous insight into what can hinder or enhance future projects.

Conclusions and Recommendations

This section presents conclusions based on all of the results. If appropriate, brief explanations are presented on how each conclusion was reached. A list of recommendations or changes in the project, if appropriate, is provided with brief explanations for each recommendation. It is important that the conclusions and recommendations are consistent with one another and with the findings described in the previous section. These components make up the major parts of a complete evaluation report.

Developing the Report

Table 11-3 shows the table of contents from a typical evaluation report for an ROI evaluation. Although this report is an effective, professional way to present ROI data, several cautions need to be followed. Since this document reports the success for a group of employees, complete credit for the success must go to the participants and their immediate leaders. Their performance generated the success. Another important caution is to avoid boasting about results. Although the ROI Methodology may be accurate and credible, it still may have some subjective issues. Huge claims of success can quickly turn off an audience and interfere with the delivery of the desired message.

A final caution concerns the structure of the report: The methodology should be clearly explained, along with assumptions made in the analysis. The reader should be able to easily see how the values were developed and how the specific steps were followed to make the process more conservative, credible, and accurate. Detailed statistical analyses should be placed in the appendix.

Selecting the Communication Media

There are many options available to communicate project results. In addition to the impact study report, the most frequently used media are meetings, interim and progress reports, the organization's publications, e-mail, brochures, and case studies.

Meetings

In addition to the meeting with the sponsor to discuss results, other meetings are fertile opportunities for communicating project results. All organizations have a variety of meetings; and, in each, the proper context and consulting results are an important part. A few examples illustrate the variety of meetings.

Staff Meetings

Throughout the chain of command, staff meetings are held to review progress, discuss current problems, and distribute information. These meetings can be an excellent forum for discussing the

Table 11-3
Format of an Impact Study Report

- Executive Summary
- General Information
  - Background
  - Objectives of Study
- Methodology for Impact Study
  - Levels of Evaluation
  - ROI Process
  - Collecting Data   } Builds credibility for the
  - Isolating the Effects of IT   process
  - Converting Data to Monetary Values
  - Assumptions
- Data Analysis Issues
- Program Costs
- Results: General Information
  - Response Profile
  - Success with Objectives
- Results: Reaction
  - Data Sources
  - Data Summary
  - Key Issues
- Results: Learning
  - Data Sources
  - Data Summary
  - Key Issues   The results with six
- Results: Application   measures: Levels 1, 2, 3, 4,
  - Data Sources   5, and Intangibles
  - Data Summary
  - Key Issues
- Results: Impact
  - General Comments
  - Linkage with Business Measures
  - Key Issues
- Results: ROI and Its Meaning
- Results: Intangible Measures
- Barriers and Enablers
  - Barriers
  - Enablers
- Conclusions and Recommendations
  - Conclusions
  - Recommendations

results achieved in a major IT project when it relates to the group's activities. Project results can be sent to executives for use in staff meetings, or a member of the IT team can attend the meeting to make the presentation.

Manager Meetings

Regular meetings with the first-level management group are common. Typically, items are discussed that will possibly help their work units. A discussion of an IT project and the subsequent results can be integrated into the regular meeting format.

Best-Practices Meetings

Some organizations have best-practices meetings or videoconferences to discuss recent successes and best practices. This is an excellent opportunity to learn and share methodologies and results.

Business Update Meetings

A few organizations have initiated a periodic meeting for all members of management in which the CEO reviews progress and discusses plans for the coming year. A few highlights of major project results can be integrated into the CEO's speech, showing top executive interest, commitment, and support. Results are reported along with operating profit, new facilities and equipment, new company acquisitions, and next year's sales forecast.

Interim and Progress Reports

Although usually limited to large projects, a highly visible way to communicate results is through interim and routine memos and reports. Published or disseminated via the intranet on a periodic basis, they usually have several purposes:

- To inform management about the status of the project
- To communicate the interim results achieved in the project
- To activate needed changes and improvements

A more subtle reason for the report is to gain additional support and commitment from the management group and to keep the project intact. This report is produced by the IT staff and distributed to a select group of managers in the organization. Format and scope vary considerably. Common topics are presented here.

Schedule of Activities

A schedule of planned steps/activities should be an integral part of this report. A brief description should be presented.

Reactions from Participants

A brief summary of reaction evaluations may be appropriate to report initial success. Also, brief interviews with participants might be included.

Results

A key focus of this report is the results achieved from the project. Significant results that can be documented should be presented in an easily understood format. The method(s) of evaluation should be briefly outlined, along with the measurement data.

Change in Responsibility

Occasionally, people involved in planning, developing, implementing, or evaluating the project are reassigned, transferred, or promoted. It is important to communicate how these changes affect responsibilities and the project.

Participant Spotlight

A section that highlights a participant can focus additional attention on results. This is an opportunity to recognize outstanding participants responsible for excellent results and bring attention to unusual achievements.

Although the preceding list may not be suited for every report, it represents topics that should be presented to the management group. When produced in a professional manner, the report can improve management support and commitment to the effort.

The Organization's Publications and Standard Communication Tools

To reach a wide audience, the IT staff can use in-house publications and electronic communication tools. Whether an electronic newsletter, intranet site, or e-mail, these types of media usually reach all employees. The information can be effective if communicated appropriately. The scope should be limited to general interest issues, announcements, and opportunities. Following are types of issues that should be covered in these communications.

Project Results

Results communicated through these types of media must be significant enough to arouse general interest. For example, an e-mail with the headline "Enterprise CRM Project Doubles Close Rate" will catch the attention of many people because they may have participated in the project and can appreciate the significance of the results. Reports on the accomplishments of a small group of participants may not receive much attention unless the audience can relate to the accomplishments.

For many IT implementations, results are achieved weeks or even months after the project is completed. Participants need reinforcement from many sources. If results are communicated to a general audience, including the participants' subordinates or peers, there is additional pressure to continue the project or similar ones in the future.

Participant Recognition

General audience communication can bring recognition to participants, particularly those who excel in some aspect of the project. When participants deliver unusual performance, public recognition can enhance their self-esteem.

Human Interest Stories

Many human interest stories can come out of major IT projects. A rigorous project with difficult requirements can provide the basis for an interesting story on participants who implement the project. In one organization, the marketing communication manager of the company's intranet participated in a demanding IT project and wrote a stimulating article about what it was like to be a participant. The article gave the reader a tour of the entire project and its effectiveness in terms of the results achieved. It was an interesting and effective way to communicate about a challenging activity.

The benefits are many and the opportunities endless for IT staff to use in-house communication tools and company-wide intranets to let others know about the success of projects.

E-mail and Electronic Media

Internal and external Web pages on the Internet, company-wide intranets, and e-mail are excellent vehicles for releasing results, promoting ideas, and informing employees and other target groups about results. E-mail, in particular, provides a virtually instantaneous means with which to communicate and solicit response from large numbers of people.

Brochures and Pamphlets

A brochure might be appropriate for projects conducted on a continuing basis, where participants have produced excellent results. It should be attractive and present a complete description of the project, with a major section devoted to results obtained with previous participants, if available. Measurable results and reactions from participants, or even direct quotes from individuals, could add spice to an otherwise dull brochure.

Case Studies

Case studies represent an effective way to communicate the results of a large-scale IT project. Therefore, it is recommended that a few evaluation projects be developed in a case format. A typical case study describes the situation, provides appropriate background information (including the events that led to the intervention), presents the techniques and strategies used to develop the study, and highlights the key issues in the project. Case studies tell an interesting story of how the evaluation was developed and the problems and concerns identified along the way.

Case studies have many useful applications in an organization. First, they can be used in group discussions, where interested individuals can react to the material, offer different perspectives, and draw conclusions about approaches or techniques. Second, the case study can serve as a self-teaching guide for individuals trying to understand how evaluations are developed and used in the organization. Finally, case studies provide appropriate recognition for those involved in the actual case. More important, they recognize the participants who achieved the results, as well as the managers who allowed the participants to be involved in the project. The case study format has become one of the most effective ways to learn about project evaluation.

COMMUNICATING THE INFORMATION

Perhaps the greatest challenge of communication is the actual delivery of the message. This can be accomplished in a variety of ways and settings, based on the target audience and the media selected for the message. Three particular approaches deserve additional coverage. The first is providing insight into how to give feedback throughout the project to make sure information flows so changes can be made. The second is presenting an impact study to a senior management team. This may be one of the most challenging tasks for the evaluator. The third is communicating regularly and routinely with the executive management group. Each of these three approaches is explored in more detail.

Providing Feedback

One of the most important reasons for collecting reaction, satisfaction, and learning data is to provide feedback so adjustments or changes can be made throughout the project. In most IT projects, data is routinely collected and quickly communicated to a variety of groups. Table 11-4 shows a feedback action plan designed to provide information to several feedback audiences using a variety of media. As the plan shows, data are collected during the project at four specific time intervals and communicated back to at least four audiences—and sometimes six. Some of these feedback sessions result in identifying specific actions that need to be taken. This process becomes comprehensive and needs to be managed in a proactive way. The following steps are recommended for providing feedback and managing the feedback process (Block, 2000).

Communicate quickly. Whether the news is good or bad, it is important to relay it to the individuals involved in the project as soon as possible. The recommended time for providing feedback is

Table 11-4
Feedback Action Plan

Data Collection Item	Timing	Feedback Audience	Media	Timing of Feedback	Action Required
1. Preproject Survey	Beginning of the Project	Participants	Meeting	One Week	None
• Climate/Environment		Team Leaders	Survey Summary	Two Weeks	None
• Issue Identification		IT Staff	Survey Summary	Two Weeks	Communicate Feedback
			Meeting	One Week	Adjust Approach
2. Implementation Survey	Beginning of Actual Implementation	Participants	Meeting	One Week	None
• Reaction to Plans		Team Leaders	Survey Summary	Two Weeks	None
• Issue Identification		IT Staff	Survey Summary	Two Weeks	Communicate Feedback
			Meeting	One Week	Adjust Approach
3. Implementation Reaction Survey/Interviews	One Month into Implementation	Participants	Meeting	One Week	Comments
• Reaction to Solution		Support Staff	Study Summary	Two Weeks	None
• Suggested Changes		Team Leaders	Study Summary	Two Weeks	None
		Immediate Managers	Study Summary	Two Weeks	Support Changes
		IT Staff	Study Summary	Three Weeks	Support Changes
			Meeting	Three Days	Adjust Approach
4. Implementation Feedback Questionnaire	End of Implementation	Participants	Meeting	One Week	Comments
• Reaction (Satisfaction)		Support Staff	Study Summary	Two Weeks	None
• Barriers		Team Leaders	Study Summary	Two Weeks	None
• Projected Success		Immediate Managers	Study Summary	Two Weeks	Support Changes
		IT Staff	Study Summary	Three Weeks	Support Changes
			Meeting	Three Days	Adjust Approach

usually a matter of days, certainly no longer than a week or two after the results are known.

Simplify the data. Condense data into an understandable, concise presentation. This is not the format for detailed explanations and analyses.

Examine the role of the IT staff and the sponsor in the feedback situation. Sometimes the IT staff member is the judge, and sometimes the jury, prosecutor, defendant, or witness. On the other hand, sometimes the sponsor is the judge, jury, prosecutor, defendant, or witness. It is important to examine the respective roles in terms of reactions to the data and the actions that need to be taken.

Use negative data in a constructive way. Some of the data will show that things are not going so well, and the fault may rest with the IT staff or the sponsor. In either case, the story basically changes from "Let's look at the success we've made" to "Now we know which areas to change."

Use positive data in a cautious way. Positive data can be misleading, and if they are communicated too enthusiastically, they may create expectations beyond what may materialize later. Positive data should be presented in a cautious way—almost in a discounting mode.

Choose the language of the meeting and communication carefully. Use language that is descriptive, focused, specific, short, and simple. Avoid language that is too judgmental, macro, stereotypical, lengthy, or complex.

Ask the sponsor for reactions to the data. After all, the sponsor is the customer, and the sponsor's reaction is critical.

Ask the sponsor for recommendations. The sponsor may have some good recommendations of what needs to be changed to keep a project on track or put it back on track if it derails.

Use support and confrontation carefully. These two issues are not mutually exclusive. There may be times when support and confrontation are needed for the same group. The sponsor may need support and yet be confronted for lack of improvement or sponsorship. The IT staff may be confronted on the problem areas that are developed but may need support as well.

React and act on the data. Weigh the different alternatives and possibilities to arrive at the adjustments and changes that will be necessary.

Secure agreement from all key stakeholders. This is essential to make sure everyone is willing to make adjustments and changes that seem necessary.

Keep the feedback process short. Do not let it become bogged down in long, drawn-out meetings or lengthy documents. If this occurs, stakeholders will avoid the process instead of being willing to participate in the future.

Following these steps will help move the project forward and provide important feedback, often ensuring that adjustments are supported and made.

Presenting Impact Study Data to Senior Management

Perhaps one of the most challenging and stressful company communications is presenting an impact study to the senior management team, which also serves as the sponsor on a project. The challenge comes in convincing this highly skeptical and critical group that outstanding results have been achieved (assuming they have), in a reasonable timeframe, addressing the salient points, and making sure the managers understand the process. Two particular issues can create challenges. First, if the results are impressive, it may be difficult to make the managers believe the data. On the other extreme, if the data are negative, it will be a challenge to make sure managers do not overreact to the negative results and look for someone to blame. Here are some guidelines for ensuring that the process is planned and executed properly:

- Plan a face-to-face meeting with senior team members for the first one or two major impact studies, as detailed in Figure 11-1. If they are unfamiliar with the ROI Methodology, a face-to-face meeting is necessary to make sure they understand the process.

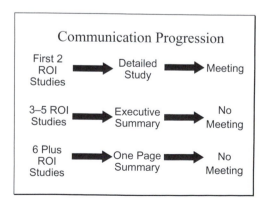

Figure 11-1. Streamline the Communication with Executives

The good news is that they will probably attend the meeting because they have not seen ROI data developed for IT or technology development initiatives in the past. The bad news is that it takes a lot of time, usually an hour, for this presentation.

- After a group has had a face-to-face meeting with a couple of presentations, an executive summary may suffice for the next three to nine studies. At this point they understand the process, so a shortened version may be sufficient.

- After the target audience is familiar with the process, a brief version may be necessary, which will involve a one- to two-page summary with charts or graphs showing all six types of measures. Table 11-5 shows a sample of a one-page summary.

- When making the initial presentation, distribution of the results should be saved until the end of the session. This will allow enough time to present the process and obtain reaction to it before the target audience sees the actual ROI number.

- Present the process step by step, showing how the data were collected, when they were collected, who provided the data, how the data were isolated from other influences, and how they were converted to monetary values. The various assumptions, adjustments, and conservative approaches are presented, along with the total cost of the project. The costs are fully loaded so that the target audience will begin to buy into the process of developing the actual ROI.

- When the data are actually presented, the results are presented step by step, starting with Level 1, moving through Level 5, and ending with the intangibles. This allows the audience to see the chain of impact with reaction and satisfaction, learning, application and implementation, business impact, and ROI. After some discussion on the meaning of the ROI, the intangible measures are presented. Allocate time to each level, as appropriate, for the audience. This helps overcome the potentially negative reactions to a positive or negative ROI.

- Show the consequences of additional accuracy if it is an issue. The tradeoff for more accuracy and validity often means more expense. Address this issue whenever necessary, agreeing to add more data if required.

- Collect concerns, reactions, and issues for the process, and make adjustments accordingly for the next presentation.

Collectively, these steps will help prepare for and present one of the most critical meetings in the ROI process.

Table 11-5
Sample Streamlined Report

ROI Impact Study

Project Title: Enterprise Customer Relationship Management Deployment
Target Audience: All Sales and Marketing (3,245)
Technique to Isolate Effects of Project: Trend analysis; quantitative data; customer satisfaction; participant estimation
Technique to Convert Data to Monetary Value: Historical costs; internal experts

Fully loaded Project Costs: $2,277,987

Results

Level 1: Reaction	Level 2: Learning	Level 3: Application	Level 4: Impact	Level 5: ROI	Intangible Benefits
93% provided action items	65% increase posttest vs. pretest Skill practice demonstration	96% conducted meetings with customers 68% report all action items complete 92% report some action items complete	Increased sales: $2,840,632 Complaint reduction: $360,276 Total improvement: $3,200,908	140%	Job satisfaction Customer satisfaction Better collaboration

Communicating with Executive Management and Sponsors

No group is more important than top executives when it comes to communicating results. In many situations, this group is also the sponsor. Improving communications with this group requires developing an overall strategy that may include all or part of the actions outlined next.

Strengthen the relationship with executives. An informal and productive relationship should be established between the IT manager (responsible for the project evaluation) and the top executive at the location where the project is taking place. Each should feel comfortable discussing needs and project results. One approach is to establish frequent, informal meetings with the executive to review problems with current projects and discuss other performance problems/opportunities in the organization. Frank and open discussions can provide the executive with insight not possible from any other source. Also, it can be helpful to the IT manager to determine the direction.

Show how IT projects have helped solve major problems. Although hard results from recent projects are comforting to an executive, solutions to immediate problems may be more convincing. This is an excellent opportunity to discuss possible future projects for ROI evaluation.

Distribute memos on project results. When an intervention has achieved significant results, make appropriate top executives aware of them. This can easily be done with a brief memo or summary outlining what the project was supposed to accomplish, when it was implemented, who was involved, and the results achieved. This should be presented in a for-your-information (FYI) format that consists of facts rather than opinions. A full report may be presented later.

All significant communications on IT evaluation projects, plans, activities, and results should include the executive group. Frequent information on the projects, as long as it is not boastful, can reinforce credibility and accomplishments.

Ask the executive to be involved in the review. An effective way to enhance commitment from top executives is to ask them to serve on a IT review committee. A review committee provides input and advice to the IT staff on a variety of issues, including needs, problems with the present project, and project evaluation issues. This committee can be helpful in letting executives know what the projects are achieving.

Analyzing Reactions to Communication

The best indicator of how effectively the results of a strategic technology initiative have been communicated is the level of commitment and support from the management group. The allocation of requested resources and strong commitment from top management are tangible evidence of management's perception of the results. In addition to this macro-level reaction, there are a few techniques the IT staff can use to measure the effectiveness of their communication efforts.

Whenever results are communicated, the reaction of the target audiences can be monitored. These reactions may include nonverbal gestures (body language), oral remarks, written comments, or indirect actions that reveal how the communication was received. Usually, when results are presented in a meeting, the presenter will have some indication of how the results were received by the group. The interest and attitudes of the audience can be quickly evaluated.

During the presentation, questions may be asked or, in some cases, the information is challenged. In addition, a tabulation of these challenges and questions can be useful in evaluating the type of information to include in future communications. Positive comments about the results are desired and, when they are made—formally or informally—they should also be noted and tabulated.

IT staff meetings are an excellent arena for discussing the reaction to communicating results. Comments can come from many sources, depending on the particular target audiences. Input from different members of the staff can be summarized to help judge the overall effectiveness.

When major project results are communicated, a feedback questionnaire may be used for an audience or a sample of the audience. The purpose of this questionnaire is to determine the extent to which the audience understood and/or believed the information presented. This is practical only when the effectiveness of the communication has a significant impact on future actions.

Another approach is to survey the management group to determine its perceptions of the results. Specific questions should be asked about results. What does the management group know about the results? How believable are the results? What additional information is desired about the project? This type of survey can help provide guidance in communicating results.

The purpose of analyzing reactions is to make adjustments in the communication process—if adjustments are necessary. Although the reactions may involve intuitive assessments, a more sophisticated analysis will provide more accurate information to make these adjustments. The net result should be a more effective communication process.

FINAL THOUGHTS

This chapter presented the final step in the ROI model. Communicating results is a crucial step in the overall evaluation process. If this step is not taken seriously, the full impact of the results will not be realized. The chapter began with general principles for communicating project results. A communications model that can serve as a guide for any significant communication effort was presented. The various target audiences were discussed, and because of its importance, emphasis was placed on the executive group. A suggested format for a detailed evaluation report was also provided. Much of the remainder of the chapter included a detailed presentation of the most commonly used media for communicating project results, including meetings, publications and electronic media. Numerous examples illustrated these concepts.

REFERENCE

Block, P. *Flawless Consulting*, 2nd Ed. San Francisco, CA: Jossey-Bass/Pfeiffer, 2000.

CHAPTER 12

Implementing the ROI Methodology

The best-designed model or technique will be worthless unless it is integrated efficiently and effectively into the organization. Although the ROI Methodology presented in this book is a step-by-step, methodical, and simplistic procedure, it will fail even in the best organizations if it is not integrated into the mainstream of activity and fully accepted and supported by those who should make it work in the organization. This chapter focuses on the critical issues involved in implementing the ROI Methodology in the organization.

OVERCOMING THE RESISTANCE TO ROI

With any new process or change, there is resistance. Resistance shows up in many ways: negative comments, inappropriate actions, or dysfunctional behaviors. Table 12-1 shows some comments that reflect open resistance to the ROI Methodology. Each represents an issue that must be resolved or addressed in some way. A few of the comments are based on realistic barriers, whereas others are based on myths that must be dispelled. Sometimes, resistance to the ROI Methodology reflects underlying concerns. The individuals involved may have fear of losing control, and others may feel that they are vulnerable to actions that may be taken if their projects are not successful. Still others may be concerned about any process that requires additional learning and actions.

Resistance can appear in all major audiences addressed in this book. It can appear in the IT staff as it resists the ROI Methodology and openly make comments similar to those listed in Table 12-1. Heavy persuasion and evidence of tangible benefits may be needed to convince those individuals that this is a process that should be

Table 12-1
Typical Objections to the ROI Methodology

Open Resistance

1. It costs too much.
2. It takes too much time.
3. Who is asking for this?
4. It is not in my job description.
5. I did not have input on this.
6. I do not understand this.
7. What happens when the results are negative?
8. How can we be consistent with this?
9. The ROI process is too subjective.
10. Our managers will not support this.
11. ROI is too narrowly focused.
12. This is not practical.

implemented—because it is in their best interest. Another major audience, the sponsor, will also experience resistance. Although most sponsors would want to see the results of an ROI project, they may have concerns about the quality and accuracy of data. Also, they may be concerned about the time commitments and the costs of the ROI process.

The managers of participants in projects may develop resistance. They may have concerns about the information they are asked to provide and about whether their performance is being judged along with the evaluation of the participants. In reality, they may express the same fears listed in Table 12-1.

The challenge is to implement the process in organizations methodically and consistently so that it becomes a routine and standard process built into all strategic IT and technology development projects. Implementation is a plan for overcoming resistance. There are four key reasons why there should be a detailed plan for overcoming resistance.

Resistance Is Always Present

There is always resistance to change. Sometimes that is a good thing, but resistance often arises for the wrong reasons. The important point is to sort out both types and try to dispel the myths. When legitimate barriers are the basis for resistance, trying to minimize or remove them altogether is necessary.

Implementation Is Key

As with any process, effective implementation is the key to its success. This occurs when the new technique or tool is integrated into the routine framework. Without effective implementation, even the best process will fail. A process that is never removed from the shelf will never be understood, supported, or improved. There must be clear-cut steps for designing a comprehensive implementation process that will overcome resistance.

Consistency Is Needed

Because this process is implemented from one impact study to another, consistency is an important consideration. With consistency comes accuracy and reliability. The only way to make sure consistency is achieved is to follow clearly defined processes and procedures each time the ROI is tackled. Proper implementation will ensure that this occurs.

Efficiency

Cost control and efficiency will always be an issue in any major undertaking, and the ROI Methodology is no exception. Implementation must ensure that tasks are completed efficiently as well as effectively. It will help ensure that the process cost is kept to a minimum, that time is used appropriately, and that the process remains affordable.

The implementation necessary to overcome resistance covers a variety of areas. Figure 12-1 shows actions outlined in this chapter that are presented as building blocks to overcoming resistance. They are all necessary to build the proper base or framework to dispel myths and remove or minimize actual barriers. The remainder of this chapter presents specific strategies and techniques around each of the building blocks identified in Figure 12-1.

PLANNING THE IMPLEMENTATION

Few initiatives will be effective without proper planning, and it is the same with ROI Methodology. Planning is synonymous with

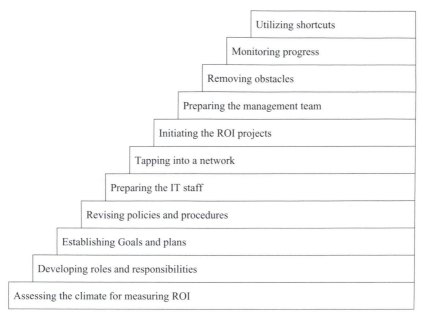

Figure 12-1. Building Blocks for Overcoming Resistance

success. Several issues are fundamental to preparation for ROI and positioning the ROI Methodology as an essential component of the IT and technology development process.

Identifying a Champion

As a first step in the process, one or more individuals should be designated as the internal leader for ROI analysis. As in most change efforts, someone must take the responsibility for ensuring that the process is implemented successfully. This leader serves as a champion for the ROI Methodology and is usually the one who understands the process best and sees the vast potential for the contribution of the process. More important, this leader is willing to show and teach others.

The ROI leader is usually a member of the IT staff who has this responsibility full time in larger organizations or part time in small organizations. The typical job title for a full-time ROI leader is manager or leader, measurement and evaluation. Some organizations assign the responsibility to a team and empower them to lead the ROI effort. For example, Nortel Networks selected five individuals to lead this effort as a team. All five received certification in the ROI Methodology.

Developing the ROI Leader

In preparation for this assignment, individuals usually obtain special training to build specific skills and knowledge in the ROI process. The role of the implementation leader is broad and serves a variety of specialized duties. The leader can take on many roles, as shown in Table 12-2.

At times, the ROI implementation leader serves as a technical expert, giving advice and making decisions about some of the issues involved in evaluation design, data analysis, and presentation. As an initiator, the leader identifies projects for ROI analysis and takes the lead in conducting a variety of ROI studies. When needed, the implementation leader is a cheerleader, bringing attention to the ROI Methodology, encouraging others to become involved, and showing how value can be added to the organization. Finally, the implementation leader is a communicator—informing others about the process and communicating results to a variety of target audiences. All the roles can come into play at one time or another as the leader implements ROI in the organization.

It is a difficult and challenging assignment that will need special training and skill building. In the past there have been only a few projects available that help build these skills. Today, there are many available, and some of them are comprehensive. For example, a project has been developed by the coauthor of this book, Jack Phillips, to certify the individuals who are assuming a leadership role in the implementation of ROI. The process involves prework and preparation prior to attending a one-week workshop. The comprehensive workshop is designed to build ten essential skills, listed in Table 12-3, needed to apply and implement the ROI process.

Table 12-2
Various Roles of the ROI Leader

Technical expert	Cheerleader
Consultant	Communicator
Problem solver	Process monitor
Initiator	Planner
Designer	Analyst
Developer	Interpreter
Coordinator	Teacher

Table 12-3
Ten Skill Sets for Certification

Skill Areas for Certification

- Planning for ROI calculations
- Collecting evaluation data
- Isolating the effects of IT
- Converting data to monetary values
- Monitoring program costs
- Analyzing data including calculating the ROI
- Presenting evaluation data
- Implementing the ROI process
- Providing internal consulting on ROI
- Teaching others the ROI process

During the workshop, the participants plan a project for ROI evaluation, develop the data collection and ROI analysis plans for the project, and present it to the team for feedback. In addition, they develop and present a plan to show how they will help implement the ROI process in their organization, addressing the issues under their control. The typical participant is charged with the responsibility of implementing ROI, or a part of it, in his or her division or organization. Sometimes participants are part of a team, and the entire team attended.

A public version was offered in 1995 when it became apparent that many organizations wanted to send one or two individuals to this type of session to develop the skills to lead the implementation of ROI, but they did not have the resources to send the entire team to an internal certification workshop.

To date, more than 4,000 individuals have attended a certification workshop, representing 3,000 organizations in 50 countries. Table 12-4 lists some of the organizations that participate in certification. Almost one-third of this group had an internal team certified. Others sent one or two individuals to a public workshop. The adoption has been widespread with certification conducted on several continents. Certification is unique, and no other process is available to satisfy these critical needs. It still enjoys internal and public success. For more information on the certification, please contact the author or visit www.roiinstitute.net.

Table 12-4
A Small Sample of Private Sector Organizations that Participate in Certification

- Accenture
- Aetna
- Air Canada
- Allstate Insurance Company
- Amazon.com
- Apple Computer
- Asia Pacific Breweries
- AT&T
- Bank of America
- Banner Health Care
- Baptist Health Systems
- Blue Cross & Blue Shield
- Boston Scientific
- BP Amoco
- Bristol-Myers Squibb
- Caltex—Pacific
- Canadian Imperial Bank of Commerce
- Canadian Tire
- Chevron/Texaco
- CN Rail (Canada)
- Commonwealth Edison
- CVS/Caremark
- Delta Airlines
- DHL Worldwide Express
- Deloitte & Touche
- Duke Energy
- Eli Lilly
- Entergy Corporation
  Eskom (South Africa)
  Federal Express
  First American Bank
  Ford Motor Company
  Georgia Pacific
  GlaxoSmithKline
  Guthrie Healthcare Systems
  Harley Davidson
  Hewlett-Packard

- Home Depot
- HSBC
- IBM
- Illinois Power
- Intel
- KPMG
- Lockheed Martin
- M&M Mars
- Mead
- Microsoft
- Molson Coors
- Motorola
- NCR
- Nortel Networks
- Novus Services
- Olive Garden Restaurants
- Overseas—Chinese Banking Corp
- Pfizer
- PriceWaterhouseCoopers
- Raytheon
- Rolls Royce
- SAP
- Singapore Airlines
- Singapore Technologies
- Sprint/Nextel
- TD Canada Trust
- United Parcel Service
- UNOCAL
- Verizon Communications
- VodaPhone
- Volvo of North America
- Wachovia Bank
- Wal-Mart
- Waste Management Company
- Wells Fargo
- Whirlpool
- Xerox

Assigning Responsibilities

Determining specific responsibilities is a critical issue because confusion can arise when individuals are unclear about their specific assignments in the ROI process. Responsibilities apply to two broad groups. The first is the measurement and evaluation responsibility for the entire IT or technology development staff. It is important for all of those involved in designing, developing, delivering, coordinating, and supporting projects to have some responsibility for measurement and evaluation. These responsibilities include providing input on the design of instruments, planning a specific evaluation, collecting data, and interpreting the results. The following are some typical responsibilities:

- Ensuring that the needs assessment includes specific business impact measures
- Developing specific application objectives (Level 3) and business impact objectives (Level 4) for each project
- Focusing the content of the project on performance improvement; ensuring that exercises, tests, case studies, and skill practices relate to the desired objectives
- Keeping participants focused on application and impact objectives
- Communicating rationale and reasons for evaluation
- Assisting in follow-up activities to capture application and business impact data
- Providing assistance for data collection, data analysis, and reporting
- Developing plans for data collection and analysis
- Presenting evaluation data to a variety of groups
- Assisting with the design of instruments

Although it may be inappropriate to have each member of the staff involved in all of these activities, each individual should have at least one or more responsibilities as part of his or her regular job duties. This assignment of responsibility keeps the ROI process from being disjointed and separate from major IT and technology development activities. More important, it brings accountability to those who develop, deliver, and implement the projects.

The second issue involves the technical support function. Depending on the size of the IT staff, it may be helpful to establish a group of technical experts to provide assistance with the ROI process.

When this group is established, it must be clear that the experts and are not there to relieve others of evaluation responsibilities but to supplement technical expertise. Some firms have found this approach to be effective. At one time, Accenture had a measurement and evaluation staff of 32 to provide technical support for the evaluation of internal professional education. When this type of support is developed, responsibilities revolve around eight key areas:

1. Designing data collection instruments
2. Providing assistance for developing an evaluation strategy
3. Coordinating a major evaluation project
4. Analyzing data, including specialized statistical analyses
5. Interpreting results and making specific recommendations
6. Developing an evaluation report or case study to communicate overall results
7. Presenting results to critical audiences
8. Providing technical support in any phase of the ROI process

The assignment of responsibilities for evaluation is also an issue that needs attention throughout the evaluation process. Although the IT staff must have specific responsibilities during an evaluation, it is not unusual to require others in support functions to have responsibility for data collection. These responsibilities are defined when a particular evaluation strategy plan is developed and approved.

Tapping into a Network

Because the ROI Methodology is new to many individuals, it is helpful to have a peer group that is experiencing similar issues and frustrations. Tapping into an international network (already developed), joining or creating a local network, or building an internal network are all possible ways to utilize the resources, ideas, and support of others.

ROI Network

In 1996, the ROI Network was created to exchange information among the graduates of the certification workshop. During certification, the participants bond and freely exchange information with each other. The ROI Network is an attempt to provide a permanent vehicle of information and support.

The ROI Network is a professional organization with about 400 members and is poised for growth. The network operates through a variety of committees and communicates with members through newsletters, websites, listservs, and annual meetings. The ROI Network represents an opportunity to build a community of practice around the ROI Methodology. To learn more about the ROI Network, visit www.roiinstitute.net.

Creating a Local Network

In some situations, it may be appropriate to develop a group of local individuals who have the same interest and concerns about the ROI Methodology. When this is the case, a local network may be feasible. For some occasions, this is a country (such as the South African ROI Network). In other situations, it is a more confined area (such as the Puerto Rico ROI Network). In Puerto Rico, a group of 30 individuals who participated in the certification process challenge each other to remain as an intact group to discuss issues and report progress. Members come from a wide variety of backgrounds but meet routinely to present progress reports; discuss problems, barriers, and issues; and plan next steps. This is an active group, typical of what can develop if the individuals are willing to share the information and support each other.

Building an Internal Network

One way to integrate the information needs of IT or technology development practitioners for an effective ROI evaluation is through an internal ROI network. The experience with networks—in organizations where the idea has been tried—showed that these communities of practice are powerful tools for both accelerating evaluation skill development and cultivating a new culture of accountability.

The concept of a network is simplicity itself. The idea is to bring together people who are interested in ROI throughout the organization to work under the guidance of trained ROI evaluators. Typically, advocates within the IT department see both the need for beginning networks and the potential of ROI evaluation to change how the department does its work. Interested network members learn by designing and executing real evaluation plans. This process generates commitment for accountability as a new way of doing business for the IT department.

Developing Evaluation Targets

As presented earlier, establishing specific targets for evaluation levels is an important way to make progress with measurement and evaluation. Targets enable the staff to focus on the improvements needed with specific evaluation levels. In this process, the percent of courses or projects planned for evaluation at each level is developed. The first step is to assess the present situation. The number of all courses (or projects), including repeated sections of a course, is tabulated along with the corresponding level(s) of evaluation presently conducted for each course. Next, the percent of courses using Level 1 reaction questionnaires is calculated. The process is repeated for each level of the evaluation. The current percentages for Levels 3, 4, and 5 are usually low.

After detailing the current situation, the next step is to determine a realistic target for each level within a specific timeframe. Many organizations set annual targets for changes. This process should involve the input of the entire IT staff to ensure that the targets are realistic and that the staff is committed to the process and targets. If the IT and technology development staff do not develop ownership for this process, targets will not be met. The improvement targets must be achievable, while at the same time challenging and motivating. Table 12-5 shows the targets established for Wachovia Bank, a large financial services company with hundreds of projects.

Using this as an example, 100 percent of the projects are measured at Level 1, which is consistent with many other organizations. Only half of the projects are measured at Level 2, using a formal method of measurement. At this organization, informal methods are not counted as a learning measure. At Level 3, application represents a 30 percent follow-up. In essence, this means that almost one-third

Table 12-5
Evaluation Targets for Wachovia Bank

Level of Evaluation	Percent of Programs Evaluated at this Level
Level 1—Reaction	100
Level 2—Learning	50
Level 3—Application	30
Level 4—Impact	10
Level 5—ROI	5

Table 12-6
Percentages and Targets for Five Years in
a Large Multinational Company

	Year 0	Year 1	Year 2	Year 3	Year 4	Year 5
Percent of Courses Evaluated at Each Level						
Reaction and Perceived Value	85	90	95	100	100	100
Learning and Confidence	30	35	40	45	50	60
Application and Implementation	5	10	15	20	25	30
Impact and Consequences	2	4	5	9	12	15
ROI	0	2	4	6	8	10

of the projects will have some type of follow-up method implemented—at least for a small sample of those projects. Ten percent are planned for business impact, and half of those are for ROI. These percentages are typical and often recommended. The Level 2 measure may increase significantly in groups where there is much formal testing, or if informal measures (e.g., self-assessment) are included as a learning measure. There is rarely a need to go beyond 10 percent and 5 percent for Levels 4 and 5, respectively.

Table 12-6 shows current percentages and targets for five years in a large Asia Pacific multinational company. This table reflects the gradual improvement of increasing evaluation activity at Levels 3, 4, and 5. Year 0 is the current status. Target setting is a critical implementation issue. It should be completed early in the process with full support of the entire IT staff. Also, if practical and feasible, the targets should have the approval of the key management staff, particularly the senior management team.

Developing a Project Plan for Implementation

An important part of the planning process is to establish timetables for the complete implementation process. This document becomes a master plan for the completion of the different elements presented in this chapter, beginning with assigning responsibilities and concluding with meeting the targets previously described. Figure 12-2 shows an ROI implementation project plan for a large software

	J	F	M	A	M	J	J	A	S	O	N	D	J	F	M	A	M	J	J	A	S	O	N
Team formed	■																						
Policy developed		■	■																				
Targets set				■																			
Network formed					■																		
Workshops developed				■	■																		
ROI project (A)					■	■																	
ROI project (B)						■	■	■															
ROI project (C)									■	■	■						■	■					
ROI project (D)												■	■	■				■	■	■			
IT staff trained											■	■											
Suppliers trained																				■	■		
Managers trained																				■	■		
Support tools developed				■	■																		
Evaluation guidelines developed	■	■	■																				

Figure 12-2. ROI Implementation Project Plan for a Large Software Development Company

development company. From a practical basis, this schedule is a project plan for transition from the present situation to a desired future situation. The items on the schedule include, but are not limited to, developing specific ROI projects, building staff skills, developing policy, teaching managers the process, analyzing ROI data, and communicating results. The more detailed the document, the more useful it will become. The project plan is a living long-range document that should be reviewed frequently and adjusted as necessary. More important, it should always be familiar to those who are routinely working with the ROI Methodology.

Revising/Developing Policies and Procedures

Another key part of planning is revising (or developing) the organization's policy concerning measurement and evaluation, which is often a part of policy and practice for developing and implementing IT and technology development projects. The policy statement contains information developed specifically for the measurement and evaluation process. It is frequently developed with the input of the IT staff, key managers or sponsors, and the finance and accounting staff. Sometimes policy issues are addressed during internal workshops designed to build skills with measurement and evaluation. Figure 12-3 shows the topics in the measurement and evaluation policy for a large technology firm in South Africa. The policy statement addresses critical issues that will influence the effectiveness of the measurement and evaluation process. Typical topics include adopting the five-level model presented in this book, requiring Level 3 and 4 objectives in some or all projects, and defining responsibilities for IT.

1. Purpose
2. Mission
3. Evaluate all project that will include the following levels:
   a. Reaction (100%)
   b. Learning (no less than 70%)
   c. Applications (50%)
   d. Impact (usually through sampling) 10% (highly visible, expensive)
   e. ROI (5%)
4. Evaluation support group (corporate) will provide assistance and advice in Measurement and Evaluation, Instrument Design, Data Analysis, and Evaluation Strategy.
5. New projects are developed following logical steps beginning with needs analysis and ending with communicating results.
6. Evaluation instruments must be designed or selected to collect data for evaluation. They must be valid, reliable, economical, and subject to audit by evaluation support group.
7. Responsibility for IT project results rests with designers, project leaders, participants, and sponsors.
8. An adequate system for collecting and monitoring IT costs must be in place. All direct costs should be included.
9. At least annually the management board will review the status and results of IT. The review will include IT plans, strategies, results, costs, priorities, and concerns.
10. Line management shares in the responsibility for IT projects. Evaluation through follow-up, commitments, and overall support.
11. Managers/supervisors must declare competence achieved through technology and packaged programs. When not applicable, IT staff should evaluate.
12. External IT consultants must be selected based on previous evaluation. Central data/resource base should exist. All external IT programs of over one day in duration will be subjected to evaluation procedures. In addition, participants will assess the quality of external programs.
13. IT program results must be communicated to the appropriate target audience. As a minimum, this includes management, participants, and all IT staff.
14. Technology staff should be qualified to do effective needs-analysis and evaluation.
15. Central database for program development to prevent duplication and serve as program resource.
16. Union involvement in total information technology plan.

Figure 12-3. Results-Based Internal IT Policy (excerpts from actual policy for a large firm South Africa)

Policy statements are important because they provide guidance and direction for the staff and others who work closely with the ROI process. They keep the process clearly on focus and enable the group to establish goals for evaluation. Policy statements also provide an opportunity to communicate basic requirements and fundamental issues regarding performance and accountability. More than anything else, they serve as a learning tool to teach others, especially when they are developed in a collaborative and collective way. If policy statements are developed in isolation and do not have the ownership of the staff and management, they will be neither effective nor useful.

Guidelines for measurement and evaluation are important to show how to use the tools and techniques, guide the design process, provide consistency in the ROI process, ensure that appropriate methods are used, and place the proper emphasis on each of the areas. The guidelines are more technical than policy statements and often contain detailed procedures showing how the process is actually undertaken and developed. They often include specific forms, instruments, and tools necessary to facilitate the process. Figure 12-4 shows the Table of Contents of evaluation guidelines for a multinational company. As this Table of Contents reveals, the guidelines are comprehensive and include significant emphasis on ROI and accountability.

Assessing the Climate

As a final step in planning the implementation, some organizations assess the current climate for achieving results. In some organizations, annual assessments are taken to measure progress as this process is implemented. Others take the assessment instrument to the management group to determine the extent managers perceive IT and technology development to be effective. The assessment process is an excellent way to clarify current status. Then the organization can plan for significant changes, pinpointing particular issues that need support as the ROI Methodology is implemented.

PREPARING THE IT STAFF

One group that will often resist the ROI Methodology is the IT staff who must design, develop, deliver, and coordinate technology solutions. These staff members often see evaluation as an unnecessary intrusion into their responsibilities, absorbing precious time and stifling their creativity. This section outlines some important issues that must be addressed when preparing the staff for the implementation of ROI.

Involving the IT Staff

On each key issue or major decision, the IT staff should be involved in the process. As policy statements are prepared and evaluation guidelines developed, staff input is absolutely essential. It is difficult for the staff to be critical of something they helped design,

---

Section 1: Policy
1.1   The Need for Accountability
1.2   The Bottom Line: Linking IT with Business Needs
1.3   Results-Based Approach
1.4   Implications
1.5   Communication
1.6   Payoff
Section 2: Responsibilities
2.1   IT Group Responsibilities: Overall
2.2   IT Group Responsibilities: Specifics for Selected Groups
2.3   The Business Unit Responsibilities
2.4   Participant Manager Responsibilities
2.5   Participants Responsibilities
Section 3: Evaluation Framework
3.1   Purpose of Evaluation
3.2   Levels of Evaluation
3.3   Process Steps for IT Implementation
3.4   Evaluation Model
Section 4: Level 1 Guidelines
4.1   Purpose and Scope
4.2   Areas of Coverage — Standard Form
4.3   Optional Areas of Coverage
4.4   Administrative Issues
4.5   How to Use Level 1 Data
Section 5: Level 2 Guidelines
5.1   Purpose and Scope
5.2   Learning Measurement Issues
5.3   Techniques for Measuring Learning
5.4   Administration
5.5   Using Level 2 Data
Section 6: Level 3 Guidelines
6.1   Purpose and Scope
6.2   Follow-up Issues
6.3   Types of Follow-up Techniques
6.4   Administrative Issues
6.5   Using Level 3 Evaluation
Section 7: Level 4 and 5 Guidelines
7.1   Purpose and Scope
7.2   Business Results and ROI Issues
7.3   Monitoring Performance Data
7.4   Extracting Data from Follow-up Evaluation
7.5   Isolating the Effects of the Learning Solution
7.6   Converting Data to Monetary Values
7.7   Developing Costs
7.8   Calculating the ROI
7.9   Identifying Intangible Benefits
7.10   Administrative Issues
7.11   Using Business Impact and ROI Data

Figure 12-4. Evaluation Guidelines for a Multinational Company

develop, and plan. Using meetings, brainstorming sessions, and task forces, the IT staff should be involved in every phase of developing the framework and supporting documents for ROI. In an ideal situation, the IT staff can learn the process in a two-day workshop and, at the same time, develop guidelines, policy, and application targets in the session. This approach is efficient, completing several tasks at the same time.

Using ROI as a Learning Tool

One reason the IT staff may resist the ROI process is that the effectiveness of their projects will be fully exposed, placing their reputation on the line. They may have a fear of failure. To overcome this, the ROI process should clearly be positioned as a tool for process improvement and *not* for evaluating IT staff performance, at least during its early years of implementation. IT staff members will not be interested in developing a tool that will be used to expose their shortcomings and failures.

Evaluators can learn more from failures than from successes. If the project is not working, it is best to find out quickly and understand the issues firsthand—not from others. If a project is ineffective and not producing the desired results, clients and/or the management group will eventually hear about it, if they haven't already. A lack of result will cause managers to become less supportive of IT. Dwindling support appears in many forms, ranging from budget reductions to refusing to let certain participants be involved in projects. If the weaknesses of projects are identified and adjustments are made quickly, not only will effective projects be developed but the credibility and respect for the function and IT staff will be enhanced.

Removing Obstacles to Implementation

Several obstacles to the implementation of the ROI Methodology will usually be encountered. Some of these are realistic barriers, whereas others are often based on misconceptions. The majority of them were presented and analyzed in the first chapter. The most common barriers involving the IT staff are reviewed here:

- *ROI is a complex process.* Many of the IT staff will perceive ROI as too complex to implement. To counter this, the staff must understand that by breaking down the process into individual components and steps, it can be simplified. A variety of tools, templates, and software is available to simplify the use of the ROI Methodology. (The resources listed in Appendix A contain many of these tools.)
- *IT staff members often feel they do not have time for evaluation.* The IT staff need to understand that evaluation can save time in

the future. An ROI evaluation may show that the project should be changed, modified, or even eliminated. Also, up-front planning with evaluation strategy can save additional follow-up time.

- *The IT staff must be motivated to pursue evaluations, even when senior executives are not requiring it.* Most staff members will know when top managers are pushing the accountability issue. If they do not see that push, they are reluctant to take the time to make it work. They must see the benefits of pursuing the process even if not required or encouraged at the top. The staff should see the ROI Methodology as a preventive strategy or a leading-edge strategy. The payoff of implementation should be underscored.

- *The IT staff may be concerned that ROI results will lead to criticism.* Many staff members will be concerned about the use of ROI impact study information. If the results are used to criticize or reflect the performance of project designers or facilitators, there will be a reluctance to embrace the concept. The ROI Methodology should be considered a learning process, at least in the early stages of implementation.

These and other obstacles can thwart an otherwise successful implementation. Each must be removed or reduced to a manageable issue.

Teaching the Staff

The IT staff will usually have inadequate skills in measurement and evaluation and will need to develop some expertise in the process. Measurement and evaluation are not always formal parts of preparing to become a facilitator, project manager, or performance analyst. Therefore, each staff member must be provided training on the ROI process to learn how the methodology is implemented, step by step. In addition, staff members must know how to develop plans to collect and analyze data, and interpret results from data analysis. Sometimes a one- or two-day workshop is needed to build adequate skills and knowledge to understand the process, appreciate what it can accomplish for the organization, appreciate the necessity for it, and participate in a successful implementation. (A list of the public two-day workshops is available from the author or at www.roiinstitute.net) Each staff member should know how to understand, use, and support the ROI Methodology. Teaching materials, outlines, slides, workbooks, and other support materials for workshops are available in a special *Field Book*.

INITIATING THE ROI PROCESS

The first tangible evidence of the ROI process may be initiation of the first project in which the ROI is calculated. This section outlines some of the key issues involved in identifying the projects and keeping them on track.

Selecting Projects for ROI Evaluation

Selecting a project for ROI analysis is an important issue. Ideally, certain types of projects should be selected for comprehensive, detailed analyses. As briefly discussed in Chapter 9, the typical approach for identifying projects for ROI evaluation is to select those that are expensive, strategic, and highly visible. Figure 12-5 lists six of the common criteria often used to select projects for this level of evaluation. The process for selection is simple. Using this, or a more detailed list, each project is rated based on the criteria. A typical rating scale uses one to five. All projects are rated, and the project with the highest number is the best candidate for ROI consideration.

SELECTING PROGRAMS FOR ROI EVALUATION

Criteria	Programs				
	#1	#2	#3	#4	#5
1. Life Cycle					
2. Company Objectives					
3. Costs					
4. Scope					
5. Visibility					
6. Management Interest					
Total					

Rating Scale	
1. Life Cycle	5 = Long life cycle 1 = Very short life cycle
2. Company Objectives	5 = Closely related to company objectives 1 = Not directly related to company objectives
3. Costs	5 = Very expensive 1 = Very inexpensive
4. Scope	5 = Very large group 1 = Very small group
5. Visibility	5 = High visibility 1 = Low visibility
6. Management Interest	5 = High level of interest in evaluation 1 = Low level of interest in evaluation

Figure 12-5. Selection Tool for ROI Impact Study

This process only identifies the best candidates. The actual number evaluated may depend on other factors, such as the resources available to conduct the studies.

Additional criteria should be considered when selecting initial projects for ROI evaluation. For example, the initial project should be as simple as possible. Complex projects should be reserved for the timeframe after ROI skills have been mastered. Also, the project should be one that is considered successful now (i.e., all the current feedback data suggest that the project is adding significant value). This helps to avoid having a negative ROI study on the first use of the ROI Methodology. Still another criterion is to select a project that is void of strong political issues or biases. Although these projects can be tackled effectively with the ROI Methodology, it may be too much of a challenge for an early application.

These are only the basic criteria. The list can be extended as necessary to bring the organization's particular issues into focus. Some large organizations with hundreds of projects use as many as 15 criteria, and the technology staff rates projects based on these criteria. The most important issue is to select those projects that are designed to make a difference and represent tremendous investments by the organization. Also, projects that command much attention from management are ideal candidates for an ROI evaluation. Almost any senior management group will have a perception about the effectiveness of a particular project. For some, they want to know the impact it is having. For others, they are not as concerned. Therefore, management interest may drive the selection of many of the impact studies.

The next major step is to determine how many projects to undertake initially and in which particular areas. A small number of initial projects are recommended, perhaps two or three projects. The selected projects may represent technology initiatives that support the various functional areas of the business such as operations, sales, finance, and engineering. It is important to select a manageable number so the process will be implemented.

Ultimately, the number of projects tackled will depend on the resources available to conduct the studies, as well as the internal need for accountability. The percentage of projects evaluated at each level, indicated in Table 12-5, can be accomplished within 3 to 5 percent of the total IT or Technology Development budget. For an organization with 200 projects, this would mean that 5 percent (10) of the projects will have ROI impact studies conducted annually, and at least 30 percent (60) will have some type of follow-up (Level 3). All of this can be accomplished with less than 5 percent of the total IT and Technology Development budget. The costs of the ROI Methodology do not necessarily drain the resources of the organization. At the same time, the projects selected for this level of analysis is limited and should be carefully selected.

Reporting Progress

As the projects are developed and the ROI implementation is underway, status meetings should be conducted to report progress and discuss critical issues with appropriate team members. For example, if a call center automation project is selected as one of the ROI projects, all of the key staff involved in the project (design, development, and delivery) should meet regularly to discuss the status of the project. This keeps the project team focused on the critical issues, generates the best ideas to tackle particular problems and barriers, and builds a knowledge base to implement evaluation in future projects. Sometimes this group is facilitated by an external consultant, an expert in the ROI process. In other cases, the internal ROI leader may facilitate the group.

These meetings serve three major purposes: reporting progress, learning, and planning. The meeting usually begins with a status report on each ROI project, describing what has been accomplished since the previous meeting. Next, the specific barriers and problems encountered are discussed. During the discussions, new issues are interjected in terms of possible tactics, techniques, or tools. Also, the entire group discusses how to remove barriers to success and focuses on suggestions and recommendations for next steps, including developing specific plans. Finally, the next steps are developed, discussed, and configured.

PREPARING THE MANAGEMENT TEAM

Perhaps no group is more important to the ROI process than the management team who must allocate resources for strategic technology projects. In addition, they often provide input and assistance in the ROI process. Specific actions to train the management team should be carefully planned and executed.

A critical issue that must be addressed before training the managers is the relationship between the IT staff and key managers. A productive partnership is needed which requires each party to understand the concerns, problems, and opportunities of the other.

Developing this type of relationship is a long-term process that must be deliberately planned and initiated by key IT staff members (Bell & Shea, 1998). Sometimes the decision to commit resources and support for key technology projects is often based on the effectiveness of this relationship.

Workshop for Managers

One effective approach to prepare managers for the ROI process is to conduct a workshop for managers, "The Manager's Role in Technology." Varying in duration from one-half day to one day, this practical workshop shapes critical skills and changes perceptions to enhance the support of the ROI process. Managers leave the workshop with an improved perception of the impact of technology and a clearer understanding of their roles in the Technology Development process. More important, they often have a renewed commitment to make IT work in their organization.

Due to the critical need for this topic in management training, this workshop should be required for all managers, unless they have previously demonstrated strong support for the IT function. Because of this requirement, it is essential for top executives to be supportive of this workshop and, in some cases, take an active role in conducting it. To tailor the project to specific organizational needs, a brief needs assessment may be necessary to determine the specific focus and areas of emphasis for the project.

Target Audiences

Although the target audience for this project is usually middle-level managers, the target group may vary with different organizations. In some organizations, the target may be first-level managers, and in others, the target may begin with second-level managers. Three important questions help determine the proper audience:

- Which group has the most direct influence on the IT and Technology Development function?
- Which management group is causing serious problems with lack of management support?
- Which group has the need to understand the ROI process so they can influence the technology transfer?

The answer to these questions is often middle-level managers.

Timing

This workshop should be conducted early in the management development process before nonsupportive habits are delivered. When this project is implemented throughout the organization, it is best to start with higher-level managers and work down the organization. If possible, a version of the project should be a part of a traditional management training project provided to supervisors when they are promoted into managerial positions.

Selling Top Management

Because convincing top management to require this project may be a difficult task, three approaches should be considered:

1. Discuss and illustrate the consequences of inadequate management support for strategic technology investments—for example, the statistics are staggering in wasted time and money.
2. Show how current support is lacking. An evaluation of an internal technology project will often reveal the barriers to successful application of IT. Lack of management support is often the main reason, which brings the issue close to home.
3. Demonstrate how money can be saved and results can be achieved with the ROI process.

The endorsement of the top management group is important. In some organizations, top managers actually attend the project to explore firsthand what is involved and what they must do to make the process work. At a minimum, top management should support the project by signing memos describing the project or by approving policy statements. They should also ask provoking questions in their staff meetings from time to time. This will not happen by chance. The IT manager must tactfully coach top executives.

Workshop Content

The project will usually cover the topics outlined next. The time allotted for each topic and specific focus will depend on the organization, the experience and needs of the managers, and the preparation of the management group. The project can be developed in separate modules where managers can be exempt from certain modules based on their previous knowledge or experience with the topic. This module concept is recommended.

The Overall Importance of IT

Managers need to be convinced that technology is a mainstream responsibility that is gaining in importance and influence in the organizations. They need to understand the results-based approach of today's progressive IT organization. After completing this module, managers should perceive IT as a critical process in their organization and be able to describe how the process contributes to strategic and operational objectives. Data from the organization are presented to show the full scope of IT in the organization. Tangible evidence of top management commitment should be presented in a form such as memos, directives, and policies signed by the CEO or other appropriate top executive. In some organizations, the invitation to attend the project comes from the CEO, a gesture that shows strong top management commitment. Also, external data should be included to illustrate the growth of IT budgets and the increasing importance of IT and technology development. Perhaps a case showing the linkage between IT and strategy would be helpful.

The Impact of IT

Too often, managers are unsure about the success of IT. After completing this module, managers will be able to identify the steps to measure the impact of IT on important output variables. Reports and studies should be presented, showing the impact of technology using measures such as productivity, quality, cost, response times, and customer satisfaction. Internal evaluation reports, if available, are presented to managers, showing convincing evidence that IT is making a significant difference in the organization. If internal reports are not available, other success stories or case studies from other organizations can be used. Managers need to be convinced that IT is a successful, results-based tool, not only to help with change but also to meet critical organizational goals and objectives.

The IT Process

Managers usually will not support activities or processes that they do not fully understand. After completing this module, managers should be able to describe how the technology development process works in their organization and understand each critical step from needs assessment to implementation. Managers need to be aware of the effort that goes into developing an IT project and their role in each step of the process. A short case that illustrates all the steps is helpful here. This discussion also reveals various areas of the potential impact of IT and technology development.

Responsibility for IT

Defining who is responsible for IT is important to the success of your strategic technology initiatives. After completing this module, managers should be able to list their specific responsibilities for IT and technology development. Managers must see how they can influence IT and the degree of responsibility they must assume in the future. Multiple responsibilities for IT are advocated, including managers, participants, participant managers, trainers, developers, and facilitators. Case studies are appropriate to illustrate the consequences when responsibilities are neglected or when there is failure to follow up by managers. One specific case is available that was designed for this purpose. In some organizations, job descriptions are revised to reflect IT responsibility. In other organizations, major job-related goals are established to highlight management responsibility for IT. Overall, this session leaves participants with a clear understanding of how their responsibility is linked to the success of strategic technology projects within their organization.

Active Involvement

One of the most important ways to enhance manager support for IT is to get them actively involved in the process. After completing this stage, managers will actually commit to one or more ways of active involvement in the future. Table 12-7 shows 12 ways for manager involvement identified for one company. The information in the table was presented to managers in the workshop with a request for them to commit to at least one area of involvement. After these areas are fully explained and discussed, each manager is asked to select one or more ways in which he or she will be involved in a strategic technology project in the future. A commitment to sign up for at least one involvement role is required.

If used properly, these commitments are a rich source of input and assistance from the management group. There will be many offers for involvement, and the IT and technology development department must follow through with the offers. A quick follow-up on all offers is recommended.

Table 12-7
Management Involvement in a Strategic Technology Project

The following are areas for present and future involvement in the IT and technology development process. Please check your areas of planned involvement.

	In Your Area	Outside Your Area
■ Provide input on a needs analysis	❏	❏
■ Serve on an IT advisory committee	❏	❏
■ Provide input on a project design	❏	❏
■ Serve as a subject matter expert	❏	❏
■ Serve on a task force to develop a project	❏	❏
■ Volunteer to evaluate an external technology project	❏	❏
■ Assist in the selection of a technology vendor	❏	❏
■ Provide reinforcement to your employees after they participate in a technology project	❏	❏
■ Coordinate an IT project	❏	❏
■ Assist in project evaluation or follow-up	❏	❏
■ Conduct a portion of the project as a facilitator	❏	❏
■ Attend a learning program on technology designed for your staff	❏	❏

MONITORING PROGRESS AND COMMUNICATING RESULTS

A final part of the implementation process is to monitor the overall progress made and communicate the results of specific ROI projects. Although it is an often overlooked part of the process, an effective communication plan can help keep the implementation on target and let others know what the ROI process is accomplishing for the organization.

Communication must be an ongoing, critical part of the process to ensure that all stakeholders are aware of their various responsibilities, understand the progress made and barriers confronted, and develop insight into the results and successes achieved. Because of the importance of communication as part of the ROI Methodology, this topic is explored in a separate chapter. Chapter 11 provides a comprehensive coverage of all the issues involved in communicating the results from projects, as well as providing routine feedback to make decisions and enhance processes. Detailed information on how to develop and present an impact study is also included in that chapter.

COST SAVINGS APPROACHES

One of the most significant barriers to the implementation of the ROI Methodology is the potential time and cost involved in implementing the process. Sometimes, the perception of excessive time and cost is only a myth. At other times, it is a reality. As discussed earlier, the methodology can be implemented for about 3 to 5 percent of the IT project budget. However, this is still a significant expense and represents additional time requirements. It is fitting to end this book with ten steps that can be used to keep the costs and time commitment to a minimum. These cost savings approaches have commanded much attention recently and represent an important part of the implementation strategy.

Take shortcuts at lower levels. When resources are a primary concern and shortcuts must be taken, it is best to take them at lower levels in the evaluation scheme. This leads to the last guiding principle.

Guiding Principle 2
When an evaluation is planned for a
higher lever, the previous level does not
have to be comprehensive.

This is a resource allocation issue. For example, if a Level 4 evaluation is conducted, Levels 1–3 do not have to be as comprehensive. This requires the evaluator to place most of the emphasis on the highest level of the evaluation.

Fund measurement and evaluation with the savings from the ROI Methodology. Almost every ROI impact study will generate data from which to make improvements. Results at different levels often show how the project can be altered to make it more effective and efficient. Sometimes, the data suggest that the project can be modified, adjusted, or completely redesigned. All of those actions can result in cost savings. In a few cases, the project may have to be eliminated because it is not adding the value and adjustments will not necessarily improve it (i.e., it was not needed). In this case, a tremendous cost savings is realized as the project is eliminated. A logical argument can be made to shift a portion of these savings to fund additional measurement and evaluation. Some organizations gradually migrate to the 5 percent of budget target for expenditures for measurement and evaluation by utilizing the savings generated from the use of the ROI Methodology. This provides a disciplined and conservative approach to additional funding.

Plan early and thoroughly. One of the most critical, cost-saving steps to evaluation is to develop project objectives and plan early for the evaluation. Evaluations often succeed because of proper planning. The best way to conserve time and resources is to know what must be done at what time. This prevents unnecessary analysis, data collection after the appropriate time, and the task of having to reconstruct events and issues because they were not planned in advance.

Integrate evaluation into IT. To the extent possible, evaluation should be built in to the IT and Technology Development projects. Data collection tools should be considered part of the project. If possible, these tools should be positioned as application tools and not necessarily evaluation tools. This removes the stigma of providing data to an evaluator and instead enables the participant or others to capture data to clearly understand the success of the project on the job. Part of this issue is to build in expectations for stakeholders to provide the appropriate data.

Share the responsibilities. Defining specific responsibilities for all the stakeholders involved in the technology initiative is critical to the successful streamlining of the evaluation process. Many individuals should play an active role in measurement and evaluation. These include performance consultants, designers, developers, facilitators, participants, participants' managers, and internal subject-matter experts. These individuals can share much of the load that had previously been part of the evaluator's responsibility. This not only has the benefit of saving time, but it also enriches the success of the process by having the active involvement of all stakeholders.

Involve participants in the process. One of the most effective cost savings approaches is to have participants conduct major steps of the process. Participants are the primary source for understanding the degree to which learning is applied and has driven success on the job. The responsibilities for the participants should be expanded from the traditional requirement of involvement in learning processes and application of new skills. Now they must be asked to show the impact of those new skills and provide data as a routine part of the process. Therefore, the role of the participant has expanded from learning and application to measuring the impact and communicating information.

Use shortcut methods. Almost every step of the ROI process model contains shortcut methods—a particular method that represents a shortcut but has proven to be an effective process. For example, in data collection, the simple questionnaire is a shortcut method that can be used to generate powerful and convincing data if it is administered properly. This inexpensive time savings data-collection process can be used in many evaluations. Other shortcut methods are available in isolation and conversion of data steps.

Use sampling. Not all projects should require a comprehensive evaluation nor should all participants necessarily be evaluated in a planned follow-up scenario. Therefore, sampling can be used in two ways. First, as described earlier, only a few projects are selected for Levels 3, 4, and 5 evaluation. Those projects should be selected based on the criteria described early in the chapter. In addition, when a particular project is evaluated, in most cases, only a sample of participants should be evaluated. This keeps costs and time to a minimum.

Use estimates. Estimates are an important part of the process. They are also the least expensive way to arrive at an issue. Whether isolating the effects of a technology investment or converting data to monetary value, estimates can be a routine and credible part of the process. The important point is to make sure the estimate is as credible as possible and that the process used to collect the estimate follows systematic, logical, and consistent steps.

Use internal resources. An organization does not necessarily have to employ consultants to develop impact studies and address other measurement and evaluation issues. Internal capability can be developed, eliminating the need to depend on consultants. There are many opportunities to build skills and become certified in implementing the process. This approach is perhaps one of the most significant time savers. The difference in using internal resources versus external consultants can save as much as 50 percent of the costs of a specific project.

Streamline reporting processing. When management understands the evaluation process, a streamlined approach to communication may be more appropriate and less time consuming. The streamline report (usually one page) is a high-level summary of the impact of the project, covering the results at various levels. A sample of this kind of document is shown in Chapter 11.

Use Web-based software. Because this process is sequential and methodical, it is ideal for software application. Comprehensive software has been developed to process data at Levels 1 through 5. Additional information on available software and how it can be used can be obtained directly from the author by visiting www. roiinstitute.net.

Build on the work of others. There is no time to reinvent the wheel. One of the most important cost savings approaches is to learn from others and build on their work. There are three primary ways to accomplish this:

1. Use networking opportunities, internally, locally, and globally (this issue was described earlier in the chapter).
2. Read and dissect a published case study. More than 100 cases have been published (see resources in Appendix).
3. Locate a similar case study in a database of completed case studies (contact the author for information).

These shortcuts are important to weave throughout the ROI Methodology to ensure that ROI does not drain the budgets and resources unnecessarily. Other shortcuts can be developed, but a word of caution is in order: Shortcuts often compromise the process. When a comprehensive, valid, and reliable study is needed, it will be time consuming and expensive. There is no way around it. The good news is that many shortcuts can be taken to supply the data necessary for the audience and manage the process in an efficient way.

FINAL THOUGHTS

In summary, the implementation of the ROI Methodology is a critical part of the process. If not approached in a systematic, logical, and planned way, the ROI process will not become an integral part of your strategic technology initiatives, and the accountability of the projects will be lacking. This final chapter presented the different elements that must be considered and issues that must be addressed to ensure that implementation is smooth and uneventful. The result would be a complete integration of the ROI Methodology as a mainstream activity in the IT and technology development process.

REFERENCES

Bell, C.R. and H. Shea. *Dance Lessons: Six Steps to Great Partnerships in Business & Life*. San Francisco, CA: Berrett-Koehler Publishers, Inc., 1998.

APPENDIX

Resources

Many additional resources have been developed to assist with the understanding, using, and implementing the ROI Methodology. A brief description of these items is included here. More detail can be obtained from the author at the following address:

ROI Institute
P.O. Box 380637
Birmingham, Alabama 35238-0637
info@roiinstitute.net

The following materials are available directly from the publishers or can be purchased at www.amazon.com.

OTHER ROI BOOKS

Show Me the Money: How to Determine ROI in People, Projects and Programs

Jack J. Phillips and Patricia Pulliam Phillips
Berrett-Koehler (2007), ISBN 978-1-57675-399-6 (hardcover)
288 pages
235 Montgomery Street, Suite 650
San Francisco, CA 94104-2916

This book offers a comprehensive, proven method for measuring and evaluating the ROI of every aspect of any organizational initiative. This book also shows how to make the business case for new projects at every stage of development—before, during, and after implementation. It includes case studies, checklists, tools, and tips to help implement this method. *Show Me the Money* clarifies and resolves the mystery surrounding the allocation of monetary values. It gives change events everything they need to provide concrete, detailed evaluations of the potential and actual financial benefits of any project or program.

Return on Investment in Training and Performance Improvement Programs, 2ⁿᵈ Ed.

Jack J. Phillips
Elsevier/Butterworth-Heinemann (2003) ISBN-13 978-0-7506-7601-4 ISBN-10 0-7506-7601-9, 388 pages
200 Wheeler Road
Burlington, MA 01803

The second edition of this bestselling book guides you through a proven, results-based approach to calculating the Return on Investment in training and performance improvement programs.

Proving the Value of Meetings and Events: How and Why to Measure ROI

Jack J. Phillips, Monica Myhill and James B. McDonough
ROI Institute and Meeting Professionals International (2007), ISBN-13: 978-0-9790285-0-2 ISBN-10: 0-9790285-0-7, 372 pages
P.O. Box 380637
Birmingham, AL 35238-0637

Essentially two books in one, this book details how to use metrics to show the value of meetings and events and provides case studies of actual application.

Proving the Value of HR: How and Why to Measure ROI

Jack J. Phillips and Patricia Pulliam Phillips
Society for Human Resource Management (2005), ISBN 1-58644-049-7, 222 pages
1800 Duke Street
Alexandria, VA 22314

The human resources function must show its contribution and prove that HR policies, practices, and solutions add directly to the organization's bottom line. This book shows how to measure ROI and provides basic, step-by-step instructions to develop the ROI of HR. It includes a CD-ROM of tools, templates, charts, graphs, a case study, and more.

The Human Resources Scorecard: Measuring the Return on Investment

Jack J. Phillips, Ron D. Stone, and Patricia P. Phillips
Butterworth-Heinemann (2001), ISBN 0-877-19367-3, 518 pages
200 Wheeler Road, 6th Floor
Burlington, MA 01803

This is the HR version for ROI and shows how the ROI Methodology has been applied in a variety of human resources settings. Beginning with a description of 12 possible approaches to measurement, the book makes a strong case for the ROI Methodology being a part of the mix. The last section of the book contains detailed case studies and ROI applications for a variety of HR programs. In essence, this is two books in one.

The Consultant's Scorecard: Tracking Results and Bottom-Line Impact of Consulting Projects

Jack J. Phillips
McGraw-Hill (2000), ISBN 0-07-134816-6, 392 pages
Two Penn Plaza
New York, NY 10121-2298

Recognizing that consulting assignments need to be subjected to accountability issues, this book applies the ROI Methodology to consulting interventions. This book is appropriate for internal and external consultants involved in large-scale projects, organization development and change programs, and technology implementation. Many examples and details from a consulting setting are featured in this unique publication.

Project Management Scorecard: Measuring the Success of Project Management Solutions

Jack J. Phillips, Timothy W. Bothell, and G. Lynne Snead
Butterworth-Heinemann (2002), ISBN 0-7506-7449-0, 353 pages
200 Wheeler Road, 6th Floor
Burlington, MA 01803

The book shows how the ROI Methodology is applied to the implementation and use of project management solutions. Using the six measures, the book shows how a project management solution, such as training and technology processes, can be measured, along with the success of a variety of approaches to improve project management.

IMPLEMENTATION BOOKS

Measurement and Evaluation Series Six Pack

Patricia Pulliam Phillips and Jack J. Phillips, et al
Pfeiffer (2007), Six Books
989 Market Street
San Francisco, CA 94103

This collection provides detailed information for developing ROI evaluations, implementing the ROI Methodology, and showing the value of a variety of functions and processes. With detailed examples, tools, templates, shortcuts, and checklists, this series is a valuable reference for individuals interested in using the ROI Methodology to show the impact of their projects, programs, and processes.

Book 1: *ROI Fundamentals: Why and When to Measure ROI*
By Patricia Pulliam Phillips and Jack J. Phillips

Book 2: *Data Collection: Planning for and Collecting All Types of Data*
By Patricia Pulliam Phillips and Cathy Stawarski

Book 3: *Isolation of Results: Defining the Impact of the Program*
By Jack J. Phillips and Bruce Aaron

Book 4: *Data Conversion: Calculating the Monetary Benefits*
By Patricia Pulliam Phillips and Holly Burkett

Book 5: *Costs and ROI: Evaluating the Ultimate Level*
By Jack J. Phillips and Lizette Zuniga

Book 6: *Communication and Implementation: Sustaining the Practice*
By Jack J. Phillips and Wendi Friedman Tush

Show Me the Money Fieldbook

Jack J. Phillips and Patricia Pulliam Phillips
Berrett-Koehler (2007), 261
Publishers Group West 1700 Fourth Street Berkeley, California
94710

Provides a Comprehensive system that enables business leaders, analysts, and consultants to implement ROI for their projects and includes case studies, checklists, tips, and tools.

ROI Fieldbook

Patricia Pulliam Phillips, Jack J. Phillips, Ron Drew Stone, and
  Holly Burkett
Butterworth-Heinemann 2007, 500 pages
200 Wheeler Road, 6th Floor
Burlington, MA 01803

Featuring tools, templates, checklists, flow processes, and a variety of job aids, this detailed guide shows how the ROI Methodology can be implemented efficiently and effectively. This is a must-have reference for those involved in any phase of implementation. The book is based on actual practices and experiences of hundreds of organizations implementing the ROI Methodology. A CD-ROM is included.

The Handbook of Training Evaluation and Measurement Methods,
  4th Edition

Jack J. Phillips
Butterworth-Heinemann (2003), ISBN 0-88415-387-8, 530 pages
200 Wheeler Road, 6th Floor
Burlington, MA 01803

This is the standard reference and college text for measurement and evaluation, detailing design issues and steps to improve measurement and evaluation. This book contains 23 chapters of information to assist in organizing, developing, implementing, supporting, and maintaining measurement and evaluation systems in an organization. This was the first major evaluation book published in the United States. An instructor's manual is available.

CASE STUDIES

Proving the Value of HR: ROI Case Studies

Patricia Pulliam Phillips and Jack J. Phillips
ROI Institute (2007), ISBN-13: 978-0-9790285-1-9 ISBN-10: 0-9790285-1-5, 232 pages
P.O. Box 380637
Birmingham, AL 35238-0637

Based on their combined experience of more than 50 years in measuring and evaluating programs, Jack and Patti Phillips have compiled some of their favorite ROI case studies in this comprehensive, easy-to-use book—an essential companion to any reference on the ROI Methodology. Explore in-depth studies in human resources, learning and development, and performance improvement fields. Some of the real-world topics detailed in this book are preventing sexual harassment, machine operator training, stress management, safety incentives, executive leadership development, eLearning, performance management training, interactive selling skills, employee retention improvement, and more!

In Action: Measuring Return on Investment, Volume 1

Jack J. Phillips, Series Editor
American Society for Training and Development (1994), ISBN
    1-56286-008-9, 18 case studies, 271 pages
1640 King Street
Alexandria, VA 22313-2043

This initial volume presents case studies from the real world. Each study details how the ROI Methodology was applied, with particular focus on lessons learned throughout the process. This book has become the all-time best-seller at ASTD and is still in great demand.

In Action: Measuring Return on Investment, Volume 2

Jack J. Phillips, Series Editor
American Society for Training and Development (1997), ISBN
    1-56286-065-8, 17 case studies, 282 pages

This follow-up volume expands the traditional training coverage to other issues, including human resources and technology. This book has become the second all-time best-seller at ASTD.

In Action: Measuring Return on Investment, Volume 3

Patricia Pulliam Phillips, Editor; Jack J. Phillips, Series Editor
American Society for Training and Development (2001), ISBN
    1-56286-288-X, 11 case studies, 254 pages

This third volume builds on the success of the previous volumes. In great detail, this book presents some of the best case studies available on the use of the ROI Methodology in a variety of human resources and performance improvement settings.

In Action: Measuring ROI in the Public Sector

Patricia P. Phillips, Editor; Jack J. Phillips, Series Editor
American Society for Training and Development (2002), ISBN
    1-56286-325-8, 10 case studies, 240 pages

This book addresses a critical need to bring additional account-ability to the public sector with the use of the ROI Methodology. This book contains case studies from the variety of settings in the public sector, with most of them involved in workforce development, training and learning, and human resources. The public sector settings vary from U.S. federal, state, and local governments to governments outside the United States. This book is published jointly by the International Personnel Management Association.

In Action: Implementing Evaluation Systems and Processes

Jack J. Phillips, Series Editor
American Society for Training and Development (1998), ISBN
    1-56286-101-8, 18 case studies, 306 pages

This book addresses the challenges organizations face as the ROI Methodology is implemented. The first half shows cases of successful integration of the ROI methodology throughout the systems, and the second half shows how the ROI methodology has been utilized with specific programs or divisions. In all, the studies detail the implementation issues confronting organizations and how they were resolved.

In Action: Measuring Intellectual Capital

Patricia P. Phillips, Editor; Jack J. Phillips, Series Editor
American Society for Training and Development (2002), ISBN
    1-56286-295-2, 12 case studies, 218 pages

Measuring and monitoring intellectual capital is a critical challenge for organizations. These case studies show how organizations have implemented measurement systems to monitor and understand the current status and identify areas for improvement in this area. Common organizational measures are discussed, as well as specific programs and processes utilized to measure intellectual capital.

In Action: Conducting Needs Assessment

Jack J. Phillips and Elwood F. Holton, III, Editors
American Society for Training and Development (1995), ISBN
   1-56286-117-8, 17 case studies, 312 pages

The initial assessment is very critical to the success of training and development. This case study book shows studies on how organizations have tackled needs assessment, showing a variety of processes in different settings.

In Action: Performance Analysis and Consulting

Jack J. Phillips, Series Editor
American Society for Training and Development (2000), ISBN
   1-56286-134-4, 18 case studies, 223 pages

Recognizing that the front-end analysis is elevated from needs assessment to performance analysis, this book focuses directly on case studies involving a detailed, up-front performance analysis. Cases are presented to show how the business needs are developed, job performance needs are analyzed, knowledge deficiencies are uncovered, and preferences are identified. The premise of each study is that a major business problem or opportunity is the driver for intervention and the studies illustrate how analysis is conducted to uncover the linkage to business need.

In-Action: Implementing E-learning Solutions

Christine Pope, Editor; Jack J. Phillips, Series Editor
American Society for Training and Development (2001), ISBN
   1-56286-292-8, 12 case studies, 200 pages

This casebook focuses on implementation of e-learning, primarily from the accountability perspective. The studies detail how e-learning is implemented and compared to other types of delivery processes. Specific ROI case studies are included in this unique publication.

SOFTWARE

Software has been developed to support the ROI Methodology described in this book and is available in different options. For more information contact the ROI Institute.

Index

Special Offer from ROI Institute

Send for your own ROI Process Model, an indispensable tool for implementing and presenting ROI in your organization. ROI Institute is offering an exclusive gift to readers of *ROI for Technology*. This 11″ × 25″ multicolor foldout shows the ROI Methodology flow model and the key issues surrounding the implementation of the ROI Methodology. This easy to understand overview of the ROI Methodology has proven invaluable to countless professionals when implementing the ROI Methodology. Please return this page or email your information to the address below to receive your free foldout (a $6 value). Please check your area(s) of interest in ROI.

Please send me the ROI Process Model described in the book. I am interested in learning more about the following ROI materials and services:

☐ Workshops and briefing on ROI   ☐ Books and support materials on ROI
☐ Certification in the ROI Methodology   ☐ ROI software
☐ ROI consulting services   ☐ ROI Network information
☐ ROI benchmarking   ☐ ROI research

Name _____   Phone _____

Title _____   E-mail Address _____

Organization _____

Address _____

Functional area of interest:

☐ Human Resources/   ☐ Learning and   ☐ Public Relations/
   Human Capital   Development/   Community Affairs/
                  Performance   Government Relations
                  Improvement

☐ Meetings and Events   ☐ Sales/Marketing   ☐ Technology/IT Systems
☐ Project Management   ☐ Quality/Six   ☐ Operations/Methods/
   Solutions   Sigma   Engineering
☐ Research and   ☐ Finance/   ☐ Logistics/Distribution/
   Development/   Compliance   Supply Chain
   Innovations
☐ Public Policy Initiatives   ☐ Social Programs   ☐ Other (Please Specify)

                                         _____

Organizational Level

☐ executive   ☐ management   ☐ consultant   ☐ specialist
☐ student   ☐ evaluator   ☐ researcher

Return this form or contact

ROI Institute
P.O. Box 380637
Birmingham, AL 35238-0637
www.roiinstitute.net

or

e-mail information to info@roiinstitute.net
Please allow four to six weeks for delivery.